Navi Radjou is a Silicon Valley-based innovation and leadership thinker who advises senior executives worldwide on breakthrough growth strategies. A Fellow at Cambridge Judge Business School, Navi has served on the World Economic Forum's Global Agenda Council on Design Innovation and contributes to *Harvard Business Review* online. In 2013, Navi won the prestigious Thinkers50 Innovation Award – given to a management thinker who is re-shaping the way we think about and practise innovation. He delivered a talk at TED Global 2014 on frugal innovation. Navi co-authored the international bestsellers *Jugaad Innovation: Think Frugal, Be Flexible, Generate Breakthrough Growth* and *From Smart To Wise*. He is a sought-after keynote speaker who is widely quoted in international media. An Indian-born French-American dual citizen, Navi lives in Palo Alto, California.

Jaideep Prabhu is Professor of Marketing and Jawaharlal Nehru Professor of Indian Business at Judge Business School, University of Cambridge. He has a BTech from IIT Delhi and a PhD from the University of Southern California. Jaideep has been published in leading international journals and his work has been profiled on BBC News24, BBC Radio 4, BBC World Service, *Bloomberg BusinessWeek*, *The Economic Times*, *The Economist*, the *Financial Times*, *Le Monde*, *MIT Sloan Management Review*, the *New York Times* and *The Times*. He has consulted for or taught executives from Bertelsmann, Barclays, BP, BT, GE, IBM, ING Bank, the NHS, Nokia, Philips, Roche, Shell, Siemens, Vodafone and Xerox, among others. He is co-author of the business bestseller *Jugaad Innovation: Think Frugal, Be Flexible, Generate Breakthrough Growth*.

Praise for *Frugal Innovation*

Long practised in developing nations out of sheer necessity, frugal innovation is now becoming a strategic business imperative in developed economies, where consumers demand affordable and sustainable products. The flow of industrial knowledge has thus become a two-way street, where the North and South, East and West learn from and exchange with each other. No business leader in the 21st century can ignore the paradigm shift fully described in this book.

Carlos Ghosn, Chairman and CEO, Renault-Nissan Alliance

Through the comprehensive set of case studies they offer in their new book, Radjou and Prabhu demonstrate that frugal innovation is one of the most critical emerging models of value creation for both businesses and the customers they serve. In a hyper-competitive, resource-constrained world, the companies that will succeed are those that can develop and market new solutions that are resource-light and cost-effective without sacrificing quality. *Frugal Innovation* provides an essential blueprint for how to approach this business imperative the right way.

Indra K. Nooyi, Chairman and CEO, PepsiCo, Inc.

Frugal Innovation distils years of thinking and experimentation into an effective and innovative how-to guide for companies large and small. It should be required reading for executives who want to get to market faster and more efficiently while delivering what customers want.

Beth Comstock, Senior Vice President, Chief Marketing Officer, GE

Frugal Innovation offers valuable insights for business leaders everywhere who are facing a familiar challenge: how to do more with less and generate sustainable value for customers, shareholders and society. To stay relevant in an increasingly digital world, organisations must embrace a frugal approach to innovation in order to increase productivity and agility, create competitive advantage and ultimately fuel growth.

Pierre Nanterme, Chairman & CEO, Accenture

Radjou and Prabhu's *Jugaad Innovation* challenged the top-down Western approach to innovation by offering an agile, bottom-up model. *Frugal Innovation* moves this further and faster forward. The practical roadmap and numerous cases in this book find the beat of the new customer-led world order – where velocity, synergy, empathy and involvement come as standard. The future will be about doing more with less, and here we see how.

Kevin Roberts, CEO Worldwide, Saatchi & Saatchi

Radjou and Prabhu show the benefits of viewing resource limitations as an opportunity. In our increasingly resource-constrained world, consumers are demanding affordable, high-quality products that are environmentally friendly and socially inclusive – and numerous innovators are already obliging them. *Frugal Innovation* insightfully articulates how Western companies can evolve to capture opportunities presented by the burgeoning "do more with less" economy.

Dominic Barton, Global Managing Director, McKinsey & Company

In a world of budget cuts where we all strive to do "more for less", Radjou and Prabhu provide real practical examples of how we can all learn the lessons of frugal innovation. They successfully draw out the wider social and environmental benefits of frugal innovation and the concept of "prosumers" in a way that is both engaging and practical. A great read.

Iain Gray, Chief Executive, Innovate UK

An excellent and bang up-to-date primer on how to do innovation cheaply, quickly, flexibly and with close attention to users and customers – approaches which are, perhaps surprisingly, diametrically opposite to the ways in which so much innovation is organised today.

Geoff Mulgan, CEO, NESTA

Frugal innovation is an idea whose time has come. Downward pressures on cost and the need to use resources sustainably demand this new approach to innovation. In this seminal book, Radjou and Prabhu explain clearly how frugal innovation works and illustrate their case with a host of practical examples from companies around the world. They have captured the wave of the future.

Sir Michael Barber, Chief Education Advisor, Pearson

Frugal Innovation offers a compelling path forward for small and large companies striving to cost-effectively develop products and services of high quality that deliver real value to customers.

Jennifer Tescher, President and CEO,
Center for Financial Services Innovation

Frugal innovation is a critical business strategy for companies to prosper in a world where customers are both value-conscious and values-oriented. It challenges Western companies to create high-quality products that are affordable and sustainable as well as desirable and meaningful for end-users.

Carol L. Cone, Global Chair, Edelman Business + Social Purpose

Radjou and Prabhu offer a clarion call for leaders in mature organisations to rethink and reinvent their fundamental approach to innovation by drawing upon the smarts of their people rather than the riches of their organisations. *Frugal Innovation* shows how established companies can stay relevant by learning to think and act like challengers again.

Liz Wiseman, Thinkers50: Top 10 leadership thinker and author of
Wall Street Journal *bestsellers* Multipliers *and* Rookie Smarts

The certainties of rising consumption in the 20th century are gone. Austerity, aspiration, personalisation and planetary limits all demand that we take a new approach to business. But what should it be? Radjou and Prabhu paint a vivid picture of how business can blend values and quality to deliver the personal and social balance that 21st-century consumers want.

Mike Barry, Director of Sustainable Business (Plan A)
at Marks and Spencer

With the cost of R&D increasing year on year, it is important for pharmaceutical companies to keep a focus on ensuring positive returns from investment in R&D and innovation. To be successful requires R&D to be organised differently, in ways that simultaneously improve both effectiveness and efficiency – an approach we at GSK are taking. *Frugal Innovation* is a timely book that provides insightful and practical guidance to firms trying to do more with less.

Stephen Mayhew, Head, R&D Strategy Development, GSK

At Thinkers50 we have been following the development of the ideas of Radjou and Prabhu for some time. They are exciting because they challenge many fundamental assumptions about how and why companies innovate; and they are important because frugal innovation is an idea of and for our times. This book will accelerate the re-invention of how we understand and practise innovation.

Stuart Crainer and Des Dearlove, founders, Thinkers50

Health care may be the global sector most urgently in need of Radjou and Prabhu's insights in *Frugal Innovation*. Aging populations and surging demand for affordable services confront health-care leaders everywhere with a stark reality: innovation must be harnessed to create massive, sustainable improvements in health delivery systems without crippling economic growth. *Frugal Innovation* sets forth a compelling roadmap for delivering better care at lower cost for more people.

Molly Coye, MD, Chief Innovation Officer, UCLA Health

Frugal Innovation is a tour d'horizon of a changing economy. The authors make a compelling case for a feedback-rich economy that is restorative and regenerative rather than extractive, heading for the "upcycle". There is real economic and business advantage to be had through a system change approach, and the authors are to be congratulated for their stimulating guide to the future.

The Ellen MacArthur Foundation

Frugal Innovation is a must-read for corporate leaders around the world facing pressure to create high-quality products using limited resources. Radjou and Prabhu convincingly show that it is possible for companies to "do better with less".

Tango Matsumoto, Corporate Executive Officer, EVP, Head of Global Marketing, Fujitsu Limited

Businesses have to innovate in an increasingly resource-constrained environment. Addressing clients' pain points and dreams in a frugal way requires a focus on simplicity and agility. This book gives many suggestions on how to do this well.

Sophie Vandebroek, chief technology officer, Xerox and president of Xerox Innovation Group

Frugal Innovation holds important insights for companies across sectors wishing to do more with less. The book is of great relevance to the financial services industry and banks like Barclays that are working with new technologies and start-ups to help customers manage their finances better.

Elisabetta Osta, Managing Director, Design Office Information, Insight & Innovation Team, Barclays Bank

In *Frugal Innovation*, Radjou and Prabhu show how the lessons from developing countries are starting to make a real impact on the innovation processes of established companies in the West. This book nicely describes these transformations and some of the difficulties encountered, and lists practical solutions for companies who want to do more innovation with less, no matter where you are in the world.

Henry Chesbrough, Faculty Director, Garwood Center for Corporate Innovation at UC Berkeley's Haas School of Business, and author, Open Innovation

Frugal Innovation proposes a breakthrough approach to solving some of the most complex issues of our global economy as it empowers human beings to use their creativity to generate economic and social value while preserving the environment. A must-read for thought leaders and practitioners worldwide.

Bruno Roche, Special Adviser to the G20 French Presidency Mission on Social Justice & Globalisation; and Chief Economist, Mars Incorporated

FRUGAL INNOVATION

How to do better with less

Navi Radjou and Jaideep Prabhu

THE ECONOMIST IN ASSOCIATION WITH
PROFILE BOOKS LTD

This edition published in 2016

First published by Profile Books Ltd in 2015 as *Frugal Innovation: How to do more with less*
3 Holford Yard
Bevin Way
London WC1X 9HD
www.profilebooks.com

Typeset in EcoType by MacGuru Ltd

Printed and bound by CPI Group (UK) Ltd, Croydon, CR0 4YY

A CIP catalogue record for this book is available from the British Library

ISBN 978 1 78125 760 9
eISBN 978 1 78283 120 4

FSC
www.fsc.org
MIX
Paper from
responsible sources
FSC® C020471

To all the frugal innovators out there who are every day making the world a better place for everyone.

Contents

Case studies

Foreword

by Paul Polman, CEO, Unilever

IN A WORLD INCREASINGLY CHARACTERISED AS VUCA – volatile, uncertain, complex and ambiguous – few things are assured. There is one thing however of which we can be relatively certain: that the insatiable demand for ever higher quality products will continue to rise while at the same time the availability of the resources needed to satisfy that demand will remain constrained.

Reconciling this apparent conflict is rapidly emerging as one of the biggest business challenges of our age. Doing more with less can no longer be a short-term response to difficult economic conditions. It has to become an essential long-term business strategy. Businesses that recognise this new reality stand to prosper. Those that continue to live in denial will surely perish.

Yet recognising the new reality and preparing effectively for it are two very different things, which is where this excellent book comes in; Radjou and Prabhu demonstrate how – and why – the concept of frugal innovation has moved seamlessly from management school slogan to boardroom priority. Through a series of case studies they provide unequivocal evidence of why the "age of austerity" can become the "age of opportunity" for those willing to approach innovation in a very different way.

They start with an innate understanding of what people want. First, quality. People are not willing to compromise on the taste or the performance of the products they buy – and increasingly they cannot afford to; having to buy an alternative or replacement product is an expensive mistake they will not make twice.

Second, value. The demand for value is greater than ever, but this need not mean low cost, as the authors show. People are willing to pay for innovations that add value rather than just giving value. Launching an innovative premium jelly bouillon into a highly competitive market at the height of austerity, for example, might not have been thought the wisest move. Yet with people eating out less, the demand for high-quality convenience products that enable people to cook at home has grown. As a result, Knorr Stock Pots are now in 36 markets and have grown at five times the rate of the overall bouillon market.

Third, purpose. Increasingly people expect companies to use their ability to innovate in a way that addresses the biggest challenges we face around social inclusion and the sustainability of our planet. Business can no longer remain on the sidelines. It has an obligation and – as Radjou and Prabhu demonstrate – a clear opportunity to use its innovative capacity to develop solutions. This is the thinking at the heart of the Unilever Sustainable Living Plan and our business agenda at Unilever. It is a total value chain approach, as highlighted in the Unilever case study (see pages 94–7), but one that finds its greatest resonance at the level of our brands, such as Dove, Lifebuoy, Domestos, Knorr, Signal and the many others infused with a strong social mission and deep sense of purpose. To address people's growing demand for quality, value and purpose, it's not enough for companies to just do more with less; they must learn to do *better* with less.

Perhaps the greatest insight from this book is the extent to which we are not just living in a VUCA world, but in a world increasingly turned on its head. Traditional business models in the West need to be revisited. Poverty is prevalent today in many parts of Europe. That's why we need to apply to European markets the principles of frugal innovation that were used to develop more affordable products at key price points for emerging and aspiring markets. In Spain, for example, our Surf detergent brand sells in packages with as few as five washes; and in Greece, our mayonnaise is available in small packets as well as large jars. Ultimately, as the authors highlight, by combining the frugal ingenuity of developing nations with the advanced R&D capabilities of advanced economies, companies can create high-quality products and services that are affordable, sustainable, and benefit humanity as a whole. This work provides the essential roadmap for those wishing to navigate this new world.

Frugal innovation is an idea – and a book – whose time has come.

Preface

FRUGAL INNOVATION is the ability to "do more with less" – that is, to create significantly more business and social value while minimising the use of diminishing resources such as energy, capital and time. In this "age of scarcity", Western companies are facing growing pressure from cost-conscious and eco-aware customers, employees and governments, who are demanding affordable, sustainable and high-quality products. Frugal innovation is therefore a game-changing business strategy. But it is more than a strategy: it denotes a new frame of mind, one that sees resource constraints as an opportunity, not a liability.

In April 2012, after four years of research, our book *Jugaad Innovation* was published. It led readers into backroom innovation labs in developing countries such as India, China, Brazil and Kenya to examine the roots of this frugal mindset. (*Jugaad* is a Hindi word meaning an innovative fix or an improvised solution born from ingenuity and cleverness.) It showed how inventive entrepreneurs and firms in resource-constrained emerging markets concoct frugal solutions such as a fridge that consumes no electricity, a bicycle that converts road bumps into acceleration energy to run faster, or a mobile-based service that allows users to send and receive money without having a bank account.

Since the publication of *Jugaad Innovation*, there has been an explosion of interest in frugal innovation for *developed* economies. Corporate leaders and policymakers in the US, Europe and Japan are eager to understand how to do better with less. This has led them to fundamentally rethink how they operate, build and deliver products and services, interact with customers and citizens, and create greater value for themselves and society while preserving the environment.

This book identifies the best practices drawn from our studies of frugal pioneers in the US, Europe and Japan across sectors including manufacturing, retail, financial services, health care and education. It takes readers deep inside developed-world businesses and industries that are already reaping the benefits of frugal innovation. Pioneering companies such as Aetna, Fujitsu, General Electric (GE), GlaxoSmithKline (GSK), Pearson, PepsiCo, Renault-Nissan, Siemens and Unilever are striving to embed frugal processes and, most importantly, a frugal mindset in their organisations.

To achieve dramatic gains in cost efficiency, speed and agility, companies need to rebuild their innovation engines. This will present different challenges for different industries and functions, but six general principles are relevant to all industries and companies. Chapter 1 provides an overview of the socio-economic factors in developed nations that have given rise to frugal innovation, and how and why Western consumers have embraced frugal thinking. Chapters 2–7 look at the six frugal principles, and how companies have adopted and profited from them:

- **Engage and iterate.** Chapter 2 lays out the first principle of frugal innovation: engage and iterate (E&I). Rather than using insular research and development (R&D) departments that rely on educated guesses about customer needs, E&I starts with customers, observing their behaviour in their natural environment, and then considers how products can be made as relevant as possible, going back and forth between the customer and the lab to refine designs. Using case studies of frugal pioneers such as Arla Foods, Fujitsu, GE, GSK, Intuit and SNCF, it shows how R&D managers and marketing executives can embed this customer-centric principle within their organisations.

- **Flex your assets.** Chapter 3 explains how customers are becoming ever more demanding. They increasingly want tailored products and services where and when they desire. It describes the trend towards mass customisation, and how new tools (such as robotics and 3D printers) and new approaches (such as social manufacturing and continuous production) can help operations and supply chain managers "flex" their production, logistics and service assets to satisfy demanding customers better and more cheaply. It draws on examples from cars (BMW and Volkswagen), pharmaceuticals (GSK and Novartis), cement (Cemex), soft drinks (Coca-Cola) and energy (GDF-Suez and GE). The goal of flexing assets is not only about saving resources, such as carrying less inventory, but also about saving time – a business's most valuable resource. Studies of Saatchi & Saatchi + Duke and W.L. Gore reveal how managers can draw out the most from their staff by creating a simpler and more agile organisation.

■ **Create sustainable solutions.** Chapter 4 demonstrates how companies can implement sustainable practices such as "cradle-to-cradle" (where components and materials are repeatedly recycled) in the design and manufacture of waste-free products. Based on case studies of Kingfisher, Levi Strauss, method, Tarkett and Unilever, the chapter provides insights into how R&D and manufacturing managers can develop self-sustaining solutions that help both businesses and the environment.

■ **Shape customer behaviour.** Drawing on research in psychology and behavioural economics, as well as on the pioneering work of organisations such as Barclays, IKEA, Khan Academy, Nest and Progressive, Chapter 5 shows how companies can influence consumers into behaving differently (for example, driving less or more safely) and feeling richer while consuming less. It also shows how marketing managers can improve brand loyalty and market share by tailoring frugal products and services more closely to the way customers actually think, feel and behave – and by properly positioning and communicating the aspirational value of these frugal solutions.

■ **Co-create value with prosumers.** Chapter 6 looks at ways consumers – especially the tech-savvy millennial generation (those born between 1982 and 2004) – are evolving from passive individual users into communities of empowered "prosumers", who collectively design, create and share the products and services they want. As a result, R&D and marketing leaders at firms like Auchan are working with do-it-yourself (DIY) and crowdsourcing pioneers, such as TechShop and Quirky, to bolster and harness the collective ingenuity and skills of consumer communities. Additionally, big brands such as IKEA are linking up with start-ups such as Airbnb to develop a "sharing economy" in which consumers share goods and services. The chapter also outlines how sales and marketing managers can build greater brand affinity and deepen their engagement with customers by co-creating greater value for all.

- **Make innovative friends.** Firms such as GE and Ford are ensuring that the R&D function is lean, flexible and highly networked. Chapter 7 shows how R&D and operations managers can develop frugal products, services and business models more efficiently by collaborating with diverse external partners (such as suppliers, universities, venture capitalists and start-ups) than by working alone.

Chapter 8 discusses how firms can foster a frugal innovation culture. It shows how leaders of companies such as Aetna, Danone, IBM, Kingfisher, Marks & Spencer, PepsiCo, Renault-Nissan, Siemens and Unilever are radically changing the culture of their organisations – and altering employees' thinking too – as they strive to implement the six principles of frugal innovation. In doing so, these pioneering companies are rewriting the rules of the game – and even changing the game entirely – in their respective industries.

The chapter contains guidelines to help senior managers identify and prioritise the principles they can implement to achieve better results faster. It provides this guidance from within a change management framework that outlines the what, how, and why of adopting a frugal innovation culture within a company. Lastly, the chapter addresses how functional leaders in charge of R&D, strategy, manufacturing, finance, operations, marketing and sales can individually and collectively foster a frugal innovation culture within their firms.

But first, let us begin by looking at the disruptive nature of a frugal strategy when implemented in a traditional multinational company used to operating in Western markets; and see why so many more established companies feel compelled to follow the same path.

Navi Radjou and Jaideep Prabhu
October 2014

1 Frugal innovation: a disruptive growth strategy

IN 1999, JEAN-MARIE HURTIGER, a senior manager at Renault, a French carmaker, was given what seemed like an almost impossible task. His boss, Louis Schweitzer, then Renault's CEO, wanted him to create a modern, reliable and comfortable car that would retail at $6,000.

Two years earlier, Schweitzer had visited Russia where, to his dismay, he had discovered that the Lada – a locally made car priced at $6,000 – was selling fast, while Renault's fancier cars – twice as expensive as the Lada – had few buyers. As Schweitzer recalls:

> Seeing those antiquated cars, I found it unacceptable that technical progress should stop you from making a good car for $6,000. I drew up a list of specifications in three words – modern, reliable and affordable – and added that everything else was negotiable.

Schweitzer instructed Hurtiger, an engineer by training with international management experience, to build a $6,000 car that matched these specifications.

Technically, Hurtiger could engineer a stripped-down version of a car for that price. But, like the Lada, this car would be clunky and uncomfortable, and customers would question its safety. Renault had a reputation for elegance and quality to protect; launching a shoddy product would be a form of brand suicide. Hurtiger therefore realised that what his boss was asking him to do was not just create a cheaper car, but one that married high quality and affordability.

This "more for less" proposition was at odds with Hurtiger's long experience. R&D engineers in the West are taught to push the frontiers of auto technology by adding features to existing products. Indeed, Western car companies invest billions in R&D to create ever more sophisticated products, in order to differentiate their brands from competitors' and charge customers more for the privilege. Schweitzer's "more for less" proposition seemed to flout the conventional "more for more" business model that had proven so lucrative in consumption-driven Western economies over the previous five decades.

Both Hurtiger and Schweitzer recognised that they would first have to change the way Renault employees think. Creating a $6,000 car required not just a new business model, but a new mental model. This would amount to an immense cultural shift in a company that was over 100 years old and for decades had designed high-quality cars – some for the premium market – primarily for Western middle-class consumers. All Renault's French engineers had grown up in a resource-rich and relatively stable economy with a "bigger is better" R&D philosophy. Schweitzer and Hurtiger needed a new breed of engineers with a different outlook who could innovate under severe constraints and turn adversity into opportunity.

They made a bold decision. Rather than build the car in France, they would do so in an emerging market, where workers were familiar with a world of limited resources. The obvious place was Romania, where in 1999 Renault had acquired a local car company called Dacia. Hurtiger assembled a cross-cultural team made up of French designers and Romanian manufacturing engineers. The French brought their high-end design sensibility to the project and the Romanians brought their cost sensitivity. Renault's Romanian engineers had grown up in a harsh communist environment. Doing more with less was second nature, and they had both the motivation and the ingenuity to succeed.

And succeed they did. They created a car that used 50% fewer parts than a typical Renault vehicle and boasted a simpler architecture. Yet the car was also spacious. To accommodate the needs of rural Romanians, the original design brief had called for a vehicle that could carry "four adults, a pig, a sink, and 100 kilos of potatoes". To achieve more with less, the engineers designed symmetrical rear-view mirrors (so they could be used on either side of the car), a flatter-than-usual windscreen (curved windscreens create more defects and cost more) and a dashboard made from a single injection-moulded piece. All this reduced the use of raw materials and avoided costly tooling on the shop floor. The engineers also limited the number of pricey electronic components, making the car easier and cheaper to produce and repair. The result was a robust saloon car with a minimalist, modern design that met stringent quality and safety standards. In 2004, Schweitzer proudly unveiled the Logan, a no-frills car priced at €5,000 ($6,000).

For Renault, the Logan was not only a technical success; it soon became a huge business success too. The carmaker initially planned to sell the no-frills saloon car to value-conscious consumers in emerging economies in eastern Europe and the Middle East. To Renault's surprise, the Logan also found a market in affluent western Europe. Especially after the recession of 2008, budget-conscious consumers in the West began clamouring for affordable products like the Logan that delivered better value for money. In 2010, a report by L'Observatoire Cetelem, which studies European consumer behaviour trends, revealed that on average 29% of Europeans (and 39% in the UK) were willing to buy a low-cost car. Suddenly, Renault could no longer keep up with demand.

To capitalise on this growing demand, Renault developed an entirely new entry-level product line under the Dacia brand. As well as the Logan saloon car, the Dacia brand now includes the Logan van, the Logan pickup, the Sandero hatchback, Duster SUV (sports utility vehicle) and the Lodgy minivan. Dacia is now the fastest-growing car brand in western Europe (including in the demanding German market). Renault's entry-level products, mostly sold under the Dacia brand, have become the carmaker's cash cow, accounting for over 40% of the company's global sales in 2013, compared with 20% in 2008.[1] These products also generate greater than average margins for Renault due to a strict no-discounts retail policy. To top it off, Dacia products are eco-friendly: 95% of the parts in every Dacia are recyclable. With its successful launch of Logan – and subsequently other Dacia-branded vehicles – Renault created a new segment of "low-cost vehicles" in the automotive industry that combine quality and affordability. In doing so, it established itself as a pioneer of frugal innovation.

Renault, however, could not afford to rest on its laurels, as it faced two major challenges. First, the huge commercial success of Renault's entry-level vehicles had whetted the appetite of Western rivals, such as Volkswagen and Opel (part of GM), which were looking to launch their own low-cost brands. Second, Renault would need to expand its entry-level segment with even more affordable vehicles than its Dacia line to meet the needs of hundreds of millions of first-time car buyers in large emerging markets like India, China and Brazil.

Carlos Ghosn, who succeeded Schweitzer in 2005, was not intimidated by these challenges. Unlike most Western CEOs, he had a truly multicultural background and a track record of tackling the intractable. A Brazilian-born French national of Lebanese descent, Ghosn had made his mark in the early 2000s by successfully turning around Nissan, a nearly bankrupt Japanese carmaker, before becoming CEO of both Renault and Nissan in 2005.

Ghosn believed that the only way Renault could compete in the entry-level vehicle segment in both developed and emerging markets was by continually out-innovating rivals. In particular, he wanted Renault to learn new, cost-effective innovation techniques from emerging markets that could serve the company well in its home market too. After several visits to India (where Renault and Nissan had joint ventures with local partners), Ghosn became intrigued by the Indian ability to innovate faster, better and cheaper. Impressed, he coined the term "frugal engineering" to describe the ability to innovate quickly and at low cost under severe resource constraints, a resourceful skill that was common in several emerging markets.

Ghosn realised that, even after the Logan's success, his Western engineers needed to master the art of frugal engineering completely if they were to continue to produce ever more affordable cars that delivered greater value at lower cost. He also realised that this was not going to be possible with an outlook shaped by resource-rich, stable Western markets. And so in 2012 Ghosn sent Gérard Detourbet, who was head of Renault's entry-level segment, to Chennai in southern India to write the second chapter in the company's frugal innovation journey. In Chennai, Detourbet leads an R&D team that is building an entirely new car platform called CMF-A, which will be shared by Renault and Nissan to develop a wide range of ultra-low-cost, high-performance vehicles aimed at India and other emerging markets.

Ghosn's ultimate aim is to bring the principles of frugal thinking, acquired and honed in resource-constrained India, to Renault's Paris headquarters and use them to develop a new generation of affordable, high-quality vehicles for Western consumers. In doing so, Ghosn is leading a frugal revolution in the West that other CEOs in other firms and sectors are also signing up to.

Before looking at the "how" of frugal innovation – that is, the tools and techniques for implementing a frugal strategy discussed in subsequent chapters – let us first consider the "what" and "why". Specifically, what are frugal innovation's unique characteristics? And why has it become today's most pressing management issue?

The rise of the frugal economy

Several profound economic changes account for the rise of frugal innovation in the developed world. First, the advanced economies have entered an age of austerity in which the notion of frugal living and consuming is becoming mainstream. Over the past decade, the middle classes in the US, Canada, Europe, Japan, Australia and elsewhere have seen their incomes stagnate and their purchasing power shrink. Adjusted for inflation, the real median household income in the US increased by merely 19% between 1967 and 2013. According to a 2014 Pew Research survey, only 44% of Americans define themselves as middle class, a nine percentage point drop since 2008. Over the same period, the number of Americans who believe that they have fallen into a lower income class has shot up from 25% to 40%. Moreover, since 2009, 95% of all income gains in the US have gone to the top 1% of earners. The richest 20% of Americans now account for over 60% of the country's consumer spending.

In parts of Europe where recession persists, deepening poverty is eroding middle-income purchasing power. Spain and Greece have been most affected, but wealthier states such as France and Germany have not been spared. For instance, only 58% of Germans now identify themselves as middle class compared with 65% in 1997. In

France, between 2008 and 2012, average salaries fell by 24%, while the cost of living rose by 30%.

As a result of these economic pressures, North American and European consumers are becoming increasingly concerned about getting value for money, and are opting for cheaper products. For example, nearly one-third of European consumers, especially young people who have only known recession in their adult lives, are now more interested in buying a low-cost rather than a premium car. Car purchases by Americans aged 18–34 fell 30% between 2007 and 2012. In Japan, where the poverty rate shot up to a record 16% in 2012, consumers are shifting from premium brands to inexpensive private-label products in retail stores. Rather than eating out, more Japanese workers now pack their own lunch, earning themselves the nickname *bento-danshi* or "box-lunch man".

These changes are here to stay. Thomas Piketty, a French economist, predicts that income inequality in developed economies will widen in the coming decades, as long-term annual growth rates remain stuck below 2%.[2] With inflation outpacing their incomes since 2007, 76% of US adults now believe their children will be financially worse off than them in the future. And well over half of consumers, surveyed by Booz & Company (now Strategy&), a global management consultancy, in late 2012, reported that they would not revert to their previous spendthrift behaviour when times improve. Booz calls these frugal buyers "permanently value-sensitive consumers".

It is not only consumers who have become more cost-conscious. Governments throughout the developed world are also watching the pennies. Ageing populations, spiralling health-care costs, the pensions burden, huge debts and deficits since 2008 have conspired to introduce a new spirit of austerity in the US, Europe and Japan.

The UK's Conservative-led government is committed to dramatic budget cuts of £81 billion ($128 billion) over four years (4.5% of 2014–15 GDP). This includes an 8% reduction in the defence budget by 2015, a 30% reduction in local government spending and a 16% decrease in the police force. In the US, Barack Obama has proposed a three-year freeze on discretionary spending, and the Pentagon is considering cutting the US army to its smallest size since the second world war. Spain, Italy and Greece are doing the same. And if the Scandinavian and Benelux countries and Germany seem relatively restrained about austerity, this is only because they underwent structural adjustments before the 2008 crisis.

However, the frugal innovation revolution is about more than austerity. Consumers in the developed world are becoming not only more value conscious but also more *values* conscious. They increasingly care about social harmony, worry about ecological degradation and the depletion of natural resources, and want businesses to play their part in making the world better. According to the 2014 Edelman Trust Barometer, an annual global study of consumer attitudes, 84% of respondents believe that business can pursue its self-interest while doing good work for society. As Carol Cone, who heads Edelman's social business practice, argues:[3]

> To increase trust levels among consumers – and earn the "licence to lead" – businesses must learn to simultaneously create more operational and societal value while also impacting less the environment. "Citizen consumers" will vote with their wallets for brands that are socially inclusive and environmentally active.

Indeed, 71% of US consumers now consider the environment when they shop, compared with 66% in 2008. Over 80% of Europeans believe that a product's environmental impact is a critical element in their purchasing decisions. More worryingly for businesses, 90% of millennials (the 70 million or so Americans in their 20s and early 30s), who spend $180 billion annually, are willing to switch to more socially and environmentally responsible brands. Despite their tight budgets, millennial consumers also expect products to be high quality and sustainable. To win the trust of these values-conscious consumers, Cone believes that companies must "move beyond transactional thinking towards a better understanding of tangible actions needed to solve critical societal issues necessary to mutual benefit". As best practices, Cone cites CVS Health's action to stop selling tobacco products from 2014; Gap raising its employees' minimum wage; and Starbucks offering employees who work at least 20 hours a week tuition reimbursement.

Governments across the developed world are also playing a role in this process. New regulations require businesses to be resource efficient. A new US law championed by President Obama requires US carmakers to improve fuel efficiency from the current average of 27.5 miles per gallon to 54.5 miles per gallon by 2025. Similarly, in 2012, the European Parliament passed a stricter recycling law that requires electronic and electrical goods suppliers and retailers to collect, and potentially recycle, 85% of electric and electronic scrap they generate by 2020. And in early 2014, the Parliament voted in favour of requiring member states to meet stricter binding national targets for 2030 to deal with climate change, including a 40% reduction in greenhouse gases (compared with 1990 levels) and at least 30% of energy to come from renewable sources. The European commissioner for the environment, Janez Potočnik, notes:[4]

> In these times of economic turmoil and rising prices for raw materials, resource efficiency is where environmental benefits and innovative growth opportunities come together.

More crucially, consumers' values are shifting, with more emphasis on quality rather than quantity. Studies show that between 15% and 28% of Americans have willingly reduced their material possessions in favour of greater self-sufficiency, with the aim of leading a simpler and more meaningful life. In Japan, a country known for long working hours, half of all consumers across generations now spend more time at home, a trend referred to as *sugomori* or "chicks in the nest". Across the developed world – from New York to Paris to Tokyo – consumers now view frugality as a means to increase not decrease their quality of life. As Simon Mainwaring, author of *We First*, points out:[5] "Consumers want a better world, not just widgets."

The silver lining in the post-crisis gloom is that citizens' search for a more balanced lifestyle is helping to create a new economic system – a frugal economy. It represents an amelioration of the more excessive aspects of 20th-century overconsumption and waste. And the "bigger is better" consumption model may slowly be sharing space with a "small is beautiful" system of consumer values.

So what are the defining features of this new frugal economy?

Recycling along the value chain

New methods of design, production and distribution allow for the continual reuse of parts and components, reducing waste and creating a so-called circular economy. In contrast to the traditional linear economy, in which products are designed, built, sold and consumed, and end up in landfills, the circular economy reuses materials, even waste. The World Economic Forum believes that the circular economy could save $1 trillion a year in major economies by 2025 by using resources better.

Mass customisation

The 20th century gave birth to three major organisational innovations: the corporate R&D lab (pioneered by Thomas Edison, who founded GE); mass production (perfected by Henry Ford); and "big-box" retail and mass distribution (developed by Sam Walton, the founder of Walmart). All three sought to centralise corporate functions – from R&D and purchasing to manufacturing, sales and marketing – with the aim of generating economies of scale. Although this centralised approach helps mass production, thus reducing unit costs, it also consumes a lot of energy and has become expensive to maintain. Worse, it reduces consumers to passive users of products and services, excluding them from a production process that typically occurs far from where they live. However, developed-world consumers are rapidly and dramatically evolving into creative producers of personalised products and services. Much of this is thanks to 3D printing and do-it-yourself (DIY) platforms such as TechShop and FabLab, which cut production costs. A new era of distributed manufacturing will be less resource intensive and will yield higher-quality, mass-customised products and services that are also affordable and sustainable.[6]

Sharing, not buying

In his book *The Age of Access*, Jeremy Rifkin, an economic thinker, sees new technologies like the internet gradually eliminating the concepts of property and ownership. The ownership of physical objects, he predicts, will be seen as an albatross around consumers' necks, as people come to prefer access and experience to ownership.[7] The sharing economy that Rifkin predicted is now upon us. An example is Zipcar (and its equivalents from around the world), a cheap pay-as-you-go car-sharing service popular among urban Americans. The service is easy to use, convenient and better for the local community and the environment. Why own a car, say its customers, when you can get wheels when you need them? Today, nearly 10 million people are less than 10 minutes' walk from a Zipcar. Similarly, why pay $400 for a night in a New York hotel when Airbnb will find you a couch to crash on in Manhattan (or 8,000 other cities the site covers) for $40?

This grassroots shift from an ownership-based consumer economy to a sharing society is propelling the growth of a peer-to-peer economic model based on frugality that involves sharing, bartering, swapping, renting or trading. Collaborative consumers do not covet the latest and fanciest products; they prefer good-enough solutions that meet basic needs. Collaborative consumption, a concept popularised by Rachel Botsman in her book *What's Mine Is Yours*, threatens to disrupt many industries. In 2013, more people used BlaBlaCar, a leading European car-sharing service, than travelled by the high-speed Eurostar train between London and Paris.[8] Airbnb now rents more room nights annually than Hilton's entire hotel chain does globally. And the peer-to-peer lending market, which bypasses banks and their hefty hidden fees, passed the $1 billion mark in early 2012. In August 2014, Zopa, a leading UK peer-to-peer lending firm, announced that its platform alone had loaned over $1 billion since its launch in 2005, with a default rate of less than 1%.

The new frugal economy is growing by leaps and bounds in the developed world not only because it meets the needs of cost-conscious consumers, but also because it responds to their aspirations to give back to society and be environmentally responsible. Companies will be able to surf this wave only by reinventing how they operate, build and deliver products, interact with customers, and create value for themselves and society.

Faster, better and cheaper

To produce affordable and sustainable products, firms must develop a faster, better and cheaper system of innovation. The frugal approach is disruptive; its intensity can be measured in terms of the following simple formula:

$$\frac{\text{Greater value (for customers, shareholders and society)}}{\text{Fewer resources (natural resources, capital, time)}}$$

This requires companies simultaneously to maximise value for all stakeholders while minimising the use of resources.

As Paul Polman, CEO of Unilever, an Anglo–Dutch multinational consumer-goods company, notes:

> Business cannot survive in a society that fails, so it is stupid to think that a business can just be standing on the sidelines of a system that gives it life in the first place.

Polman believes that Unilever's frugal innovation initiatives, many of which are described in this book, are not altruistic but simply common sense.

Meanwhile, frugal innovation seeks to reduce not just the financial cost of doing business but also its environmental cost. Frugal innovation also seeks to minimise time, especially important in such situations as bringing a promising new drug to market.

Frugal innovation is not a management technique like Six Sigma and total quality management (TQM), which aim to reduce cost and waste. Rather, cost efficiency is a means to achieve the larger goal of greater customer value, as is manifest in $30 computers, $40 tablets, $800 electrocardiogram (ECG) machines and $6,000 cars.

It is also possible for firms to be frugal in how they develop and market new products and services, while exercising discretion over whether or not they pass these savings on to consumers. And so frugal innovation practices can coexist with, and even enhance, high-end brands. For instance, Fujitsu, a Japanese technology company, has applied frugal innovation in its manufacturing processes to build one of the world's most advanced supercomputers. This also differentiates frugal innovation from low-cost innovation – an approach that enables a company to develop and market products and services of average quality at low prices. Frugal innovation yields products that are not necessarily cheap or of the highest quality. Rather, they are well-designed, good-quality products that are developed cost-effectively and sold at affordable prices to deliver best customer value.

What does customer value mean? Frugal innovators strive to create products and services that score high on three, seemingly contradictory, attributes that are increasingly valued by Western customers: affordability, quality and sustainability. A high-quality product (say, an over-engineered, beautifully designed, gas-guzzling car) is generally expensive and not always sustainable. Rather than seeking a trade-off or dealing with each of the three attributes independently, frugal innovation seeks to integrate them. For example, over 70% of a product's life-cycle costs and environmental footprint is determined during its design phase. Hence, rather than tackling quality and sustainability later in the manufacturing or distribution process, when doing so becomes more costly, frugal innovation factors in these aspects earlier in the R&D phase. When Renault developed its $6,000 Logan car, its R&D team incorporated elegant design, reliability, safety, comfort and fuel efficiency early on in the development phase. The result was a best-selling, attractive, dependable, energy-efficient and affordable vehicle. This was not easy to achieve: one engineer described it as like trying to change the car tyres while driving at full speed on a road that is still being built.

Doing better with less

Frugal innovation is not just about "doing more with less" but about "doing better with less", and finding ways to reduce complexity in all aspects of the business. But when done right, companies will find that they are better placed to do the following.

Capture underserved markets at the bottom of the pyramid

In his book, *The Fortune at the Bottom of the Pyramid*, C.K. Prahalad, a management guru, argued that low-income people in developing economies such as India, Africa and Brazil collectively represent a huge, untapped market. But a bottom of the pyramid exists in *developed* economies too, and is not negligible. According to Accenture, a multinational management consulting and services company, low-income Europeans represent a €220 billion ($280 billion) untapped market. Western companies have traditionally ignored them, focusing instead on high-income earners or middle-class consumers. For instance, according to the Federal Deposit Insurance Corporation (FDIC), over 68 million Americans – nearly one-quarter of the US population – have little, if any, access to financial services. Traditional financial institutions are not adequately meeting their unique needs. Yet, according to the Center for Financial Services Innovation (CFSI), underbanked Americans collectively earn around $1 trillion in annual income and represent an untapped market worth nearly $90 billion. With frugal products, they could be reached. As Vianney Mulliez, CEO of Auchan, a French international retail group, puts it:[9] "There are many 'emerging markets' within Western economies that we are eager to serve."

Comply with new regulations, aimed at promoting inclusive growth

Governments in North America and Europe are pushing new measures and regulations that aim to reduce social inequality and promote inclusive growth. In the US, where 50 million citizens lack health insurance, President Obama championed the Affordable Healthcare Act in an effort to rein in health-care costs that are expected to rocket to $4.6 trillion in 2020. By adopting frugal business models, makers of drugs and medical devices and health maintenance organisations (HMOs) could make their products and services more affordable and accessible to more Americans while maintaining the same levels of quality.

Cope with an ageing workforce

According to a 2013 Stanford University study, by 2020 workers aged 55 and older will account for 25% of the US labour force, compared with just 13% in 2000. Meanwhile, more than one-quarter of German and Japanese manufacturing workers will retire by 2020. Large industrial countries will soon have to adopt frugal processes to deal with having a smaller workforce to draw upon.

Attract and retain younger staff

Most young people in the developed world prefer to work in socially and environmentally responsible companies. Frugal innovation can boost staff engagement and productivity. This change is sorely needed. According to Gallup, a US research company, in its 2013 *State of the Global Workplace Report*, only 13% of employees worldwide feel actively engaged at work, implying that at the global level, work is more often a source of frustration than one of fulfilment. In the US, among the 100 million people who have full-time jobs, 50 million people are not engaged and another 20 million are totally disengaged, costing the economy up to $550 billion annually in lost labour and output. This dissatisfaction can, however, be turned around by involving staff in projects that make full use of their talents, skills and ingenuity. According to a 2012 study funded by the John and Catherine T. MacArthur Foundation, workers who are able to make a social or environmental impact on the job are twice as satisfied and motivated as those who are not. This is particularly true of millennials, who are more sceptical of big business and less loyal to their employers compared with earlier generations. Over half of the millennials surveyed by Deloitte, one of the big four professional services firms, believe that innovation and social development, rather than maximising profit and shareholder value, should be the primary purpose of business. Yet the majority also believe that business is collectively most able to solve pressing social problems. Large, frugal companies now have a means to attract this values-conscious generation.

None of this suggests that the transformation will be easy. As they attempt to adopt frugal innovation, Western corporations especially are likely to encounter deeply entrenched thinking and processes. Some of the worst of these include the following.

The pursuit of technology for its own sake

R&D engineers like to push technological boundaries for no particular commercial reason. Many think about innovation in terms of "bigger is better" – more features and newer technology – rather than the purpose their products are meant to serve. Traditionally, large Western firms spend vast sums to achieve this objective. For instance, the world's

1,000 largest corporate R&D spenders (most of which are Western) invested a record $647 billion in R&D in 2014. It is hardly surprising that R&D teams in these companies view complexity as progress, and doing more with less as a step back. Moreover, because of the way budgets are allotted, there is little incentive to think otherwise.

Branding worries

Marketers are concerned that consumers will equate frugal solutions with poor quality. For them, quality must always command a market premium. A product's quality is typically rated according to the number of features, so low-cost products, with fewer features, suggest poor quality. Managers fear that frugal products will damage the corporate brand, and so think in terms of money for value rather than value for money.

The cannibalisation conundrum

Business strategists and sales executives fear that frugal products will eat into their more expensive goods, and even destroy their more profitable product lines. Sales teams typically are urged and incentivised to sell the firm's big-ticket items. Why would, say, medical-device company sales staff, on 5% sales commission, pitch portable, low-cost ECG devices priced at $5,000 to hospitals, when they could sell high-end ECG machines for $100,000?

Market pressures

Board members are concerned that shareholders and analysts will hammer their stock price if they start producing more frugal products and services. Even if senior managers are amenable to a strategic shift, they may be unable to get it past the board. Board members will typically oppose lower-margin products even if sales volumes and profits rise.

Distorted views of sustainability

Western companies rarely take a balanced view of sustainability: it is either something that is "nice to do" or a compliance cost. Frugal innovation marries these two outlooks. It is a source of competitive advantage, but also provides a firm with a licence to operate that is essential for market success. However, changing existing mindsets about sustainability can be a major undertaking.

Unusual frugal competitors

Despite these obstacles, companies do not have the luxury of waiting and watching. Frugal competitors are already in the market.

Rivals from emerging markets

Emerging-market companies are already having an impact on Western markets. Haier, a Chinese home appliance manufacturer, is now a leading supplier to the US of wine coolers, once a premium product for the affluent. Likewise, India's Tata Motors plans to sell its $2,500 Nano car in Europe and the US within a couple of years. Although it will be priced somewhat higher, it will still be the cheapest vehicle in its different markets, and will especially appeal to young adults who cannot afford Western cars, and whose share of the new-car market in the US has already dropped from nearly 38% in 1985 to around 27% today. Moreover, Western versions of Tata cars might also be the most environmentally friendly: Tata Motors has licensed from MDI – a French company that makes eco-friendly, affordable vehicles and power generators – compressed-air engine technology that it plans to integrate into its compact cars.

Digital disrupters

The iPhone 4 contains more technology than the Apollo spacecraft of the 1970s. Facebook has over 1.3 billion monthly active users. This massive computing and communication power literally at everyone's fingertips is spawning a virtual R&D platform that is permanently switched on. Aspiring entrepreneurs, whom Forrester Research refers to as digital disrupters, are now using this nearly free, online R&D platform to innovate faster, better and cheaper, and create affordable products and services that leverage social-media and mobile technologies.[10] In doing so, these start-ups are disrupting the lucrative business models of well-established bricks-and-mortar companies.

For instance, the Khan Academy, founded by Sal Khan, offers

free maths and science courseware as bite-sized videos via YouTube, creating panic among academic publishers who charge a fortune for textbooks. Or take Plastyc, a start-up that claims to put the "power of a bank in your cell phone" by providing affordable 24-hour access to FDIC-insured virtual bank accounts that can be accessed from any internet-enabled computer or mobile device. These accounts are tied to prepaid Visa cards; consumers cannot go overdrawn and they incur no late fees. Plastyc's low-fee, no-frills, online banking services are appealing to the nearly 70 million underbanked, or unbanked, Americans who cannot afford to pay large bank fees. And in the sharing economy, firms such as Airbnb (sharing homes), RelayRides (sharing cars) and ParkatmyHouse (sharing parking spaces) are taking advantage of the internet and social media to enable ordinary people to monetise their idle household assets. Many of these disruptive digital ventures are being launched by millennials (popularly known as generation recession), who can raise capital on crowdfunding sites such as Kickstarter, KissKissBankBank and MedStartr.

Digital disrupters are not all young bootstrap entrepreneurs. Technology heavyweights including Apple, Google, Cisco and IBM are investing heavily in driverless cars, smart grids, connected homes and consumer medical devices. A massive shakeout in the automotive, construction, energy, health-care and other mature industries seems imminent. When asked who her company's main competitor would be in five years' time, a senior executive at a large US industrial firm answered: "Google."

Ingenious "prosumers"

Deterred by high prices for commercial products and services, and empowered by new tools, many Western consumers are becoming "prosumers"; that is, producing the goods and services they need themselves, thereby unleashing a DIY revolution. In *Jugaad Innovation* several ingenious emerging-market "MacGyvers" (named after a US TV character known for his improvisational skills) were profiled. These are small entrepreneurs who find frugal solutions to meet local community needs. This bottom-up innovation phenomenon is now taking root in the US and Europe.

When his daughter Lily was born, Rupert Plumridge was reluctant to invest in a $300 branded video baby monitor. So he built his own, using Google Android devices, a night-vision webcam and open-source platforms. His DIY invention cost $80. Thousands of Europeans and Americans are also rolling up their sleeves and building products in their kitchens. In his book *Makers*, Chris Anderson, a former editor of *Wired*, chronicles this MacGyverisation of the US economy, which is taking root thanks to the proliferation of such inventions as 3D printers and events such as the Maker Faire which celebrate the DIY ingenuity of ordinary people. Michael Bloomberg, a former New York mayor, has designated the last week in September as the city's "Maker Week".

Big-box retailers

Walmart, a US multinational retail corporation, is rapidly becoming a leading provider of affordable financial services. It has opened hundreds of Walmart Money Centers across the US to serve the basic financial needs of low-income consumers. Similarly, Costco, a US membership-only warehouse club, is now selling private-label medical devices at a fraction of the cost of branded products. Costco's hearing aid is priced at $500, one-quarter of the cost of the branded competitor, and is an especially attractive option for retiring baby-boomers who lost out in the financial crisis.

Conclusion

Having addressed the "what" and "why" of frugal innovation, let us now turn to the "how" and begin with the first of our six principles: engage and iterate.

2 Principle one: engage and iterate

A customer is the most important visitor on our premises. He is not dependent on us. We are dependent on him. He is not an interruption in our work. He is the purpose of it. He is not an outsider in our business. He is part of it. We are not doing him a favour by serving him. He is doing us a favour by giving us an opportunity to do so.

Mahatma Gandhi

IN 1983, SCOTT COOK, who had worked in marketing at Procter & Gamble, a multinational consumer-products company, co-founded Intuit, a start-up that aimed to replace paper-and-pencil personal accounting with software applications that could run on personal computers. Cook was inspired to launch the applications after hearing his wife complain about the hassle of tracking and settling household bills. But he did not immediately get started on a solution. Instead, he first investigated the challenges that others faced with their finances. Cook's sister-in-law helped him conduct hundreds of phone surveys. These customer insights enabled him to design Intuit's first product, Quicken, an affordable, easy-to-use, computer-based personal-finance program, which was launched in 1984.

At that time, there were 46 rival software products already in the market, but all were complex to use. Cook chose not to compete on technological features, but focused on ease of use. In many ways Quicken's main rival was the pencil. Rather than create and meet new needs, Cook wanted to address a well-defined existing need to reduce the hassle of book-keeping. He wanted to offer a simple solution whose value lay in saving precious time by getting things done quickly (hence the product's name). Quicken was designed with a familiar, cheque-book style interface, and its intuitive features were easy even for novice computer users. To demonstrate this, Cook recruited the Palo Alto Junior League to be Intuit's first beta testers. With its affordable price, Quicken became a runaway bestseller: within two years of its launch it had risen from 47th in the personal-finance software market to first.

But Cook did not stop there. He knew that customers' needs are never static and that his products needed to keep evolving if they were to remain relevant. So he came up with an ingenious idea to keep track of their changing requirements and identify unmet needs. He began hanging out at Staples office-supplies stores, and offered to go home with customers to observe how they actually used the software. The goal of this "follow me home" strategy was to identify the challenges that customers faced in installing and using Quicken and find ways to improve their experience.

Today Intuit has annual revenues of $4 billion and its market capitalisation is more than $23 billion. Under CEO Brad Smith's leadership the company has accelerated its innovation efforts and has been called a 30-year-old startup.[1] The company still uses its "follow me home" approach in developing and improving its products; Intuit's employees conduct more than 10,000 hours of follow-me-homes annually. Thirty years later this customer-driven innovation is still how Intuit uncovers important and unsolved problems. Intuit rallies its employees around the mantra "fall in love with the problem, not the solution". CEO Brad Smith says:

> *If you never lose sight of the customer problem, how you attack the solution can remain more flexible and iterative and ultimately be more likely to succeed.[2]*

The company has also pioneered a method, which it calls Design for Delight, to create better ways to deliver what's most important to customers. Design for Delight encompasses deep customer empathy, going broad with ideas before narrowing and rapid iteration with customers or prospects. These customer interactions can be humbling experiences. It is sometimes demoralising to discover, for example, that the product you have spent so much time developing leaves customers cold, and that the features your R&D team feels most proud of are of little value to users. But these interactions can also be enriching. To identify customers' real challenges, and then develop the right solutions, can be inspiring and motivating. Intuit's formula for success, according to Cook, who is still active at the company and chairman of the executive committee, is:[3]

Both the engineering and business sides infused the same principles into product development. When we design and build products, we start with, and focus on, the customer.

Cook is a frugal innovator. Specifically, he is frugal in his focus. Rather than dispersing his energies (and his fledging firm's limited resources) in solving many big problems, he channelled all his efforts into solving a single, well-defined problem: making personal finance less tedious. He gained that laser-like focus not by sitting in an insulated R&D lab, but by engaging with real-life customers in their natural settings to identify their actual needs. He also kept honing that focus by continually iterating the design of his software to match his customers' evolving needs. As Tom Peters, a management guru, says:[4] "Excellent firms don't believe in excellence – only in constant improvement and constant change." Intuit has become excellent because its innovation model is based not on pushing new technologies onto customers, but on starting with customer insights, and looking for ways to solve their actual problems. This is the engage and iterate (E&I) principle.

E&I is the first and perhaps most critical of the six principles of frugal innovation. This is mainly because it aims to bring greater value to customers and does so in a continually evolving, iterative manner. As this chapter argues, there is no better way to create value. It shows how firms in the developed world can unlearn the insular and costly R&D practices that have been built on long and linear development cycles with little, or at best arm's length, customer involvement. Specifically, it shows how companies can make their innovation process frugal with more market-focused, cost-effective and agile R&D activities, saving precious time in the process. It also discusses new techniques to keep customers engaged at every stage of the product or service life cycle. In short, shifting from "technology push" to dynamic "market pull" can help firms innovate faster, better and cheaper.

A costly and rigid R&D model

During the 20th century, large corporations such as General Motors (GM), General Electric (GE) and AT&T invested huge sums in R&D labs that aimed to industrialise the innovation process. These labs hired thousands of engineers and scientists charged with pushing technological boundaries in order to invent "the next big thing". These firms' sector dominance allowed them to push their new products and services onto relatively passive customers. They employed large sales forces and spent heavily on mass marketing, especially TV and print media, to stimulate demand. Successful as this model was for decades, its useful life is ending. The industrial R&D model, based on big science and technology push, is increasingly maladapted to the 21st century's fast-paced digital economy. In a world of growing financial constraints, resource scarcity and increased competition, involving highly empowered, cost-conscious and eco-aware customers, there are several reasons why the industrial R&D model is losing its effectiveness.

High investment for low value

According to Booz & Company (now Strategy&), the world's top 1,000 corporate R&D spenders invested a staggering $647 billion in R&D in 2014 alone.[5] Although 90% of this occurs in the world's most technologically advanced markets – North America, Europe and Japan – many Western firms struggle to generate commercially successful innovations. In the consumer-products sector, for example, 80% of new products fail at launch. In the global life-sciences industry, the cost of developing a new drug rose by 18% between 2010 and 2013, to $1.3 billion. As a result, biopharmaceutical firms expect to boost R&D spending by 3% to $201 billion in 2014. And yet, according to Oliver Wyman, a management consultancy, the value generated by pharmaceutical R&D investments has fallen by more than 70% in recent years. A 2011 Oliver Wyman report shows that the industry generated only $75 million in fifth-year sales for every $1 billion it spent on R&D.[6] And returns on R&D investment keep falling: from 10.5% in 2010 to 4.8% in 2013. The reasons for this include more late-stage trial failures – costing the top 12 life-science companies $243 billion between 2010 and 2013 – and more "me too" drugs that fail to stand out in a super-competitive market. As Jerry Cacciotti, a partner at Oliver Wyman, puts it:[7]

> Most [drug companies] have maintained strong net income levels. But ... in the activity that counts the most – bringing valuable new drugs to market – the industry is in worse shape than has been publicly acknowledged.

Time-consuming and inflexible R&D

Big-ticket R&D projects in asset-intensive industries such as pharmaceuticals, semiconductors, aerospace and automotive have long development cycles. It can take up to 15 years to develop a new drug, over five years to design and build a new aircraft, and three years on average to conceive of and launch a car. This is because of linear and sequential R&D processes that fail to collaborate across business functions. Unfortunately, the longer a company takes to develop a new product, the more money it wastes. Worse, a launch delay can mean missing an all-too-brief market opportunity. Moreover, inflexible processes are unable to accommodate changing customer requirements, further undermining the value of a new product. For example, the CEO of a large European industrial conglomerate noted how his company lost a government contract to build public-transport systems because its R&D engineers took too long to develop a solution. As it was several months late and hundreds of millions over budget, the government cancelled the deal.

Rewarding innovation quantity over quality

Cacciotti says of the pharmaceutical sector: "Now that the industry has clearly entered a different era (of austerity), R&D needs a new mindset for drug development." His view applies to most industries in the

US, Europe and Japan. Firms must fundamentally rethink how they perceive, measure and value innovation. Today's R&D functions are typically measured by, and rewarded for, the quantity of their inputs (that is, R&D spending) and outputs (number of patents and new product features), rather than the quality of these inputs (customer insights) and outputs (customer value). However, a company's success does not depend on how much it spends on R&D but how well it uses its R&D investments. As Barry Jaruzelski, a senior partner at Strategy&, says:[8] "When it comes to innovation, *how* you spend is much more important than how much you spend."

Complex, expensive and environmentally unfriendly products

R&D engineers in the developed world are trained to associate complexity with quality. They seek to push scientific and technological boundaries by designing sophisticated products with complex features and functions that customers do not really need. For instance, most people only use 10% of functionality in feature-rich productivity apps such as Microsoft Word, and 90% of customers use merely 10–15% of features in computer networking devices. This complexity costs both companies and their customers dearly, because over 70% of a product's total life-cycle costs result from R&D design decisions. The more complex its design, the more costly it is to build, sell and service a product. This in turn makes the product more expensive for the customer to buy, use and maintain.

Furthermore, products are designed with planned obsolescence, forcing customers continually to upgrade – an expensive proposition at best. Mobile phones, for instance, are designed to make them hard to disassemble. This complexity and planned obsolescence is a cost to customers and increases environmental waste. Cramming cars with more microchips, for instance, makes them heavier and less fuel efficient. Similarly, American consumers typically replace their mobile phones every two years, which may cheer up Apple and mobile operators, but 125 million obsolete phones end up in landfills every year as a result.

Alienating customers

Ask the CEOs of North American, European or Japanese corporations if their companies engage customers, and most will emphatically respond with a loud "yes", and point to the vast sums they spend on marketing and social-media campaigns. And yet customers rarely feel engaged with these companies or their products. According to a 2013 survey by NetBase, a social-media analytics company, 93% of customers consider marketing ads (across all media channels) disingenuous. They also feel that, far from engaging customers and genuinely trying to understand their needs, companies are simply pushing products their way. Furthermore, over 80% of customers say they are more likely to buy products and services from brands that actively listen to them and design products with their input; and 32% have no idea that brands are even listening to them.

To be fair, business-to-consumer (B2C) companies in the advanced economies do commission market surveys and focus groups in an attempt to listen and identify market needs. Unfortunately, these traditional market-research tools are often ineffective. Christine Overby, a vice-president at Forrester Research, notes damningly that they are "too biased, too expensive, too slow, too imprecise, and often misdirected". Market surveys that, for instance, ask customers about their interest in new products can get unhelpful responses, since the questions are asked out of context and do not take adequate account of where and how these products will be bought and used. For example, based on initial market surveys, Kimberly-Clark, a US personal care company, spent $100 million developing pre-moistened wipes on a roll. But the product, Cottonelle Fresh Rollwipes, failed at launch because customers found the wipes impractical. Concept testing is another expensive but misleading technique since it asks customers to validate an existing product idea, rather than discover unmet needs for a potential product. As Arun Prabhu, innovation and insights director at Lion Dairy & Drinks, Australasia's leading food and beverage company, puts it:[9]

> *Concept testing is a waste of time and money. Why are you asking consumers to make your product decisions for you? Don't you, as the marketing manager, have the experience to make that decision*

yourself? You shouldn't be seeking customers' approval of how clever you are. Instead, you should be trying to get under their skin to identify their real needs and using those insights to co-create new solutions with them.

In business-to-business (B2B) sectors, companies may not use focus groups but rely instead on their sales and customer-service departments to identify new market needs. And yet personnel in these departments are not trained and encouraged to "pull" new requirements from customers but rather to use every customer interaction to "push" more products and services onto them. And when they do gain crucial customer insights, this information often fails to get to the R&D team in a timely and actionable way because of the disconnected nature of large firms' departments. Or, even when such information is readily available, the R&D team may not trust or value it because it comes from the field, or because the team lacks the incentives or tools to act swiftly on the insights by, say, quickly redesigning an existing product.

In sum, it is no surprise that the industrial R&D model, which sustained firms' growth during the 20th century by pushing ever more complex and expensive technology-led innovation onto customers, is beginning to crumble in the 21st century. The growth of new market forces – cost-conscious and eco-aware consumers and agile competitors – is rapidly exposing the shortcomings of the old system. It is increasingly too costly, too resource intensive and, most importantly, too disconnected from market realities and customer needs. To systematically design and launch affordable, eco-friendly solutions of value to customers at lower cost, companies must rebuild their R&D engine so they can innovate faster, better and cheaper. What firms need is a market-focused, agile R&D model.

A market-focused, agile R&D model

As outlined above, the industrial R&D model has at least three inherent weaknesses:

■ It is market-blind and excludes customers from the innovation process.

- It relies on time-consuming and rigid development processes.
- It values perfect solutions above general usefulness.

To overcome these weaknesses – and become the core enabler of frugal innovation within corporations – the R&D function must cultivate several new capabilities.

Engage customers throughout product and customer life cycles

Rather than relying on second-hand market data or on the outcomes of others' focus groups, engineers and scientists must engage directly with customers, specifically in their natural settings – their homes, factories and offices – to unearth new or unmet needs. As well as engaging existing customers, R&D teams should interact with users in new market segments by actively involving customers in new product design processes, as well as tracking customers' use of the product after purchase. The focus on customer needs will enable R&D to replace its costly and scattershot approach to product development with more efficient, user-focused investment.

Adapt rapidly to unexpected changes

In today's unpredictable business environment, customers' requirements are constantly changing and new competition is emerging seemingly from nowhere, as are new technologies and market opportunities. R&D teams, and their rigid, time-consuming design and development processes, are ill-equipped to deal with the unexpected. But by adopting dynamic portfolio management techniques and agile design processes, they can re-prioritise projects and re-allocate resources frequently, and therefore better anticipate and respond to market shifts. With faster innovation and improvisation, a new, nimble approach will also help firms to constantly improve existing solutions as well as develop new solutions.

Seek cheaper, good-enough solutions

R&D teams too often reinvent the wheel and end up with over-engineered products (at great cost to the firm) that are too complex for customers. Customers, however, are more likely to be impressed by products that solve their problems than by mere technological prowess. R&D should be guided first and foremost by customer insight, and produce easy-to-use offerings that may lack bells and whistles but are good enough, especially if they come at a lower price. Moreover, the good-enough approach will be simpler and cheaper for companies too, to say nothing of lessening the environmental impact.

This is not an easy transition to make. Companies will need to reorganise their entire innovation process at both the front end – where market opportunities are identified and products are conceived, funded and tested – and the back end, where promising ideas are developed and tested in the market. According to 2013 research by Booz & Company, the developed world's largest R&D spenders tend to underinvest in the front end (often seen as a fuzzy art) and spend too much time, effort and money on the more structured, measurable back end of the innovation process. As a result, big companies have become highly efficient at executing the *wrong* ideas faster, better and cheaper, and launching products that customers neither want nor need.

Companies must first recognise the strategic nature of the front end of their innovation process. Decisions made at this stage can hugely influence the overall cost and speed of developing and marketing new products over their life cycle. This part of the process can also be managed methodically, and customers can be engaged systematically.

Involve customers from the outset

Actively engaging customers at the front end of innovation is likely to result in products that they prefer, thus increasing their loyalty while reducing product cycle times and waste. Yet the Booz study estimates that only 8% of large R&D budgets are spent on digital tools that, among other things, track changing customer needs and help firms work with customers to create solutions.[10] It is an obvious way to improve front-end innovation performance and, thanks to plummeting technology costs, affordable digital tools and techniques now exist to improve the depth and breadth of customer engagement.

Deploy crowdsourcing and social media

Crowdsourcing is a cost-effective technique for collecting customers' ideas and ascertaining specific, explicit needs. For instance, SoapBox, a Toronto-based online crowdsourcing site, provides companies with a platform for individuals to talk about their ideas and gauge initial public reactions through its thumbs-up or thumbs-down voting system. Ideas that garner sufficient support are packaged with supporting data and sent to the relevant managers, who in turn signal their view of its potential to executives responsible for taking such ideas forward.

Cisco, a multinational networking equipment designer and manufacturer, has used SoapBox for its Smart + Connected Communities project to identify citizens' most prevalent problems and help municipal leaders understand and respond to their constituents' most pressing needs. Meanwhile, GSK Canada, a pharmaceutical and consumer health-care company, has used SoapBox to support an internal idea-generation initiative to improve health care. The tool has also given employees a way to voice their concerns to senior management.

Social-media networks, where customers reveal and share preferences, can also yield a wealth of market insights. For instance, FGI Research's SmartScan uses social-media mining to help firms understand their consumers better. SmartScan collects user-generated content from news, blogs and social-networking sites, such as Facebook, Twitter and YouTube, and uses it to "pinpoint unmet needs, previously unknown problems, and areas that require deeper research" and "discover reactions to newly launched products, price points, marketing campaigns, or business decisions".

Use immersion techniques to identify latent needs

In many cases, customers may be unaware of what they want or unable to articulate their needs. Companies like Intuit can study customers in their natural settings to unearth these latent needs. Such ethnographic research enables R&D teams to pinpoint customers' "pain points" and design solutions that are most relevant for each situation. For instance, in Japan, two Fujitsu R&D engineers, Tomihiro Yamazaki and Daisuke

Kawai, got their hands (and feet) dirty by working closely with mandarin farmers at Sawa Orchards in Wakayama. They spent days in the field, sharing agricultural tasks with farmers. Their aim was to find ways to increase mandarin yields. Japan's agricultural workforce is ageing (currently averaging 65), so Fujitsu decided to investigate how technologies such as mobile phones and wireless sensors could raise productivity and output, and capture farmers' tacit knowledge of agricultural practices to pass on to future generations.[11]

Things started badly for the two engineers. They undertook backbreaking manual labour and were unable to understand the technical terms used by the farmers. But after several weeks they began to empathise with the farmers. They saw that the existing technology was too complex and ill-suited to the real-life operating environment. For example, farmers wearing thick gloves could not operate smartphones; they could not see the screen when it was sunny; and the non-waterproof phones were useless when it rained. As Yamazaki recalls:

> I was always tired when I got home after working on the farm all day. I figured that farmers would hate having to spend another 10 or 20 minutes doing data entry when they got home from work.

Moreover, farmers used indicators that were often hard to quantify when carrying out certain tasks. "They base their decisions on things like the softness of the soil or the colour of the leaves," said Yamazaki. The farmers relied on paper to plan everything, including when and where to plant crops and how much water to use. These decisions could directly affect both the quantity and taste of the mandarins produced.

Armed with these insights and their first-hand experience, Yamazaki and Kawai created an easy-to-use decision-support system that relies on accurate data collected regularly from multiple sources, including sensors, on the temperature, precipitation and soil moisture levels across Sawa Orchards. The data are cross-referenced with the producer's observational records. Farmers are then advised how much water to use and for how long certain agricultural tasks must be performed. The system calculates the actual cost of producing mandarins, which in turn helps the farmers price their fruit more accurately. It also collects the intuition and knowledge of experienced farm workers so that this can be shared with future generations.

Using the same amount of labour, Sawa Orchards significantly increased output while also optimising the use of water in accordance with the season. Most importantly, the mandarins tasted better. Yamazaki and Kawai became convinced that only by immersing themselves in the environment were they able to fully appreciate the problems and, with the farmers, develop an easy-to-use solution.

Of course, R&D teams are not always required to undergo 14-hour days of backbreaking work to feel their customers' pain. Sometimes new tools and technologies let them experience their customers' challenges from a distance. For example, Cambridge University's Inclusive Design team has developed remarkable tools for this purpose, including glasses that replicate the vision of the visually impaired, and heavy gloves that reproduce the difficulties that arthritic customers experience when handling everyday tools such as can openers.

Share prototypes with end-users

Rather than develop over-engineered products in their ivory tower, R&D teams can now quickly design good-enough prototypes that they can share with customers, and then adapt them based on early customer feedback.

New digital tools enable interactive prototyping to take place online, thereby increasing the reach and reducing the cost and time of engagement efforts. For instance, Affinnova, an online market research company, uses a technology platform powered by optimisation algorithms and predictive analytics to help companies iteratively improve designs by drawing on online customer feedback and validation. Specifically, the company's IDDEA (Interactive Discovery & Design by Evolutionary Algorithms) is a quantitative method that generates and presents a number of design options to customers. They indicate their preferences, which are then used to generate new designs via a computer program exploiting a genetic or evolutionary computational technique. The process can be repeated rapidly for as many cycles as needed. Affinnova's digital tools are used by well-known brands such as Procter & Gamble, Nestlé and Unilever.

Not all product categories lend themselves to online discussion. Often high-quality customer engagement needs to happen in the physical world. Customer immersion labs – such as the customer demonstration lab at Caterpillar, a US construction and mining equipment manufacturer – invite customers to play with new prototypes or models and give instant feedback directly to R&D teams. Unlike concept testing, which requires people explicitly to articulate to researchers what they need and want, immersion labs allow researchers to observe customers as they play with prototypes and infer what needs to be done to improve product design and the user experience.

Make use of big data analytics

Consumer and industrial products of all kinds are increasingly connected to the internet. Mobile phones and the Internet of Things (identifiers for different physical objects) allow researchers to collect large amounts of detailed data to predict customer needs and respond with tailored solutions.

This approach, called predictive analytics, has particular power in industrial contexts. Philips Lighting, which produces commercial lighting systems for large installations, provides a good example of its capabilities. The company fits (with the customer's permission) each light fixture with sensor switches and motion detectors that gather data, such as hours used and dimming levels, and sends it back to a central information system. Bob Esmeijer, head of Philips Professional Lighting Solutions, comments:[12]

> Eventually, we will be able to use that information to develop lights that do the work themselves – that can sense the amount of light coming in from outside and how much activity is in the room, and adapt accordingly.

Predictive analytics can also assist service companies in anticipating and mitigating risks. For instance, Aetna, one of the world's leading health insurers, and Newtopia, a personalised health coaching provider, are piloting a system that uses an individual's unique genetic profile to assess their health risks, such as metabolic syndrome, that can lead to diabetes, stroke, or coronary heart disease.

Based on this assessment, the individual is offered personalised advice to help reduce those risk factors. Similarly, mobile network operators use Alteryx's predictive analytics tool to identify high-value customers with high attrition risk and take proactive marketing steps to fulfil their unmet needs and retain them.

In sum, companies have numerous ways in which they can engage customers in the R&D process in a systematic manner to identify market needs. But although it is crucial to engage customers early on, this is not by itself sufficient to ensure that companies can come up with faster, better and cheaper solutions. To do that, companies must also revamp the back end, or execution stage, of their innovation processes.

Back-end innovation: improving execution agility

Like a convoy, the front end and back end of innovation must move at a similar pace. Unfortunately, the back end of innovation in firms often fails to keep up, and R&D needs tools to help it on its way. Specifically, R&D's focus must shift from the pursuit of efficiency to a quest for greater flexibility. Firms can achieve greater back-end agility in a number of ways.

Use dynamic portfolio management tools

Given their limited resources, R&D teams can benefit from using portfolio management tools to identify and prioritise product ideas that deserve the most attention and funding at different times. As markets change, the R&D project portfolio needs to be continually managed, allocating resources according to which projects are most relevant to customers at any particular time. This even applies in science-driven industries such as chemicals and pharmaceuticals. DuPont, a US chemical company, takes this market validation process a step further. As part of its "market-driven" innovation process, the company's long-term scientific research projects are reviewed regularly by business-unit leaders, who reshuffle priorities for potential applications and alter the project scope to reflect new market realities.

Use just-in-time design

Rather than over-engineering products with just-in-case features, companies should adopt just-in-time design. This starts with a good-enough product and incrementally adds new features based on customer feedback in a just-in-time fashion. Approaches such as agile development methodology and lean start-up, which teach companies how to fail fast, fail early and fail cheaply, can enable such just-in-time design in large firms with big R&D teams.[13]

Beware supply chain constraints

Delays and cost escalation in innovation projects often occur because R&D teams design products without considering supply chain capabilities. As a result, new products are often designed using components that are hard to find, too costly, or too complex to manufacture and maintain. These supply chain realities then send R&D teams back to the drawing board to redesign the original product. But by using supply chain visibility tools that reveal important procurement, manufacturing and maintenance requirements, R&D teams can design products that can be brought to market faster, better and cheaper – and serviced cost-effectively.

Ultimately, better front-end and back-end processes must fuse into a single, well-integrated system. This in turn will enable a nimble R&D team to systematically engage customers. But for this to happen, companies also need a market-focused business strategy and a business model that can be fully integrated with R&D initiatives. Companies cannot transform R&D without regard to the rest of the company, and this is where the CEO must implement fundamental change across the entire organisation.

Recommendations for managers

Chief executives and senior managers have an important role to play in making the entire company more agile and market-focused. In particular, relations between R&D and other business functions, such as sales and marketing, business development and operations, must be carefully managed. In B2B industries, R&D managers might lead the changes. In other sectors, such as B2C industries, customer-facing departments such as marketing may champion these initiatives, alongside R&D colleagues. The following guidelines can help senior managers promote the E&I process within their firms.

Align R&D strategy with corporate strategy

A firm's R&D strategy reflects its corporate strategy, and CEOs should make sure that the two are aligned. When Andrew Witty took over as CEO of GlaxoSmithKline (GSK) in 2008, he was concerned about ballooning budgets, long time frames and exposure to change and risk. So he led a comprehensive review of the firm's R&D strategy, structure and culture. First, he shifted attention away from the industry's obsession with creating blockbuster drugs. He urged his researchers to look for "many more potential drugs, both small and large", to build the firm a more reliable pipeline. Second, he moved the firm from its developed-world prescription-drug focus, and encouraged a more diversified revenue stream, in particular in emerging markets, which hitherto had been viewed more as charity than business. Third, he demanded that the company work more closely with customers such as the UK's NHS and the US's pharmacy-benefit managers and insurers, asking them what products they would be willing to pay for in the future. Lastly, he restructured GSK's R&D division to focus on customers and diseases, rather than on products and suppliers, giving researchers more freedom to innovate.

As Stephen Mayhew, GSK's head of R&D strategy development, describes it:[14]

> *The idea was to look more closely at R&D processes and the operating model. The focus was not so much on the product portfolio but more about how to organise, what processes and tools to put in place to create value, and how to increase the firm's ability to be flexible from a corporate allocation of capital perspective.*

Break up big-ticket R&D programmes

A focused R&D strategy does not mean investing in just one big project. Indeed, from a financial risk management perspective, it may be more prudent to invest in several promising smaller projects that can eventually be tapered rather than focusing all corporate R&D investment on a few big-ticket projects with high pay-off but high risk.

For example, Witty sought to turn GSK's drug-discovery efforts into "a nimble fleet of destroyers, rather than two or three vulnerable battleships", reducing the firm's exposure to "sudden torpedoes" like lawsuits and regulatory crackdowns. Mayhew describes the process:

> The discovery business in GSK now constitutes about 40 biotech-like entities. Each unit is based around a particular scientific problem as opposed to having a single department that looks at everything. The intent is to flexibly move in and out of new areas of science. If an area of science looks like it will flourish, then we can increase the investment. If it doesn't hold promise for a particular therapeutic use, we can close that unit down and redeploy those people in other units. In this way, we avoid making large, fixed infrastructure investments. Instead, we seed across a number of business opportunities and areas of science such that we get to an inflexion point and build out our investment once we have the confidence to do so.

Break out of silos and reduce bureaucracy

The old industrial model of R&D thrives on the existence of large specialised teams working separately: R&D, business development, marketing and sales are all different functions, each with their own incentives, culture and values. Such a set-up prevents effective and agile innovation. As the CEO of the French subsidiary of a US multinational laments:

> Even after our global CEO has approved a highly promising product project, we still need over 60 sign-offs from various functions to implement this new idea.

Since over 70% of a product's total development costs are determined by R&D's design decisions, researchers must find ways to collaborate with their supply chain and marketing partners, rapidly redesigning offerings to accommodate time-to-market and budget constraints. When Whirlpool, a multinational home-appliances provider, launches a new R&D project, it simultaneously configures the global supply network to build and deliver the innovative goods.

Perhaps the best way to encourage cross-functional integration is to create smaller, more networked teams. Again, GSK provides a useful example. Worried that the firm's R&D culture resembled that of a police state, Witty led a cultural transformation away from an excessively regimented approach towards a simpler culture that trusts staff to do the right thing. This transformation was supported by R&D's new structure. Mayhew notes:

> An industrial approach to drug discovery and development was all about putting as much volume of science through the system as possible and seeing what came out at the other end ... In the smaller, more networked model, there is a greater opportunity for spontaneous interactions to bring different disciplines together, as well as to use incentives and rewards to drive innovative behaviour from an organisational perspective.

Similarly, Paul Cornillon, senior vice-president of R&D at Arla Foods, recalls:[15]

> R&D used to be very much a service function within the firm. But now we have transformed it into being more of a business partner. We have brought marketing into R&D. Two to three marketers now work on long-term initiatives that are not affected by the P&L but are based on consumer needs. This helps us to remember that the consumer is always king. Increasingly we try to keep this perspective in mind even with technical stuff.

In 2004, Jørgen Vig Knudstorp, chief executive of Lego Group, a Danish toy manufacturer, created a cross-functional team (called the executive innovation governance group) to lead the company's innovation activities. It formulated innovation strategy, selected the product portfolio and co-ordinated efforts across groups, delegating authority, allocating resources and evaluating results to make sure they supported company strategy. As a result, Lego's managers considered not only new products but also pricing plans, business processes and channels to market.

Integrate technical and business design

A specific form of cross-functional integration that is crucial to innovation is that between technical and business design. As Matt Bross, former chief technology officer at BT, a British multinational telecommunications company, noted:[16] "There are no breakthrough technologies, only breakthrough market applications." R&D's inventions, ground-breaking or otherwise, which are not backed by sound business models, are more likely to be axed by growth-seeking business leaders.

To turn sceptical senior managers into sponsors, R&D teams must hone their business-development skills to quantify their invention's market value and offer a profitable go-to-market strategy. For instance, the R&D teams at companies like Yahoo!, Google and Microsoft have all included microeconomists to help design business models, pricing strategies and alliances for disruptive innovations. And with the rise of emerging economies like India, China and Brazil, R&D solutions should be fine-tuned to meet the unique market conditions and customer needs in different regions. For instance, at PepsiCo, a multinational food and beverage corporation, the R&D team is deeply attuned to the business needs of its different geographical areas, having set up regionally focused R&D centres of excellence in China, Mexico and the US. At each, it develops products that are created specifically for the tastes and needs of consumers in that region.

No business model is set in stone. Every model needs to be fine-tuned continuously, based on ever-changing customer requirements and market conditions. And R&D initiatives need to mirror these business model changes. Integrating R&D with business development and design can help achieve these important objectives.

Change the incentive system

In many large organisations, R&D personnel are not trained or encouraged to engage the customer. Their training is typically science-oriented and their interests lie in technology, not markets. Thus any attempt to alter this outlook is likely to face resistance, and even risks alienating valuable scientific personnel. For instance, a market-based approach might seem too commercialised and suggest that the firm lacks technical ambition. Attempts to shift R&D away from its technology culture must be aided by new measurements and key performance indicators (KPIs). Just as high-tech start-ups use stock options to align the work of scientific staff with the firm's financial performance, so too large firms can link R&D staff bonuses to market breakthroughs rather than just scientific discoveries. Large firms should also consider measuring R&D performance based on speed to market and customer value. Lastly, incentives should encourage cross-functional collaboration, something GSK's Witty has attempted by rewarding R&D personnel for drugs that get Food and Drug Administration (FDA) approval and sell well.

Create new roles and titles for customer engagement

A powerful way to change entrenched behaviour is to create new roles and titles that focus explicitly on customer engagement. This can be done with either existing or new personnel who are placed in important positions within R&D where they can effect change. Firms can also build new, multi-skilled teams to help change existing practices within R&D. This might involve building teams with both marketing and technical skills to reduce traditional barriers between R&D, sales and customers. It may not even be necessary for all R&D personnel to change or take on a more customer-focused role: just having one in five in an R&D team being more customer-focused might be enough. For example, IBM, a US multinational technology and consulting corporation, set up its On Demand Innovation Services (ODIS) in 2004 to improve the connection between its labs and its service clients. ODIS draws on over 3,000 experts within IBM Research who work closely with clients to devise tailored business solutions. Since ODIS's inception, hundreds of IBM clients have benefited.

Customer-engagement personnel could also draw important insights from potential customers in other sectors, regions or markets. Scouts can play a valuable role by seeking out ideas from other markets. Lastly, by changing roles and titles, a firm can signal and legitimise these changes in values, so that rather than rejecting ideas as "not invented here" they celebrate ideas "proudly found elsewhere".

Create global R&D networks

If it proves too hard to begin the frugal transformation process in established, Western R&D labs, firms might find it easier to get the ball rolling in their emerging-market subsidiaries. Emerging markets, being new to R&D, have the advantage of starting afresh (rather than being weighed down by corporate convention), and are used to working in changeable markets and with fewer resources. Many large developed-world companies have already established R&D labs in India, China, Brazil and Africa, and are even making these labs global centres for frugal innovation. Some firms are now moving to the next phase in the process and integrating these frugal innovation hubs with their developed-world R&D centres, so their market insights and ideas now flow to developed markets too.

In the automotive sector, Renault-Nissan is using its Indian operations to learn about frugal engineering and applies the ideas across the firm's chain of R&D operations including in France and Japan. In food and agribusiness, PepsiCo has located its Global Value Innovation Centre in India with the aim of spreading disruptive innovation around the world. In health care, GE is creating a whole new generation of affordable medical devices in its Indian and Chinese R&D centres for sale not just locally but in western markets too. Furthermore, GE Healthcare has changed its global structure. Previously managed in Europe, the US and Japan, with emerging economies as sub-regions, the firm now has six equal regions that include India and China, each with a CEO who reports to the global GE CEO. By giving emerging markets a louder voice in global decision-making, the company is effectively globalising the frugal approach.

Seek inspiration from start-ups

Large firms across sectors often find it hard to respond to new-market opportunities quickly and cheaply. As Jacob de Geer, founder of iZettle, a Swedish start-up that offers a payments service in Europe and Latin America, puts it:[17] "Innovation isn't part of their DNA. Banks and carriers have focused on creating solutions for problems that don't exist." Start-ups, however, lacking legacy issues and hungry to make their mark, typically have no such difficulty.

Just as large corporations can look to emerging markets for a way to do frugal innovation, they can also get inspiration from start-ups in their home markets. As Beth Comstock, chief marketing officer at GE, a multinational conglomerate, puts it:[18]

> We're constantly tinkering with our business models to get leaner and more agile and to get closer to our customers – to act small even though we're big.

Comstock believes that GE has learned four main lessons from start-ups:

- Keep things simple. Although GE may seem complicated from the outside, its laser-like focus on its core activity – technology – gives the company a unified sense of purpose.
- Work fast. GE has drawn on the lean start-up ethos to develop FastWorks, a set of tools and principles to help the firm do things more quickly and efficiently (see Chapter 7).
- Find solutions through multiple partnerships and ask the wider community when the firm lacks relevant expertise.
- Don't be afraid of uncertainty. Many GE start-ups did not turn out as originally planned, but were useful nonetheless. The Durathon battery, for example, marketed today as a green back-up power source for mobile phone towers, started life as a hybrid locomotive battery.

CASE STUDY 1

SNCF: high-speed innovation[19]

In 2008, SNCF, France's national railway company, faced a massive challenge: European passenger railways were due to be liberalised in 2010, and the company's French monopoly on domestic and European routes was about to end.

Over decades, the company had built a global reputation for technical innovation. Its R&D engineers were famous for developing increasingly sophisticated high-speed trains, such as the Train à Grande Vitesse (TGV), which set a new world speed record of 574.8 kilometres per hour. In 2008, however,

SNCF's leaders recognised that producing ever-faster TGVs would not attract and retain value-conscious European travellers, who would soon have their pick of train operators. They realised that the value of a high-speed train depends mainly on the quality of services during the entire travel experience. So SNCF began thinking about service innovation.

SNCF's R&D department had always relied on a rigorous product development process that took 5–10 years. Such long cycles were inappropriate for quick testing and launching new services for a rapidly shifting market. SNCF, an industrial giant employing over 180,000 people in 120 countries, desperately needed a new, more agile innovation engine that could churn out and test new services in months, if not weeks.

In 2008, with the help of ExploLab, an innovation and strategy consultancy, SNCF set up TGV Lab, a small unit responsible for identifying, prioritising, piloting and validating innovative service ideas that carried a high risk but also great revenue potential. SNCF recruited Laurence Ternois to run TGV Lab. An outsider, Ternois had spent years in leadership positions at fast-paced internet companies such as AOL and Voyages-sncf.com (SNCF's e-commerce business). She was well placed to execute the TGV Lab mandate within just six months.

TGV Lab is lean, with a modest budget and run by only two dedicated project managers supported by one or two ExploLab consultants. Each year it carries out 6–8 pilot projects. Every six months, the department's managers meet SNCF Voyages business-unit heads to identify and prioritise potential high-stake projects. Business units assign a sponsor to each project selected for trial, and work closely with the TGV Lab staff over a six-month period to pilot the project. Once they are ready, the teams present final results and recommendations (go or no go) to the appropriate business-unit heads, who may then scale up the project depending on the results of the pilot project.

Given TGV Lab's limited resources and time constraints, Ternois says, it has no choice but to practise frugal innovation techniques, using rapid prototyping to design good-enough solutions, rather than over-engineered offerings, and working throughout with internal experts, customers and a variety of technology partners (including tech start-ups). As a result, TGV Lab is able to innovate faster, better and more cost-effectively than SNCF ever could. The lab is also allowed to carry out riskier projects, guided by the Silicon Valley innovation philosophy: fail early, fail fast and fail often. TGV Lab does the failing, so SNCF does not have to.

Yet the Lab's success rate is relatively high. Of its 30 pilot projects launched since 2008, over half have been successfully implemented and scaled up by

SNCF. Its smartphone-based productivity tools are used by 10,000 TGV ticket inspectors. Its TGV Family scheme, in collaboration with Disneyland Paris and others, provides 600 train carriages for the exclusive entertainment of families. One particularly frugal success is an SMS-based system that enables train crews to communicate with hearing-impaired passengers. SNCF had originally planned to refit all its TGV train carriages with video monitors, which would have taken years to implement and cost millions of euros. But the SMS-based system tested and proposed by TGV Lab cost just a few hundred thousand euros and was implemented across the entire train fleet in a matter of months.

Conclusion

All these initiatives point to one overriding imperative: the R&D function – the engine-room of innovation – of large corporations must focus on the customer. This must happen at the front end of the innovation process (greater engagement with customers) as well as the back end (continually improving the product). Getting this right is no easy task for established organisations, but it is a precondition for the other five principles of frugal innovation.

The next chapter looks at the more tactical aspects of these themes, and how these ideas apply not just to R&D, but also to production, distribution, marketing and customer service.

3 Principle two: flex your assets

The Nestlé supertanker couldn't become faster and bigger. So the only way was to break it up into a very agile fleet of independent boats, with a common supply chain afterwards. The challenge is how you manage that without losing coherence and strategic direction.[1]

Peter Brabeck-Letmathe, chairman, Nestlé

VOLKSWAGEN, ONE OF THE WORLD'S largest carmakers, is retooling all its factories using a process called *Modularer Querbaukasten* (MQB). MQB calls for more standardised production techniques so individual factories can manufacture multiple models using the same assembly line. Rather than maintaining a few large, centralised plants with too many dedicated production lines (all of which add energy and logistics costs), MQB allows Volkswagen to operate multiple, smaller but nimbler plants with versatile production capabilities. When fully deployed across its factories in the US, Europe and China, Volkswagen will be able to manufacture any vehicle that local customers want close to where they live, and do so faster, better and more cost-effectively. In this way, Volkswagen hopes to live up to its name, the "people's car", by delivering what people want, cost-effectively. Nissan, Toyota and others are following suit. MQB is a harbinger of frugal manufacturing.

Novartis, a global pharmaceutical company, is also investing heavily in next-generation manufacturing techniques. It has co-funded an $85 million centre at The Massachusetts Institute of Technology

(MIT) that focuses on research into continuous manufacturing, led by Bernhardt Trout. The continuous manufacturing process represents a major technology leap for the pharmaceutical industry, enabling drugs to be produced in smaller volumes in a continuous flow in one small, fully integrated facility, rather than mass-manufactured in large batches using a multi-step process distributed across many large factories. Compared with the traditional batch-based system, the end-to-end continuous manufacturing process enables companies to produce pills faster (ten times faster in MIT's experimental lab), rapidly scale up and down production to deal with uncertain demand, and use the same equipment to make multiple drugs. For pharmaceutical companies, continuous manufacturing delivers speed and agility, reduces both capital and operating expenditure by up to 50%, increases operational asset effectiveness, reduces the use of natural resources, cuts the environmental footprint by up to 90%, and improves quality by lessening the chance of products going out of spec. All this will enable such companies to deliver higher-quality drugs to consumers faster and at a lower price.

In a presentation made at MIT, Joseph Jimenez, Novartis's CEO, showed how in a pilot project the company was able to leverage the continuous manufacturing process developed at MIT to produce Diovan, a drug for blood pressure and heart failure, in merely six hours rather than the 12 months it takes with the conventional batch method. "This will change the way medicine is made around the world," said Jimenez. Trout believes that Novartis could leverage the continuous manufacturing platform both to strengthen its existing business model – by producing traditional drugs faster, better and cheaper – and to manufacture and deliver personalised medicine – the holy grail of health care – cost-effectively in the long term. Novartis's rivals, such as Amgen, Genzyme and GSK, are also investing heavily in continuous manufacturing. Yet Trout believes that Novartis's early engagement and strong senior management-level commitment to reinvent its entire drug development value chain to support continuous manufacturing give it a significant first-mover advantage. Novartis plans to launch a commercial-scale continuous manufacturing plant in 2017, well ahead of its rivals.[2]

By adopting MQB and continuous manufacturing, Volkswagen

and Novartis respectively are reshaping 21st-century manufacturing. The industrial era of the 20th century was characterised by mass production, in which manufacturers focused on making more of the same at increasingly lower cost, and achieving ever-greater economies of scale. This goal was reinforced by the fact that firms' factories and warehouses were literally fixed assets, and dedicated to doing only one thing at a time, repeatedly. For many decades, this rigid, monolithic mass-production system worked well: resources were abundant and customers' needs were fairly homogeneous.

Today, however, the world is facing growing resource scarcity and demographic diversity. This new reality is exposing the limitations of mass production. The old model has become inflexible and wasteful for three reasons: it requires giant, energy-hungry, purpose-built factories; huge inventories to feed these giant plants; and expensive logistical infrastructure to transport goods to thousands of retail stores worldwide. The system is ill-equipped to meet the diverse needs of an increasingly heterogeneous customer base in a flexible and resource-efficient manner.

This chapter shows how frugal approaches can be applied to all aspects of a business, including its manufacturing, distribution, services and people. This can be achieved by the simple process of making the most of existing assets.

The rise of frugal manufacturing

The recession notwithstanding, customers in the developed world are increasingly seeking greater variety and personalisation in their purchases. These customers do not form a homogeneous group and so their needs are diverse. Some firms are meeting these needs. Captivated by Amazon's same-day delivery service, for example, customers now want their products and services delivered to their doorstep at the click of a mouse. And these finicky customers seem to have little brand loyalty. Their allegiance is increasingly to firms that can meet their changing needs faster, better and cheaper.

Some manufacturers are already shifting to a new frugal manufacturing model that enables mass customisation at lower cost, with fewer resources. Their next-generation factories are taking advantage of several revolutionary technological innovations. They are using new materials such as carbon fibres and nanoparticles to cut costs, enhance performance and reduce waste simultaneously. They are using new manufacturing tools such as robots, computer-aided software and 3D printing to enable mass customisation at a fraction of the normal cost. And they are adopting new approaches such as social manufacturing, continuous processing and decentralised production.

New materials

Materials used in products – whether in mobile phones or cars – are a major source of cost and waste, at the start and throughout a product's life cycle. For example, a car's fuel efficiency depends on its weight, and therefore its materials. As a result, carmakers are increasingly employing "lightweighting" – that is, the use of lighter yet stronger materials. BMW, a German carmaker, favours aluminium and carbon fibre over steel in its BMW i8 electric car. Its drive train and chassis use aluminium, which reduces the weight by 30% compared with steel, and the passenger cabin is almost entirely carbon fibre. The instrument panel sits in a lighter, magnesium frame. As a result, the BMW i8 weighs 1,490kg, which is in line with conventional sports cars, despite its heavy battery. The car has lower emissions and fuel consumption while increasing performance and driving pleasure.

Carbon fibre, combined with resin, is half the weight of steel but just as strong. It is increasingly used in planes and space travel, and can be produced in large single-piece sections, eliminating the need to rivet individual components together, and making overall construction more robust and secure.

New tools for manufacturing

3D printers are responsible for a major breakthrough in manufacturing. When combined with computer-aided design and other digital tools, 3D printers can dramatically reduce manufacturing costs while increasing the capacity to customise products.

3D printers' additive manufacturing involves adding several successive layers of a material until the product in question is finalised.

This resource-efficient approach contrasts with the subtractive method used since the 19th century, in which a larger block of material, usually hard metal, is reduced, hammered, shaved or twisted into shape. Subtractive processes use more energy and waste at least half of the materials used. In contrast, because the same 3D printer can be used to print a large number of designs, it can mass customise at a fraction of the conventional, subtractive cost. 3D printing is also less dependent on wage costs, potentially changing some basic economic assumptions that companies operate by.

3D printers boast other, important capabilities. They work with an expanding range of materials including plastic, stainless steel, ceramics and glass. They can print mechanical objects with moving parts, thereby producing fully functional components in one go. They can be used to make small household items from jewellery to confectionery, but they can also produce larger, more complex products such as prosthetic limbs, concept cars, houses, electronic gadgets and orthodontic appliances. A large number of open-source initiatives and crowdfunded projects are drastically bringing down the cost of 3D printers, making personalised manufacturing more affordable and accessible to more people. For instance, in May 2014, in an effort to make 3D printing accessible "to billions", Autodesk, a design software provider, released Spark, an open-software platform that aims to make 3D printing simpler and more reliable. The same month, M3D, a start-up, raised a whopping $3.4 million on Kickstarter to produce a $300 super-easy-to-use 3D printer.

One particularly impressive product of 3D printers is spare parts for fighter aircraft. In December 2013, BAE Systems, a British multinational defence and aerospace company, tested Tornado jets that had several 3D printed metal components in them. The company is now developing ready-made parts for four squadrons of Tornado GR4 aircraft. BAE Systems engineers believe that some components will now cost less than £100 ($158). Overall, 3D technology could reduce the Royal Air Force's service and maintenance costs by £1.2 million ($1.9 million) over the next four years. Mike Murray, head of airframe integration, notes:[3]

You can manufacture the products at whatever base you want, providing you can get a machine there, which means you can also start to support other platforms such as ships and aircraft carriers. And if it's feasible to get machines out on the front line, it also gives improved capability where we wouldn't traditionally have any manufacturing support.

Based on over 20 years of its own research, GE also believes that these tools will help launch a new industrial revolution. The company has built a full-scale facility in Cincinnati, Ohio, to develop and scale up new alloys, processes and parts for use in additive manufacturing. GE has a global team of 600 engineers at 21 sites that is focused on additive manufacturing. Moreover, GE is committed to developing parts and components using additive techniques in several of its business lines and scaling up in a smart way based on early successes. For instance, GE Aviation plans to manufacture 100,000 additive parts by 2020. One application will be a fuel nozzle for the company's CFM LEAP jet engine. In health care, GE researchers can print ultrasound transducers faster and more cheaply than using standard manufacturing techniques. GE does not do all this in-house. It works with innovators outside the group, with a view to building a global additive manufacturing ecosystem to spread the use of the technology. The main challenge is developing sufficient capacity for large- and small-scale industrial needs; if achieved, this will create many new manufacturing businesses and jobs.

In addition to 3D printing, the plummeting cost of industrial robots – such as Baxter, a $25,000 humanoid robot sold by Rethink Robotics – is unleashing a wave of automation in factories that could not only boost manufacturers' productivity and quality but also their agility. SRI International, a research institute based in Silicon Valley, is working on a project funded by DARPA (Defence Advanced Research Projects Agency) to develop nimbler, smaller and lighter robotic arms that will be ten times cheaper and consume 20 times less energy than existing industrial robots, and yet perform complex tasks in dynamic settings more reliably. Low-cost robotics is used particularly in Germany and Japan, where factory workforces are ageing rapidly. Indeed, Japan is already a robotics world leader, with over 300,000 robots operating in its factories. It is predicted that over 1 million industrial robots will be in use in the country by 2025. Given that a single robot can perform the work of ten humans, these 1 million robots would be equivalent to 15% of Japan's 2012 workforce (approximately 65.3 million, according to World Bank data). "Robots are the cornerstone of Japan's international competitiveness," says Shunichi Uchiyama, head of manufacturing policymaking at Japan's trade ministry.

Robots are also quicker learners than humans and more versatile. For this reason, carmakers Ford and GM are using robot-powered assembly lines with interchangeable tooling that can be programmed to switch rapidly between car models.

New approaches to manufacturing

New digital tools, including 3D printing and affordable robotics, are enabling frugal approaches such as social or collaborative manufacturing, continuous processing and decentralised production.

Social or collaborative manufacturing goes beyond the factory to include consumers and end users in the manufacturing process. For example, Quirky, a consumer-goods start-up that operates from a New York warehouse, takes the best ideas submitted by its online user community and converts them into products. A section of Quirky's office-cum-design studio contains all the equipment that the factory needs: milling machines, a laser cutter, a booth for spray painting and several 3D printers. Prototypes are rapidly made in Quirky's machine shop. The inventors remain close to the process and suggest colours and modifications; in some cases, they even set prices. External manufacturers then produce the prototypes, and the end products are sold online or in stores.

An important aspect of the company's business model is that the inventors themselves stand to make money from the process. Quirky claims that 10% of its direct revenues are shared with its online community; in 2013, inventors and online influencers shared a pot of $3.8 million. According to Ben Kaufman, the company's CEO, two consumer products are developed every week. Quirky has launched several products based on crowdsourced ideas, including a flexible power strip, an egg separator and a smartphone-controlled air conditioner. Kaufman uses this as evidence to explain to corporate leaders he meets that the most innovative ideas do not necessarily come from the boardroom or from within the company, but from consumers and the general public.

Increasingly, inventors do not even need access to companies like Quirky. Armed with a laptop, high-speed broadband and design software, individuals can manufacture one-off products and make a profit. One company that helps such inventors is Shapeways, a Dutch start-up now based in Manhattan. Peter Weijmarshausen, its CEO, describes the company as "a service where people can make, buy and sell anything they want".[4] Customers upload their product design to the Shapeways website; Shapeways produces it in its 3D printing factory, and consumers sell the product on the web.

Another firm helping to democratise innovation and manufacturing is littleBits, an open-source library of electronic modules that snap together with tiny magnets for prototyping, learning and fun. Just as Lego enables users with limited knowledge of construction to build complex structures, littleBits enables non-engineers to use small, simple, intuitive blocks to build sophisticated electronics simply by snapping together specially designed magnets. Each piece has a specific function such as sensing, producing light or sound, acting as a button or a motor and so on. The system involves none of the soldering, wiring or programming required by most electronics manufacturing.

Decentralised manufacturing is another approach that can help companies dramatically cut costs and boost agility. Today, manufacturers rely on a highly centralised production model that looks like a pyramid. At the top, there are a few dozen big factories that mass-produce goods, which are then shipped in containers by air or sea to a few hundred warehouses around the world; from there they are delivered by trucks to thousands of supermarkets, where millions of consumers shop. This pyramidal model is highly efficient and delivers great economies of scale, but it requires a lot of capital assets, resources, space and energy to maintain, and it cannot respond flexibly to customers' rapidly evolving and personalised needs. Decentralised production collapses the hierarchical pyramid into a distributed network of potentially hundreds or even thousands of micro-factories, located close to points of consumption, which can produce customised, small-dimension goods in low volume using locally sourced parts. Conceived by Japan's Mechanical Engineering Laboratory (MEL) in 1990, micro-factories are now a hot trend supported by academic research and government and corporate-funded R&D programmes worldwide.

Micro-factories, which can fit inside a container, can easily be set up anywhere. And their modular design allows them to be reassembled rapidly in different configurations. Thus they represent a sustainable manufacturing model that promises to deliver greater value for companies and customers – in terms of agility, customisation and cost-effectiveness – while drastically minimising the use of resources. Recent advances in miniaturisation technologies are bringing micro-factories closer to reality. For example, SRI is working on a project to create ant-like micro-robots (known as "labs on a chip") that are built from simple, low-cost magnets propelled electromagnetically. These tiny, nimble micro-robots can reliably handle a wide range of liquid and solid materials, including electronics. Working together as a swarm, this mobile army of tiny robots can roam around in a micro-factory to manufacture parts of any size with high precision and quality. And they can do so faster, cheaper and more reliably than today's bulky and expensive machine tools.

Large corporations are also investing in micro-factories. In partnership with Local Motors, an open-source hardware innovator, GE has opened its first micro-factory, FirstBuild, in Louisville, Kentucky. It will engage local community members as well as a global network of innovators to co-create next-generation consumer appliances more rapidly and cost-effectively, using agile techniques such as digital prototyping, 3D printing, rapid iteration and small-batch production. GE's micro-factory will also enable local community ideas to be rapidly converted into viable options.

Beyond the traditional industrial sector, frugal manufacturing – enabled by innovations like micro-factories – promises to transform the dynamics of other sectors such as energy. Since the second world war, the trend in developed economies has been to build ever-larger power-generation units. Today electricity is generated in a small number of centralised mega units and transmitted over hundreds of miles to customers' homes and offices. This centralised power system is asset- and resource-intensive, costly to maintain and vulnerable to catastrophic events such as terrorist acts or blackouts (as occurred in North-eastern America in 2003).

Increasingly, however, distributed – or decentralised – energy systems are emerging, based on smaller power-generation units that can be placed closer to major points of consumption. This miniaturisation of power generation is made possible thanks to advances in renewable energy technologies, which are making small-scale energy production affordable and accessible. A typical electricity power station generates 1 gigawatt (GW), compared with a wind turbine's 2–3 megawatts and a solar panel's few kilowatts. It is now possible, therefore, to generate power at one-millionth of the scale. These smaller units are in turn giving rise to mini power-generation units that can be distributed and quickly deployed during a sudden spike in demand (for example, during extreme winters) or a power outage (for example, in the aftermath of a natural disaster such as Hurricane Sandy). In 2012 alone about 142GW of distributed power capacity was installed, accounting for nearly 40% of total capacity additions. Investment in distributed power technologies is expected to grow from $150 billion in 2012 to over $200 billion in 2020. Sensing a huge market opportunity, GE launched a new business unit in early 2014 called GE Distributed Power to supply distributed power systems to utilities as well as directly to end-customers such as municipalities or large manufacturers. GE predicts that between now and 2020 distributed power will increase 40% faster than global electricity demand.

GDF Suez, a leading European energy firm, headed by Gérard Mestrallet, is stepping up its investment in distributed energy-production systems. Mestrallet believes that the global energy sector is primed for a 4D revolution: deregulation, decentralisation, digitisation and deceleration. He believes that, much like the telecoms sector after its liberalisation, Europe's energy-sector deregulation will create competition, and push firms towards more frugal, distributed energy systems. Digitisation involves the convergence of energy technologies and digital tools that help to create connected homes and buildings. This convergence, Mestrallet believes, will help customers use energy more responsibly and cost-effectively (thanks to smart meters) and even enable some to produce their own energy (with advanced home-energy storage technologies).

Deregulation is not the only reason utility firms such as GDF Suez are investing in decentralised and digitised energy-production systems. The bigger motivation is to respond to a structural economic trend not seen since the first world war: the deceleration of energy consumption in developed countries. In Europe, in particular, primary energy consumption declined by 8% between 2006 and 2012. Since then, most EU member states have experienced stagnation or a further decline in energy use. This reduction is the result of lower energy-intensive economic activity and increased efficiency due to new technologies and heightened environmental awareness. On current trends, the EU might even meet its target of reducing energy consumption by 20% by 2020. Of course, this is not great news for utility firms, which may be left with excess generation capacity. They have little choice but to adopt frugal techniques. Describing how the market favours consumers, Mestrallet notes:[5]

The relationship the customer has with energy is radically changing. Before, she was a passive user. She simply plugged her devices into a socket without worrying about the cost and origin of electricity. But now, she has become an active player. She wants to know where and how this electricity is produced. She wants to change her consumption patterns. She wants to negotiate and even sometimes produce her own electricity. We at GDF need to adapt to this new socio-economic reality.

Creating a frugal supply chain

Today's supply chains lack efficiency and flexibility because of the vast distance between where a product is manufactured and where it is consumed, and because of delays in how changing information is shared along the supply chain. The geographic gap increases distribution costs and makes it harder to respond to changing customer needs. Costs also rise because manufacturers must hold extra inventory in case of unexpected market changes. These inventory costs can add billions of dollars in multi-tiered industry value chains such as automotive and electronics. Together, these two obstacles can be called the "value gap", and they prevent firms from meeting demand faster, better and cheaper.

Some firms, however, have been able to bridge the value gap in the following ways.

Reshoring

After several decades of unbridled offshoring to low-cost destinations from China to Mexico, manufacturing is now returning to the developed world, as a way to cut costs. Much of the savings involve a product's physical distribution. The 20th-century industrial model worked only as long as cheap labour and economies of scale outweighed shipping costs. This is no longer always the case.

Emerging-market wages are rising. By the end of 2014, wages in China are likely to have increased by 10%, compared with 2013. Shipping costs have also risen: shipping a 40-foot container from Shanghai to San Francisco cost $3,000 in 2000; the price was $8,000 in 2008. Locating production closer to the main market also cuts carbon emissions, and allows producers to respond more quickly to changing market needs. And in a 2012 survey by the Boston Consulting Group, 37% of companies with annual sales above $1 billion said they were planning or actively considering shifting production facilities from China to the US.

Zara, a Spanish clothing retailer, has made substantial cost savings by near-shoring operations to countries like Portugal, close to its main European markets. This allows Zara to vary the styles in its stores constantly, keeping its fashions fresh.

Onshoring is gathering strength in the US too. In 2013, Caterpillar announced the expansion of its US operations with the construction of a 600,000 square foot hydraulic excavator manufacturing facility in Victoria, Texas. Once operational, the plant will employ more than 500 people and triple its US-based excavator capacity. Gary Stampanato, a vice-president at Caterpillar, says:[6]

> Victoria's proximity to our supply base, access to ports and other transportation, as well as the positive business climate in Texas, made this the ideal site for this project.

In late 2009, NCR, a US electronics company, announced it was bringing its ATM (automated teller machine) production back to

Columbus, Georgia, to decrease time to market, increase internal collaboration and lower operating costs. Even low-value toy manufacturers are going this way. In 2013, Wham-O returned half of its frisbee and hula hoop production from Mexico and China to the US.

Local sourcing

The business world is now witnessing a shift from low cost to local sourcing. Western multinationals are already sourcing from local suppliers in emerging markets as part of localisation strategies; apart from meeting local sourcing requirements, this also allows firms to create more affordable products. This trend is becoming more evident in mature economies too, where sourcing smaller quantities from smaller firms located near factories and R&D facilities reduces costs and risk. Motorola, a multinational telecoms company, chose to manufacture all its Moto X smartphones in Texas so that its manufacturing engineers in Texas and its R&D team in Illinois and California could work more closely with local suppliers and respond more quickly to demanding US consumers. (Chinese tech giant Lenovo acquired Motorola's handset business in early 2014.)

These large manufacturers are taking their lead from big retailers. In 2010, for instance, Walmart, the US's biggest importer, committed to doubling the sales of locally sourced products in the US by 2015. Waitrose, a UK supermarket chain, sources nearly 70% of its food from suppliers located within a 30-mile radius of a store.

Sharing resources

Rather than keeping their production and distribution assets idle, some manufacturers now allow other firms, including rivals, to use them. It has long been common in Africa and India for competing telecoms providers to share mobile-phone towers, and Western telecoms companies are now doing the same. For instance, Ericsson and Philips recently unveiled a project that combines city streetlighting with mobile-phone infrastructure. The two companies will incorporate mobile-phone antennae into energy-efficient LED streetlights that can be placed in parts of cities where carriers want to increase their network coverage.

Western firms are also learning from health-care firms in Africa which piggyback on Coca-Cola's "cold chain" (a temperature-controlled supply chain) as a cost-effective way to preserve life-saving medicine and have it delivered rapidly to remote villages. Rival chocolate-makers Hershey and Ferrero, for instance, have agreed to share warehousing and transport assets and systems across North America, thus reducing the number of distribution trips. And Mars, a global food manufacturer, has developed a sustainable distribution network of consumer goods in Germany through co-operation with competitors that allows for joint use of vehicle fleets. In many respects, these developments are the business-to-business equivalent of the sharing economy, in which companies trade and share supply chain assets.

Distributing to the last mile

Fulfilling orders for customers in far-flung locations is a particular challenge. The so-called last-mile challenge exists because it is costly for companies to deploy physical distribution (such as bank branches or retail stores) in places with few users. Innovative distribution models, which make use of trusted locals and networks, are often used in emerging markets. These include using corner shops for financial services (for example, M-Pesa in Kenya) and community personnel to sell consumer goods (for example, Unilever's Project Shakti and Essilor's door-to-door ophthalmic-lens salespeople in rural India). US and European companies can use such proximity networks to solve the last-mile problem in Western markets as well.

Integrating manufacturing and logistics

In the mass-production model, companies first make their products and then move them to customers. These processes have been managed separately, but several manufacturers are now creating a hybrid make/move model to shorten order-to-delivery cycles. These include mix-in-transit processes in which products are completed en route to a customer, and made-to-order formulation and packaging in custom batches near the point of consumption. Such techniques represent a supply chain strategy called postponement or delayed differentiation, which postpones customisation of a product until the point when local customer preferences are most discernible. This is a frugal approach to mass customisation through flexible logistics and supply chain. It is being championed in fast-moving industries such as apparel, food and beverages and electronics, as well as sectors such as chemicals and pharmaceuticals with unpredictable demand. For instance, a 2010 study in the *International Journal of Production Economics* describes how the adoption of postponement in the soluble coffee supply chain could lead to:[7]

> *significant cost savings by delaying the labelling and packaging processes until actual orders from retailers are known. These savings include the reduction of inventory carried as safety stock and obsolete stock unsold from promotional events.*

Kevin O'Marah, chief content officer at SCM World, a global community of supply chain professionals, observes that by integrating manufacturing and logistics activities companies can "manage complexity closer to customers".[8] This is less expensive and faster to do when production occurs closer to the customer.

As well as reducing geographic distance between supply and demand, manufacturers can shorten the time between supply and demand in other ways.

Using real-time demand signals

Supply chain experts flippantly refer to demand forecasts as "stale food"; planning future production based on past sales, they say, is akin to driving while only looking in the rear-view mirror. Firms need to replace lagging indicators with leading indicators. New technologies allow consumer-goods companies to receive point-of-sale and inventory-level data from retailers in real time so they can anticipate future demand better. Procter & Gamble (P&G) and Ford also mine social-media content for insights into customer preferences. As manufacturers shift from mass production to mass customisation, collecting real-time demand signals becomes a vital part of keeping supply chain costs low and fulfilling changing customer needs.

Sharing data with partners

Collecting real-time demand signals is useless without also sharing those insights with suppliers and distributors. This is especially important in heavily outsourced multi-tiered supply chains. Otherwise, firms risk playing a game of phone tag that leads to mis-communication and distorted demand signals being perceived by upstream suppliers. This is why Cemex, a cement supplier, has integrated its supply chain management (SCM) and customer relationship management (CRM) systems to respond better to customer inquiries, co-ordinate distribution processes with partners, and streamline operations at its distribution terminals. Cemex estimates this SCM/CRM integration – implemented with its technology partner, SAP – has saved it millions of dollars since 2005 through lower freight costs, fewer calls to the customer care centre and higher productivity during peak hours at its terminals. Cemex now even provides customers with a delivery time to the hour when taking orders, says Ven Bontha, the company's vice-president for customer experience. The company has managed 29% more customer transactions with the same headcount, delivered over 99% of its orders on time without problems (up from 95%), and halved the volume of calls regarding account information.

More and more manufacturers are also investing in tools that provide end-to-end supply chain visibility. This helps them detect changes and disruptions at all stages of production and distribution, and then alert partners. Supply chain management tools have always been good at providing order management, order status and total cost; with outsourcing, though, companies also want their external partners and customers to have this information. According to KPMG's 2013 *Global Manufacturing Outlook*, nearly 50% of the manufacturers surveyed lack visibility beyond their tier 1 partners, and less than 10% can evaluate the impact of supply chain disruptions within hours.

As a result, businesses now want tools that help them to monitor tier 2, 3 and 4 suppliers. Noha Tohamy, a vice-president and analyst at Gartner, a technology research consultancy, points to the varied tools available, from those that enhance visibility and collaboration with external partners, to those that manage a company's various trading relationships. All these tools benefit companies and customers.

"It's usually good news for the customer because they're getting their products or services quicker and at a lower price," she says.[9] Levi Strauss & Co, a clothing company, uses advanced technology to manage its supply chain – which includes product development, demand and supply planning, manufacturing and logistics – to ensure real-time visibility of products that move through its complex, multi-tiered supply chain network. In this way, the company can accurately forecast demand and supply, react faster and better to market conditions, maintain lower stock levels and keep costs down.

A frugal services revolution

Companies are finding new, highly effective and affordable ways to deliver services or services bundled with products. Such business models include: software as a service (SaaS) in computing; power by the hour in aircraft engines; massive open online courses (MOOCs) in education; hub-and-spoke and yield management models in airlines; online retailing; and cloud computing.

By flexing their assets, airlines such as Southwest Airlines, easyJet and Ryanair have created a new, low-cost market segment for flyers within the US and Europe, and have succeeded in challenging long-haul incumbents. First, the low-cost carriers rebased the existing airline business model by maximising the time that their most valuable assets – their aircraft – spend in the air, and reducing the time they spend on the ground. Second, they use a hub-and-spoke model that maximises reach while minimising the typical journey distance. Third, they use new digital technology to understand, anticipate and influence consumer behaviour and ticket pricing to squeeze as much revenue as possible from their main, perishable resource: seats on flights. To do this, they have had to hand more control to customers, for instance in booking and checking in, and this has improved overall efficiency and reduced costs.

In retailing, Amazon has from the outset sought ways to flex its assets. The company first used its book distribution platform to sell music and household goods as well. It then used its installed customer base for peer-to-peer sales, as on eBay. Amazon then made and sold consumer electronics such as the Kindle (on which to read its books) and market-research tools such as mTurk, to captive customers. Lastly, it used its server space for cloud computing, which it sells as a service. Given its interest in drones as a mode of product delivery, Amazon might one day expand into travel and transport.

Meanwhile, a wave of creative destruction is crashing through the education industry and, by extension, the textbook publishing world. The arrival of MOOCs has threatened higher-education models. Start-ups such as Coursera, Udacity and EdEx in the US and FutureLearn in the UK are now offering courses on an ever-widening range of subjects to students worldwide. Often taught by star professors, these courses are free and reach a far larger audience than any university does. Users can study where they live, when they wish and at their own pace. Perhaps the most powerful aspect of the experience is that users can learn from one another through online forums and discussion boards. While testing and evaluating remains a challenge, it is surely only a matter of time before this issue too is resolved.

More generally, the rise of digital technologies has put pressure on newspapers, magazines and book publishers. Philip Parker, a professor of marketing at INSEAD, a graduate business school, has developed a particularly disruptive publishing business model. He has found a way to reduce the cost of writing and printing to 12 cents a book while charging hundreds of dollars for niche titles. Some 95% of Parker's automatically generated books are sent out electronically, and the rest are printed on demand as self-published paperbacks, targeting the long tail of extremely specialised topics. Probably the most prolific author there has been, Parker claims to have written over 200,000 books, with titles such as *The 2009–2014 World Outlook for 60-milligram Containers of Fromage Frais* and *Webster's English to Italian Crossword Puzzles: Level 1*. Although this is still a niche, it may be only a matter of time before mainstream publishers adopt such frugal approaches to writing, printing, selling and distributing books.

The world of advertising and promotion has also been profoundly affected by the frugal service revolution. The spread of mobile phones, broadband and social media has made it possible for firms to do more effective marketing more affordably. The old interruption-based model that made heavy use of broadcast media has given way to a permission-based model in which consumers who are interested in a brand's messages opt in to receiving them. As a result, advertising now targets these self-selected groups. TiVo, SkyPlus and Apple TV have given viewers more discretion and power, but marketers also know more about who is watching what and when, and can direct and schedule their messages accordingly. The internet and social media also allow closer tracking and more focused targeting of customers and user communities.

An example is the "Share a Coke" integrated marketing campaign in Australia in 2011. Coca-Cola, a soft drinks company, began the campaign by featuring 150 of the most popular Australian names on millions of Coke bottles in stores across the country, creating a considerable buzz on the internet. It then recruited fans to become the campaign's face. On the highest-rated media weekend, Australians were invited to "Share a Coke". Messages such as "If you know a Kate, share a Coke with Kate, or Mel or Dave" were everywhere, including on digital and interactive media such as Sydney's Coke billboard. Blogs were buzzing. Thousands of requests poured in for more names to be added to the list. The company then set up kiosks where people could print a name on a can, which attracted long queues. After receiving 65,000 suggestions, Coca-Cola released 50 new names on its bottles. In just three months, this relatively simple, inexpensive tweak to a Coke can resulted in 5% more people drinking Coke; sales rose by 3% and volume by 4%. A similar UK campaign was also a big hit. Coca-Cola's Facebook community expanded by 3.5% in the UK and 6.8% globally, and the hashtag #shareacoke was used over 29,000 times on Twitter. Crucially, the campaign used digital tools and social media to achieve two frugal outcomes – mass-market penetration and personalisation – outcomes previously considered mutually exclusive.

Frugal solutions are not only being used to deliver intangible services like news, education and advertising; increasingly, manufacturers are also grappling with the service aspects of physical products. For instance, BMW's business used to be simply selling cars. It now sells a package of services with every car. This is because any mid-level car, such as a Volvo Gold, is similar to a BMW. Thus BMW no longer asks "how do we make and sell cars?", but "how do we engage users through our cars and services?" BMW is also asking how it can be part of innovative car-related services such as ZipCar and ParkatmyHouse and offer related financial services.

Although it is important to flex a firm's physical and service assets, it is more crucial to make greater use of a company's most valuable assets: its staff.

Frugal organisations

In 1958, Bill Gore, a chemical engineer with 16 years' experience as a research scientist at DuPont, decided to go it alone. With his wife Vieve, Bill founded W.L. Gore & Associates, a company devoted to developing products such as electrical cables from fluoropolymers such as polytetrafluoroethylene (PTFE to scientists and Teflon to consumers).

Starting from the family home's basement, within a decade the company had built a factory in Delaware, and wire and cable plants in Arizona, Scotland, Germany and Japan. Its products were used in high-performing computers and some even made it to the moon. In 1969, the company made another giant leap when Bill's son Bob, also a chemical engineer, found a way to stretch PTFE into a waterproof, breathable, lightweight and almost cold-proof fabric, called GORE-TEX. Annual revenues are now over $3 billion, and the firm employs 10,000 people worldwide.

What makes W.L. Gore so distinctive is not its technical prowess, but how it is organised and managed. Gore was an innovator in this too, and is likely to be remembered for three novel management ideas: the lattice organisation, "un-management" and the human-sized factory.

Inspired by Douglas McGregor's *The Human Side of Management*, Gore adopted a lattice-style organisation, with no explicit hierarchy, in which staff could make up their own job titles. (Two later maverick innovators, Larry Page and Sergey Brin, would try something similar at Google.) The idea was to reduce bureaucracy and create an environment in which every employee could communicate and work directly with every other. Teams were self-forming; leaders were not appointed beforehand, but arose through the force of their ideas, commitment or personality. Without corporate bureaucracy, new ideas were shared sooner, decisions made faster, and new products developed more quickly than at competitor firms that required executive approval. The flexible set-up not only meant that W.L. Gore could innovate more quickly, but it also freed employees to think up yet more ideas.

But Gore did not stop there. He soon came up with yet another breakthrough idea: the human-sized factory. He noticed how his firm's rapid growth made it hard to contain bureaucracy. The bigger his factories became, the more his workers shirked, and the less they helped one another. It was as if there was a threshold beyond which staff considered colleagues as "them" not "us". Gore felt that this threshold began when the factory exceeded 150 workers. Beyond that, people rapidly lost track of colleagues, and with it any sense of community. So he capped the size of his new factories and broke up older plants that exceeded that limit.

Gore was a frugal innovator because he found ways to get more from his people with less investment. His lattice organisation, the "un-management" approach and his human-sized factories allowed him to flex his firm's most valuable assets: its employees.

Gore's approach is profoundly different from that which most fast-growing firms take when faced with increasing market complexity. Most firms respond by increasing internal complexity. But, as Gore showed, they should do the opposite – simplify things to get more from their people. This is a lesson adopted by Boston Consulting Group's Yves Morieux, a passionate advocate for organisational simplicity. He argues that today's businesses have become so "dizzyingly complex" that they make staff "miserable and disengaged". Despite all the technological advances, productivity remains low as a result. Morieux believes that older thinking about organisational design, through structure and process, leads managers to add even more structure and process. For instance, faced with poor co-ordination between front and back offices, firms create a middle office, thereby creating two dysfunctional systems when there was previously only one.

Morieux thinks the old convoluted and monolithic organisational model is dead, and he offers rules for "smart simplicity". First, he advises, "understand what your colleagues actually do". He argues:[10]

The solution is not drawing more boxes with connecting lines ... The solution is co-operation. When people co-operate, they use fewer resources. When we don't co-operate we need more time, more equipment, more services, more stock, more inventory. And who pays for this: shareholders? Customers? No. Employees, who experience burnout, get stressed and disengage.

Ultimately, a company that has learned how to flex its organisational assets – by eliminating bureaucracy, empowering employees and cultivating a flexible mindset in its workforce – might be the most frugal company of all.

Recommendations for managers

There are a number of things that companies wishing to flex their manufacturing and supply chain assets should do.

Digitise processes and assets

Over 40% of manufacturers worry that their R&D teams and supply chain partners are not sufficiently integrated. They can improve this situation by using inexpensive technologies to digitise manufacturing, supply chains, sales, marketing and customer-support systems, and then integrating these processes with external partners. For example, car designers used to exchange computer-aided design (CAD) drawings with suppliers via delivery services such as FedEx. Today's advanced simulation software enables them to do virtual prototyping in collaboration with suppliers, which speeds up product development cycles. Similarly, factory equipment and delivery trucks can be monitored online, and their roles and activities adjusted almost immediately. Cisco estimates that just 4% of the world's shop-floor devices are connected to the internet. And research by the American Society for Quality (ASQ) shows that only 13% of manufacturers have digitally integrated their factory tools and equipment. ASQ has also found that digitally networked manufacturers boosted productivity by 82% and customer satisfaction by 45%.

Maribel Lopez, CEO of Lopez Research, which advises *Fortune* 500 companies on digital strategies, recommends that manufacturers should use ever-cheaper wireless and sensor technologies, not to enhance their old factory processes, but rather to radically transform them to gain "exponential agility".[11] For example, Harley-Davidson's motorcycle factories are "self-aware" and "self-regulating". Most equipment is digitally wired and the performance of machine tools (such as the speed of fans in the painting booth) is continually monitored by software. When the system detects any deviation from key indicators, such as humidity, temperature or fan speed, it automatically readjusts the machinery, thus avoiding costly interruptions.

Manufacturers should also continually collect and analyse such industrial data to improve performance and anticipate maintenance issues. The US Department of Energy reckons that this predictive maintenance approach can reduce maintenance costs by up to 30%, machine breakdowns by 75% and downtime by 35–45%, while increasing production by 25%.

Decentralise supply chains with smaller, nimbler factories

Decentralised supply chains, whereby production happens as close as possible to the point of consumption, will help bridge the supply–demand gap. One way to do this is by shifting production from big factories with rigid manufacturing processes to smaller, nimbler plants that are flexible and versatile. Danone, a French multinational food-products company, was able to build in Bangladesh a yogurt-making micro-factory only 10% the size of Danone's existing factories and much cheaper to build. Impressed, Danone's chairman Franck Riboud asked his R&D and supply chain leaders to find out how Danone could build such low-cost micro-factories in other markets, including in Europe.

Bayer, a global chemical and pharmaceutical company that makes aspirin, is taking flexible manufacturing to a new level in its F3 (flexible, fast and future) factories based on a "plug-and-produce" philosophy. Inspired by Germany's famous bratwurst (sausage) food trucks, F3s will use mobile and modular production units that can produce and deliver in small volume a wide range of custom chemicals at the customer's own location. Bayer Technology Services, which is part of

Bayer, is leading a consortium of 25 corporate and academic partners from nine European countries to accelerate the development and adoption of modular F3 factories in the chemical industry.

Adapt R&D

R&D engineers also need to take full advantage of digitised and flexible supply chain assets and processes when designing products. Three conditions should be in place:

- Products must be factory-agnostic; in other words, it should be possible to produce them in any factory in the manufacturer's global supply chain. For instance, John Deere, a US agricultural and construction machinery manufacturer, has an operating model, Design Anywhere Build Anywhere (DABA), which allows it to shift production quickly and seamlessly from one factory to another, depending on relative capacity.

- R&D should use fewer, more standard components so they can be assembled faster on the shop floor.

- R&D should adopt techniques such as modular design and design for postponement so that products can be mass customised cost-effectively, either at the factory or at the point of distribution (or, even better, at the point of consumption). For example, Benetton's designers initially produce all knitted sweaters in white and then dye them into various colours the moment the customer's preferences become known.

Weigh up procurement priorities

Purchasing managers and sourcing experts must choose suppliers for flexibility, not just cost. Some suppliers can compensate for higher cost with greater agility. Sourcing experts should use the supply chain operations reference (SCOR) model to choose new suppliers and assess existing suppliers. Specifically, they should use the model's five key performance indicators (KPIs) – costs, assets (which measures efficiency), reliability, responsiveness and agility (which measures adaptability) – to do so, giving equal weight to all five.

Companies also need to flex their service assets. They can use predictive maintenance methods to anticipate and deal with customer needs, even before they occur, saving money and boosting loyalty. For instance, Northrup Grumman, one of the world's largest defence contractors, has built a predictive maintenance system that enables US Air Force technicians to predict cracking on their aircraft weeks before these cracks even become visible to the naked eye – thus avoiding costly repairs and potentially saving the lives of military pilots.

Focus on the core

KPMG's 2013 *Global Manufacturing Outlook* reports that 40% of manufacturers plan to end unprofitable, non-core product lines and business units over the next two years. For example, Nestlé, a Swiss multinational food and beverage company, will focus on "wellness" businesses and run them as a collection of autonomous units. And GM intends to cut the number of distinct vehicle architectures from 30 in 2010 to 14 in 2018.

Sometimes firms need a shock to make this change. In 2004, Lego nearly went bankrupt after several failed innovations. The new CEO, Jørgen Vig Knudstorp, then asked a basic question: "Why does Lego Group exist?" His answer was: "To offer our core products, whose unique design helps children learn systematic, creative problem solving – a crucial 21st-century skill." He added, "We wanted to compete not by being the biggest but by being the best".[12]

Similarly, when Steve Jobs returned to Apple in 1997, the company was, he said:[13]

> [making] a zillion and one products ... It was amazing ... I started to ask people, why would I recommend a 3400 over a 4400? Or when should somebody jump up to a 6500, but not a 7300? And after three weeks, I couldn't figure this out! And I figured if I can't figure it out working inside Apple with all these experts ... how are our customers going to figure this out?

So Jobs focused his turnaround efforts on simplifying the company's offerings. Every product team had to convince him that their product was essential to Apple's strategy. If a product was not profitable, it had to go. Gil Amelio, his predecessor, had begun by cutting Apple projects from 350 to 50. Jobs finished the job by cutting them down to ten. The idea was to focus on a few "insanely great" products. And it did.

*

Frugality comes from flexing not just physical or service assets, but also human assets. To achieve this, companies should consider the following.

Simplify organisational structures

As Bill Gore found, smaller, modular teams are more cohesive, more co-operative and have a greater sense of purpose, which in turn increases efficiency and creativity. Large firms need to find ways to keep teams small and tight-knit, flatten organisation and reduce internal complexity. They should try to replace pyramids with networks that link people according to their roles. Doing so will increase job satisfaction, reduce burnout and improve work performance.

Empower employees

A top-down management culture can be powerful in a crisis, but it will not make a company flexible and agile. Given that creative and skilled employees have increasing job options, firms must seek frugal ways to attract and retain them. One way is to let employees make and implement their own decisions.

Following Lego's 2004 turnaround, Jørgen Vig Knudstorp realised that the company "required a looser structure and a relaxation of the top-down management style imposed during the turnaround". As he recalls:[14]

> I stopped participating in weekly sales-management and capacity-allocation choices and pushed decisions as far down the hierarchy as possible.

When leaders cannot dictate, employees must be able to co-operate to get things done. Of course, the company can help by rewarding co-operation. "Blame is not for failure but for failing to help or ask for help," notes Knudstorp.

Another way to empower staff is to create an unstructured playground where creativity does not violate company rules. (Disruptive innovation, after all, requires people to be disruptive.) Henry Ford, founder of the eponymous motor company, was anything but playful – you would be hard-pressed to find a smiling photo of the man. He was most famous for standardising and automating manufacturing and creating hierarchical structures to achieve economies of scale by mass-producing cars. Yet Ford is now undergoing a cultural transformation initiated under its former CEO, Alan Mulally, in 2006 and maintained by his successor, Mark Fields. Mulally understood that customers want affordable, eco-friendly cars of all shapes and colours (not just black). He believed that creative humans – not robots – make great cars, and wanted to draw out their potential. He set out to create an unstructured environment where employees could express their ingenuity without risk, and pursue even wild ideas, unencumbered by bureaucracy, that might eventually succeed.

Ford has partnered with TechShop, a provider of the Maker platform. Together, they have converted a Detroit warehouse into an innovation playground where employees can spend their spare time experimenting with 3D printers and other DIY technologies. Ford engineers feel empowered to develop ideas that would not make it in its more strait-laced R&D labs. Thus Ford has increased its patentable ideas by over 100%, without investing more in R&D. The quality of ideas has also improved: engineers seem to produce more ground-breaking solutions working at TechShop than at the corporate R&D lab. The lesson is that innovation is more likely to happen in a messy, freewheeling, autonomous environment.

Recruit for a purpose

Agile organisations recruit employees with deep expertise in one field, but also basic skills in several others too. Such "T-shaped" individuals can relate to others beyond their function, and this facilitates cross-functional co-operation.

Firms need recruitment strategies for the long term. For example, Saatchi & Saatchi, an advertising agency, hires staff in pairs. With a 15% annual employee churn rate, it can change half its staff every three years, revitalising itself in the process, while maintaining continuity. This increases creativity, though not at the expense of efficiency.

Simon Francis, CEO of Flock Associates, a marketing company, and former head of Aegis Europe, a research network, asks:[15]

> *How do you get genuine creativity in an organisation? Firms like Dyson in the UK and Apple in the US are design led. They value people who are creative. In other, less creative organisations, people who are creative might get hammered down for being different.*

CASE STUDY 2

Saatchi & Saatchi + Duke: agile advertising[16]

Advertising agencies are undergoing profound change. As digital technologies such as social media disrupt the industry, agencies have lost their advertising monopoly and have seen their influence over consumers' purchasing decisions diminish. Consumers' main source of product information now comes from social networks, and purchasing decisions are determined mainly by recommendations from friends and family.

According to Elie Ohayon, former CEO of Saatchi & Saatchi + Duke, advertising agencies are unprepared for these technological and socio-economic changes. They continue to work according to 1950s structures and methods – that is, highly specialised functions that fail to communicate with one another, with sequential and time-consuming development processes. This Taylorist model (named after a system of scientific management advocated by Frederick Taylor) worked well in the past when promoting, say, a detergent through just four channels: TV, radio, press and display. In today's more complex and dynamic world, a brand touches dozens of different markets and promotional messages are sent through hundreds of channels, many of which are enabled by social media. It is no longer enough for advertisers just to influence consumers; they must also engage them in conversation – no simple task when there are thousands of possible points of contact and millions of possible conversations.

But it is possible. During his tenure as CEO between 2011 and 2014, Ohayon shook up Saatchi & Saatchi's staid culture and made it more agile. Teams now work on the same project in cross-functional collaboration, enhancing communication between functions. Creative directors, for example, have a better understanding of the overall business objectives of a project from the start. This structure also allows the agency to compress development cycles and quickly test concepts in the market and gain instant feedback.

Through its merger with Duke, a boutique digital marketing company, Saatchi & Saatchi can anticipate and respond better to technological changes. Its new creative technologists scout for promising software or start-ups that can be integrated into the company's offering, and leverage social networks and mobile platforms in their ad campaigns. Ohayon concludes: "Ten years ago we didn't have managers in charge of social networks; today, we couldn't do without them."

In an industry in which opportunities are often ephemeral, and speed and agility are competitive advantages, such a reorganisation allows the agency to execute campaigns much faster. This is why Ohayon was explicit about adding "Duke" to the company name:

> When I meet my clients, I do not introduce my company as an advertising agency but as an ideas development platform that is open and agile. This openness to both consumers and external partners is essential; otherwise we cannot innovate quickly. Design will remain our core business but we are going more and more to open the execution part to talented outside experts in order to gain in agility.

Conclusion

Flexing assets is about saving money, resources and time. By flexing their production, distribution, service and organisational assets, companies are able to make and deliver tailored products and services to customers, where they live and work, and when they want them, faster and more cheaply. But they will face additional limits to what they can achieve because of the shortage of natural resources. As Unilever's CEO, Paul Polman, points out, if the emerging economies are to catch up with the West in the way that the West became prosperous, we will need the resources of two planets do so.

Companies have only recently started to put sustainable growth at the centre of their business strategies. But many have discovered that, far from being a business cost or a fancy marketing slogan, sustainability turns out to be a brilliant frugal strategy when implemented over the longer run. This third principle of frugal innovation is discussed in the next chapter.

4 Principle three: create sustainable solutions

Nothing is lost, nothing is created, everything is transformed.

Antoine-Laurent de Lavoisier, French chemist

TARKETT IS A MULTINATIONAL COMPANY that equips homes, offices, hospitals, schools and stores with vinyl, wood and laminate flooring, carpets and tiles, and fits artificial grass in sports stadiums. With roots going back to 1880, it has established itself as a global leader in its sector. In the late 2000s, it was growing at an annual rate of over 10%. Most firms would be delighted by such performance. But Tarkett's CEO, Michel Giannuzzi, who took over the company in 2007, worried that its rapid growth was a ticking time bomb. To sustain this speed of expansion, the company would need to consume more and more resources every year. Producing 14 million square feet of flooring daily requires a lot of raw material, including oil, water, wood and minerals. These non-renewable resources were getting scarcer and costlier, and the environmental harm they created was increasing. Tarkett's production model was financially and environmentally unsustainable.

Tarkett had always seen itself as a responsible corporate citizen that respected wider society and the planet. So it reinvented its business model. Instead of selling a product to be used by a single customer for a few years and then discarded, Tarkett began selling eco-friendly products that could be reused or recycled, repeatedly. Doing so prolongs the life of the product and extends its usage across multiple customers, so helping both customers and the environment.

The firm has radically changed the way it designs, makes, sells and maintains all its products, embedding environmental sustainability in every stage of its product life cycle:

- It has adopted eco-design principles by creating products that use only good materials; that is, those that are abundant and easily replenished, do not harm people or the planet, and can be 100% recycled or decompose naturally. For instance, only 2% of materials in Tarkett's tiles produced in Brazil are petroleum based. It prefers to use rapidly renewable materials such as oyster and walnut shells, linseed oil, wood flour, pine resin, jute, wood or cork. It also uses pre- and post-consumer recycled plastic material that comes from used windscreens and structural safety glass. Its R&D team excludes substances categorised as being of "very high concern" by European and US environmental protection agencies. The Germany-based Environmental Protection and Encouragement Agency (EPEA) assesses all its materials for safety in respect of people and the environment.

- It has re-engineered its manufacturing processes and facilities so they consume less water and energy. By installing closed-loop water circuits in its production sites, Tarkett has reduced fresh and potable water consumption by 12% in 2013, compared with 2010. Between 2010 and 2013 it also reduced by 37% the industrial waste it sends to landfill, by reintroducing this waste into its own manufacturing processes. Today, 75% of its wood plants use sawdust to generate electricity. Moreover, it has increased its renewable energy share from 6% in 2010 to 22% in 2013 using, for example, biomass boilers to produce hot water to heat its ovens.

- It has ensured that its indoor products for homes, schools, offices and hospitals are not harmful. Improving indoor air quality is crucial, given that on average Americans spend 90% of their time indoors, and typical European students spend on average 6,700 hours at school before the age of 14. Tarkett now designs almost all its products with very low emissions of total volatile organic compounds (TVOC). Its vinyl products' TVOC emissions are one-tenth to one-hundredth of those prescribed by European regulations, and its flooring products are certified as "asthma and allergy friendly" by the Asthma and Allergy Foundation of America (AAFA). Tarkett has also developed flooring products that can be maintained over their 20-year life cycle using fewer chemical ingredients and energy-efficient cleaning technologies such as dry-buffing cleaning systems. Its iQ products can be cleaned using nearly 20% less electricity and water, and 2.3 times less detergent than rival products. This translates into a 40% reduction in resources and environmental impact over 20 years.

- It strives to apply a cradle-to-cradle (C2C) design philosophy whereby it recycles all its products at the end of their life to make new products. In 2013, as part of its take-back programme, Tarkett collected and recycled 17,400 tonnes of post-consumer and post-installation materials, a 51% increase over 2012. Interestingly, its Tandus flooring recycling centre, the first in the industry to be third-party certified, processes not only its own products but also those of other manufacturers.

Anne-Christine Ayed, Tarkett's head of research, innovation and environment since 2009, explains that while customers value products that are eco-friendly, they also want high-quality options that are affordable and well designed, and contribute to their well-being. For instance, Tarkett's eco-friendly flooring products are designed not only to improve air quality but also to reduce noise. This approach is particularly important in public facilities like schools and hospitals. Likewise, Tarkett's FieldTurf, a 100% recyclable artificial grass deployed in sports stadiums, is designed to provide greater safety and comfort to players while saving millions of gallons of water and many tonnes of fertiliser and pesticide. A 2012 study by FIFA, football's international governing body, deemed FieldTurf to be as good as natural grass, and the 2012 Super Bowl was played on a FieldTurf field in Indianapolis. In an effort to enhance customer experience, Tarkett now offers modular flooring solutions that give customers more design choices and are easier and faster to install, repair, replace and recycle. This modularity allows Tarkett to be more agile (a subject covered in Chapter 3), and helps the firm keep up with the rapidly evolving tastes of clients such as retailers and hotel managers who regularly change the flooring in their establishments.

Tarkett's offerings are also financially sustainable, thanks to its innovative business model. It provides custom value-added services to customers during the entire life of a product. For instance, as part of its FieldTurf TotalCare offering, Tarkett takes care of the installation, maintenance, disposal and replacement of synthetic turf in sports fields. Its product removal and replacement process is also environmentally sustainable. For instance, Tarkett can replace existing field turf by reusing and cleaning as much of the existing infill as possible. Similarly, it minimises the amount of glue used when installing carpets so they can be removed without chemical adhesives.

Ayed credits Tarkett's entrepreneurial culture for its ability to continually innovate products and processes and reinvent its business model before rivals do:

The only non-depletable resource in the world is human ingenuity. We use sustainability as a powerful lever to unleash all our employees' ingenuity.

Not surprisingly, Tarkett invests heavily in training its 11,000 employees, and collaborates extensively with suppliers, distributors and customers, as well as universities, trade associations, scientific labs and environmental protection agencies in the US and Europe.

Shareholders are also happy. In 2013, Tarkett's sales grew by nearly 10% and net profits rose 8.5%. As Giannuzzi, who believes strongly that sustainability is a key growth lever, notes:

Far from being a business constraint, corporate sustainability is an opportunity to continuously improve our operations, and to innovate and differentiate our brand in a highly competitive marketplace.

Giannuzzi now wants Tarkett "to become the industry benchmark for achieving high standards in sustainability". In 2013, it became one of the first global companies to join the "Circular Economy 100" programme. Initiated by the Ellen MacArthur Foundation, this programme regroups over 100 companies committed to supporting the development of a sustainable economic growth model based on the reuse of materials and the conservation of planetary resources.[1] By 2020, Tarkett aims to use 75% of renewable and recycled materials, eliminate industrial waste going to landfill, make sure that all flooring products are made from phthalate-free plasticisers and have low TVOC emissions, and double the 2010 volume of collected post-installation and post-consumer products.

Tarkett's story is remarkable for touching on so many aspects of frugal sustainability. But it is not unique, and many established companies will be able to draw on its experiences to make similar transformations. This chapter shows how companies can drastically reduce their consumption of scarce natural resources in their value chain by designing, making and selling products and services with a lower environmental impact. It describes how to implement sustainable practices such as cradle-to-cradle and the circular economy (where components and materials are repeatedly recycled) to design and manufacture waste-free products of value to customers. It shows how the sharing economy – in which customers share products as pay-as-you-go services rather than own and consume them – can boost customer loyalty and generate new sources of revenue. And it explains how some pioneering firms are using techniques such as upcycling to combine and integrate the principles of the sharing and circular economies, thus paving the way for the "spiral economy": a virtuous system that generates ever more value while reducing waste and the use of natural resources.

Essential – not optional – sustainability

For many years, companies only paid lip service to sustainability as part of their corporate social responsibility (CSR) and philanthropic activities. Recently, however, several factors have forced developed-world companies to take a more strategic approach to sustainability.

Resource scarcity threatens the viability of businesses

Paul Polman of Unilever notes that the world consumes 1.3 times more than the planet can replenish.[2] Given current rates, by 2030 we would require two planets to supply the resources we need and to absorb our waste. With 3 billion new middle-class consumers worldwide projected over the next two decades, demand for energy, food, water and materials will drive up prices for natural resources. The discovery of shale gas may bring some relief to oil-dependent firms, but there will still be chronic shortages of water, wood and other natural resources. "We will run out of water long before we run out of fuel," predicts Nestlé's chairman, Peter Brabeck-Letmathe, who champions water conservation.[3] IKEA, a Swedish company that designs and sells ready-to-assemble furniture, consumes 1% of the world's commercial wood supply and frets about its continuing availability, even as it plans to double revenues to €50 billion ($63 billion) and customers to 1.5 billion by 2020. Steve Howard, IKEA's chief sustainability officer, reckons:[4]

> Sustainability will be a decisive factor in terms of which businesses will be here in 20 or 30 years' time. It is the future of business.

Customers demand eco-friendly and healthy solutions

Customers are now more environmentally conscious and want products and services that are less damaging to the planet. Moreover, they realise that the planet's health affects their own. For instance, 61% of EU citizens worry that pollution is damaging their well-being, and 42% are concerned about the harmful effects of poor air, food and products. According to the World Health Organization, air pollution caused one in eight deaths worldwide in 2012. Indeed, research shows that 90–95% of new cancer cases are caused by lifestyle and environmental factors, mainly air pollution and chemicals in the food chain.

Regulators demand greater sustainability from companies

Governments in the US, Europe and Japan demand that companies create cleaner and healthier products. New US standards for mileage and emissions require carmakers to deliver a fleet by 2025 that will halve greenhouse-gas emissions and save billions of dollars at the pump. Japan – which has banned diesel engines from Tokyo – is ratcheting up its already strict environmental standards. Its top eight carmakers are now working together to develop eco-friendly diesel engines by 2020 that will cut carbon-dioxide emissions by 30% from 2010 levels.

The EU has been even more aggressive. In September 2012, the European Parliament passed the Energy Efficiency Directive aimed at cutting EU energy consumption by 20% by 2020. As a result, large European companies will have to make their supply chains more energy efficient. In the same year, the European Parliament also passed a stricter recycling law that requires electronic and electrical goods suppliers and retailers to collect, and potentially recycle, 45% of all electric and electronic scrap by 2016, increasing to 65% by 2019. Janez Potočnik, the EU commissioner for the environment, noted:

> *In these times of economic turmoil and rising prices for raw materials, resource efficiency is where environmental benefits and innovative growth opportunities come together.*

Policymakers are also pressuring companies to reduce water consumption. In 2013, California experienced its driest ever year. With the looming prospect of drought, it passed a law to reduce per-head urban water consumption by 20% by 2020 and is demanding that agribusinesses produce more using less water.

Regulators also want companies to reduce chemical usage in their supply chain. In 2007, the EU Registration, Evaluation, Authorisation and Restriction of Chemicals (REACH) regulation to control and reduce the use of chemical substances in industrial processes and everyday products, such as cleaning products, clothes, furniture and electric appliances, came into force. The US Food and Drug Administration has proposed a ban on transfats, and in New York a campaign by a former mayor, Michael Bloomberg, helped to ban the sale of sugary drinks in school vending machines.

Employees want their companies to care for the environment

More than 12 peer-reviewed academic studies and a host of business surveys show that especially younger job seekers prefer to work for environmentally friendly firms. Once hired, these employees tend to be more productive and stay longer. A 2012 UCLA (University of

California, Los Angeles) study found that productivity is 16% higher in companies with green practices and standards. Employees also want a sustainable work environment. And a 2006 survey by Mortgage Lenders Network USA found that 94% of Americans prefer to work in energy-efficient and ecologically sound buildings.

The dictionary offers three definitions for the verb "to sustain":

- to undergo or suffer (something unpleasant);
- to cause to continue or be prolonged for an extended period or without interruption;
- to strengthen or support physically or mentally.

The first captures many developed-world perceptions of sustainability; that is, the sense that business is compelled to comply with environmental standards (and that this is a sunk cost). Sustainability is deemed to be incompatible with profitability. Some pragmatic business leaders adhere to the second definition, recognising how resource scarcity could constrain growth, and so are willing to adapt to protect existing business models. Based on the authors' research and consulting work, it is estimated that some 90% of US and European companies fall into these two categories.

However, one in ten companies have embraced the third definition, and are adopting sustainable business practices to boost performance. Firms like Tarkett are rebuilding their entire value chain and reinventing their business models around sustainability. They are doing so not just to reduce the use of costly and hazardous materials, but also to fire up growth and customer loyalty.

These enlightened leaders transcend the sustainability-versus-profitability debate, seeing sustainability as a competitive advantage. Underlying their business models are two defining operating principles: the circular economy (the indefinite reuse and recycling of materials); and the sharing economy (where products and services are shared rather than owned).

The rise of the circular economy

The dominant model of production and consumption in the 20th century was linear. Firms made products, and consumers used and disposed of them. More recently, however, firms and consumers have started to reduce, recycle and reuse products, thus giving rise to a circular economy (thanks in large part to ideas from the Ellen MacArthur Foundation). According to McKinsey & Company, adopting circular economy principles could save the global consumer-goods sector alone $700 billion annually. This is perhaps a modest estimate, given that the $3.2 trillion consumer-goods sector accounts for 60% of total consumer spending, 35% of material inputs, 90% of agricultural output and 75% of municipal waste, and that only 20% of materials in this value chain is currently recovered and reused or recycled. In 2014, the World Economic Forum estimated that circular business models could increase the value of the global economy by $1 trillion annually by 2025, and create 100,000 jobs over the next five years.

An early adopter of the circular economy was method, a cleaning-products supplier founded in 2000 by two childhood friends, Adam Lowry and Eric Ryan, who disliked the poorly designed, smelly, ineffective and toxic cleaning products sold in shops. Seeing a ready source of recyclable materials in the estimated 46,000 pieces of plastic floating in every square mile of ocean, they decided to shake up the cleaning world with good-looking, eco-friendly products made with non-harmful ingredients. The company developed a 2-in-1 dish plus hand soap packaged in a well-designed bottle made from recycled ocean plastic. The cleaning product inside is 100% natural, totally biodegradable and "cleans like heck and smells like heaven", says method.

Since then, the company has launched many "best-smelling" products, crafted by its "green chefs" (or formulation chemists and designers) to be innovative, eco-safe and effective. Its products include a plant-based laundry detergent that is eight times the normal concentration (and hence able to do better with less). All method's products are made with 100% natural and biodegradable ingredients, fully disclosed and certified, and come in 100% recycled plastic bottles. None of the products are tested on animals (a practice that won Lowry and Ryan PETA's Person of the Year award in 2006), and all are competitively priced.

Method soon disrupted the staid world of cleaning products. This eco-chic company is literally cleaning up. In 2006, Inc. magazine ranked it as the US's seventh fastest-growing private company, and in

2011 method reported revenues of $100 million. In September 2012, method was acquired by Ecover, a large European manufacturer of planet-friendly cleaning products, to form the world's largest green cleaning-products supplier with combined annual sales of $200 million. In 2007, method became a founding Benefit Corporation or B Corp. This is a new type of company that uses the power of business to solve social and environmental problems. In 2013, method was ranked number one for making the most positive environmental impact among 650 B Corps worldwide.

Lowry and Ryan were successful because they adopted an R&D approach that integrates the three core tenets of frugal innovation: quality, affordability and sustainability. Hence every method product is designed from the outset to be safe, effective, eco-friendly, good-looking and reasonably priced. There is no compromise or trade-off.

Indeed, sustainability lies at the heart of its product development strategy. It has embraced a variant of the circular economy, cradle-to-cradle design (C2C for short), popularised by William McDonough and Michael Braungart in their 2002 book *Cradle to Cradle*.[5] Inspired by nature's remarkable capacity to renew itself without waste, C2C calls for waste-free design and manufacturing, in which all raw materials are as natural as possible and reused continuously. C2C therefore stands in direct contrast to the traditional "lab-to-landfill" (L2L) approach, with artificial materials created in an R&D lab ending up in a landfill after a single use.

C2C is not just a warm and fuzzy CSR practice; it is a game-changing business practice – the cornerstone of the circular economy. Indeed, C2C is essential for truly frugal innovation. By embedding it into the business model, companies can create self-sustaining products and services and drive up profits.

Although method was born a circular company, older and more established companies can also make the transition from linear to circular models with C2C, as Levi Strauss & Co, founded in 1853 and known for its Levi's denim jeans and Dockers khakis, has done.

Levi Strauss recently adopted the design-for-sustainability principle to create jeans that can be manufactured using fewer natural resources. For instance, its Levi's Water<Less collection, launched in 2011, uses up to 96% less water for some styles than regular jeans do

during the finishing process. Each pair is processed using only 1 litre of water. Levi Strauss has already produced 62 million items using the Water‹Less process, which it claims has saved over 770 million litres of water (enough to fill 308 Olympic-sized swimming pools). In 2013, Levi Strauss also launched Waste‹Less, a denim collection that incorporates post-consumer waste, specifically recycled plastic bottles and food trays. At its launch, each pair of Waste‹Less jeans included a minimum of 20% post-consumer waste, on average eight plastic bottles. Levi Strauss estimates that its spring 2013 Waste‹Less collection uses over 3.5 million recycled plastic bottles.

In 2013, Levi Strauss also set up a world-class water recycling system in one of its Chinese supplier's factories. This system has since helped produce 100,000 pairs of women's jeans with 100% recycled water, saving 12 million litres of water. The company is currently spreading this water recycling system to other suppliers and collections. In 2014, Levi Strauss's Dockers brand launched the Wellthread collection, a new line of clothing designed explicitly for long-term durability – the opposite of disposable, fast fashion. All Wellthread products are made of 100% cotton fabrics, thread and pocketing, and their dyeing process uses less energy and water. The garments are designed with reinforced pockets and buttonholes to extend their lifespan, and there are locker loops and overlapped shoulder seams on T-shirts to support hang drying instead of machine drying.

Commenting on Levi Strauss's commitment to sustainable design, Michael Kobori, vice-president of global sustainability, notes:[6]

We don't want to create separate, dedicated "green" product lines. Rather, we invest in innovative technologies like Water‹Less and processes like Wellthread that can be applied across multiple product lines, making sustainability a core design principle for all our products. We want to gradually build a rich design-for-sustainability toolkit that we would share with our suppliers, and even our competitors. The hypercompetitive apparel sector is known for its race to the bottom. We want to initiate a race to the top by uplifting the sustainability standards of the entire industry.

As well as saving on production costs, Levi Strauss's sustainably designed products are generating greater customer goodwill and boosting employee morale. Employees in its stores – especially those in their 20s and 30s – rave about the Water‹Less, Waste‹Less and Wellthread products, which they find cool. Levi Strauss can be sure its brand is winning when employees willingly promote a product they genuinely care about.

A growing number of global *Fortune* 1000 companies, including Nike, Herman Miller, Heineken and Philips, are adopting C2C. Many are getting their products cradle-to-cradle certified by McDonough Braungart Design Chemistry (MBDC). MBDC has already certified 60 method products. Tarkett intends to become a C2C company – and to get most of its products C2C certified – by 2020. Certification is becoming the gold standard for environmental sustainability and helps differentiate products in hypercompetitive industries such as consumer goods.

Another sustainable strategy is biomimetics, also known as biomimicry, which seeks to imitate the well-adapted models and systems of nature and living organisms. These models and systems, which have evolved over many millennia through natural selection, can inspire resilient and resource-efficient technologies and solutions. For instance, inspired by the lotus flower's rough surface, which repels dust and dirt and keeps its petals clean, Ispo, a coating supplier (now owned by Sto Corp), has developed Lotusan, a self-cleaning paint that wards off dust particles, thus reducing the need to wash the surfaces of houses and buildings. Similarly, the shimmer of butterfly wings inspired engineers at Qualcomm, a global semiconductor company, to design Mirasol, a reflective display technology used in e-reader and tablet screens that delivers brighter colours while consuming less energy. By reusing materials again and again, through multiple production cycles, and by adopting the resource-efficient design principles of biomimicry, companies are able to significantly reduce their supply chain costs and pass these savings on to customers.

Widening the sharing economy

In a circular economy, a product undergoes multiple incarnations – with its materials being recycled and reused again and again – thus sustaining its value over multiple lifetimes. During any particular lifetime, however, the product is most likely to be owned and used by just one customer. But what if, during even a single lifetime or incarnation, the same product could be consumed by many users? Then the same inputs could be made to create greater value for more and more users. That is the underlying premise of the sharing economy – also known as collaborative consumption – in which participants aspire to share access to goods and services rather than to have individual ownership.

Sharing economy firms include Airbnb (sharing homes), RelayRides, BlaBlaCar and easyCar (sharing cars), ParkatmyHouse (sharing parking spaces), BringBee (sharing trips to the grocery store), Wishi or Wear It Share It (choosing clothes), Eatwith (sharing your dinner), yerdle.com (sharing household equipment with neighbours), Skillshare (sharing skills and knowledge) and TaskRabbit (outsourcing small jobs and errands). As we saw in Chapter 1, these services typically take advantage of the web and social media to enable ordinary people to monetise their time, space, knowledge or skills.

The sharing economy contributes to environmental sustainability because it reduces individual consumption by allowing, for instance, four people to share the same car rather than having to buy four different cars. The sharing economy also reduces waste by making excess capacity and unused resources available to those who need them most. By enabling products and assets to be fully utilised, the sharing economy increases their value.

Although sharing in the UK accounts for only 1.3% of GDP, and an even smaller proportion of the US economy, it is expected to grow exponentially in coming years, especially given the preference of young consumers to share everything from flats to cars to books. Nearly 50% of Europeans believe that, within a decade, cars will be consumed as a "shared" good rather than being individually owned, and 73% of them predict rapid growth of car-sharing services. Even in car-crazy Germany, Europe's biggest market, new car purchases by people aged under 30 fell from 6% in 1999 to 2.7% in 2013. Sharing-economy pioneers are also profiting from this growing trend. In March 2014, Airbnb was valued at $10 billion, making its founders the first sharing-economy billionaires.

Sensing an opportunity, and fearful of losing out to these start-ups, traditional companies are adapting their business models accordingly. As described in Chapter 3, BMW once just made and sold cars; it now thinks about "how to engage users through our cars and services". Its DriveNow car-sharing programme serves city dwellers who do not own a car but sometimes need one, offering customers an opportunity to share cars in a systematic way. BMW owns all the cars in its DriveNow fleet. Customers register on the DriveNow website and use a smartphone app to reserve, use and park cars within a certain area for the next customer to use. Customers pay per minute of use. Describing the service, Erich Ebner von Eschenbach, head of BMW Group's Financial Services Segment, said:[7]

In addition to helping us engage with new business models, DriveNow also gives us access to a new, younger and more cost and environmentally conscious customer group – one that is different from the core BMW buyer.

After a successful launch in Germany, BMW plans to roll out the service in Europe and North America. It also plans to add the i3, a purpose-built electric car with a carbon-fibre body, to the DriveNow fleet. "Shared electric cars offer a compelling, convenient and environmentally friendly proposition to city dwellers of the future," says von Eschenbach.

Kingfisher, Europe's largest home-improvement retailer and a founding member of the Circular Economy 100, has long been concerned about its dependence on natural resources such as timber (Kingfisher's annual wood consumption is equivalent to a forest the size of Switzerland). Its Net Positive plan aims to achieve net forest restoration to secure long-term raw-material supplies. As part of this plan, Kingfisher is pioneering closed-loop innovation, which cuts out waste. Closed-loop products are made mostly from recycled or renewable materials and consume only renewable energy during their manufacture and use. When they break or get old, materials and parts from these products can be collected to make new products. Starting with 1,000 products in 2020, Kingfisher wants its entire 40,000 products portfolio to reach closed-loop status.

The company is also piloting numerous product-sharing initiatives. One, titled Project Box, allows customers to rent rather than buy the DIY tools they need for home-improvement projects. Tools such as power drills are typically used for less than 30 minutes over their entire lifetime, making them particularly suited to a rental model. As James Walker, former head of innovation at Kingfisher, explains:[8]

> *Instead of spending £300 on buying the wrong tools, that they may use only once anyway, customers can rent the right tools from us for less.*

Focus groups suggest that women like the concept more than men. Women typically complain that their husbands never have the right tools and end up doing a terrible job, or returning to the store to buy more tools; and men respond positively, because they do not have to work it all out themselves. So everyone is happy and less stressed, and there are fewer fights, Walker says.

A product that gets recycled, however, may not necessarily become a better product. Similarly, someone who picks up a shared car will not get more value from this car than the previous customer. But what if a product, service or asset gains in value as it is transformed, reused and shared across multiple users? Then its value circle would become a value spiral and the circular and sharing economy would become a "spiral economy".

From the circular to the spiral economy

Pioneering companies can use several techniques to create value spirals around their products.

Turn waste into wealth

The digital age promises to make us more productive and connected, but it is also prone to pollution. Indeed, electronic waste (or e-waste) is growing three times faster than any other type of waste. In the US, it accounts for 70% of heavy metals in landfills. In their book *Resource Revolution*, McKinsey consultants Stefan Heck and Matt Rogers predict the rise of what they call "global recovery of waste (GROW)" companies.[9] These use eco-friendly, energy-efficient processes to recover high-value materials from e-waste. Heck and Rogers cite the case of ATMI, a company that literally turns waste into gold. ATMI has developed a proprietary, water-based, non-toxic solution that extracts tiny bits of gold encrusted in electronic circuits. The extraction process is undertaken by a machine the size of a shipping container that can be sent to any location where e-waste needs to be treated. The machine can recycle an entire city's e-waste and churn out a bar of gold every two days. And because ATMI's water-based process does not damage the chips in the circuits, the chips can be reused in other electronic products, thus extending their life and value.

While ATMI uses sophisticated science and technology, other companies are leveraging the power of design to transform non-precious waste into high-ticket items. These design-savvy modern-day alchemists can transmute waste into aspirational products. FIAM Italia, founded in 1973 by Vittorio Livi, produces high-quality glass furniture by combining traditional craftsmanship and cutting-edge industrial processes. Its products, such as the Ragno monolithic curved glass table, are avidly bought by top-tier hoteliers, architects and corporations worldwide.

In 2012, Daniele Livi, the founder's son and current CEO, had a brainwave: to collect glass waste from FIAM's factory and use it to make beautiful, aspirational products. He challenged several up-and-coming designers to beautify glass waste. They would not be paid, but Livi promised to make them world-famous. Within a few months, the designers created several stunning pieces of furniture made entirely from glass waste, which FIAM exhibited at the 2013 Milan Furniture Fair to rave reviews. In 2014, a limited collection, branded REMADE IN FIAM, sold out within days, turning its lesser-known designers into overnight celebrities. Livi reflects:

> Using waste, it is hard to get something of high quality. But our key strength is that we work with artists. We give them a platform to discover and try new things. Artists don't have limits, and know how to turn constraints into creative opportunities and integrate sustainability and beauty.

FIAM's project is classic upcycling, whereby waste is not merely recycled into something of similar or lower value but transformed through design into a product with high aesthetic appeal. Sometimes, the frugal producer can even charge more, suggesting that frugal innovation is not just about reducing cost and making products more affordable but also creating aspirational value. This may explain the growing success of "fashion trucks", such as Caravan Shop in Paris, that sell trendy apparel and accessories using recycled materials created by local designers.

Design multipurpose products

Qarnot Computing, a French high-performance computing services provider, makes digital radiators which contain microchips that can download and process computational jobs, such as scientific calculations or 3D rendering, submitted by developers and scientists anywhere in the world. The heat harvested from the microprocessors is then used to warm homes and offices. Qarnot's founder, Paul Benoit, an engineer by training who quit his job in the financial sector to launch a start-up to "do good", explains that the digital radiators act as mini supercomputers for one set of customers – offering them high-end computation services at low cost – while providing free heating for others.

Digitally enrich physical products

Analogue products can be upgraded into digital products, thus allowing them to do more. For instance, Berg, a design company, hacked a Zanussi washing machine to make it a connected device, thus dramatically improving the user experience. Smart companies are increasingly tapping into user communities to generate new digital content that can improve their products. Ford has extensively open-sourced the electronics of its cars' telematics systems so that third-party developers (including DIY customers) can upgrade them as they wish, thus prolonging the life of the car and increasing its value. (Chapter 7 discusses how Ford is engaging makers and tinkerers to create more value for car users without spending more on R&D.)

Create products that adapt to evolving customer needs

Bouygues Immobilier, one of Europe's largest property developers, is building apartments that can evolve with their inhabitants at different stages of their life. The modular design enables effortless reconfiguration of space so the same room can serve, say, as a private gym and later as a place to receive at-home care. As Eric Mazoyer, deputy CEO of Bouygues Immobilier, explains:[10]

> Our customers tell us their #1 need is flexibility. To meet this need, we apply innovative techniques like modular design to build Lego-like apartments and homes that can be easily reconfigured to adapt to tenants' changing requirements over time.

Get ecosystems to embrace sustainability

Visionary firms such as Timberland, a US clothing manufacturer, are building coalitions of employees, suppliers, retailers and even competitors to cultivate value spirals within their industry. The firm has teamed up with 60 other apparel and footwear manufacturers to create an environmental index called the Higgs Index, the likely future industry standard for measuring the environmental performance of branded apparel. This benchmarking tool could move other apparel-makers towards more sustainable design and supply chain practices.

Recommendations for managers

At a strategic level, senior managers wishing to create sustainable solutions in their firms can do the following.

Set "big, hairy audacious goals"

To inspire and galvanise all employees to achieve breakthrough innovation, senior managers must set the bar high by committing the entire company to a big, hairy audacious goal (BHAG), such as "100% of all our products will carry an external sustainability certification within ten years" (the BHAG of Marks & Spencer's extended Plan A announced in 2010) or "to have zero environmental footprint by 2020" (a BHAG that Interface, a leading carpet-maker, has set for itself as part of its Mission Zero). The BHAG must be highly ambitious, otherwise the initiative risks ending up as a series of minor, incremental and insignificant changes. Elisabeth Laville, founder of Utopies, a sustainability consultancy, advises clients to run big marketing campaigns that emphasise these BHAGs to encourage organisation-wide commitment and stimulate major cultural change, with the risk of losing face if the publicly announced goals are not met. BHAGs also help create positive constraints that shift perceptions of sustainability from being painful to being a source of disruptive and meaningful innovation. A sense of urgency also helps. If necessity is the mother of invention, then scarcity is its grandmother.

Use key performance indicators (KPIs) to measure progress against the big goal

KPIs should measure the company's progress in doing things better, not simply less badly. Laville calls the former "absolute KPIs" and the latter "relative KPIs". She says:[11]

Behaving a little less badly, for example reducing electricity consumption in your factory by using more energy-efficient equipment, doesn't make you good. To be good, you would have to redesign the entire production system so it runs totally on renewable energy.

Companies' KPIs should be holistic and extensive and include their impact on suppliers and customers. For example, Kingfisher's closed-loop calculator is used across the company to assess how existing and new products meet ten criteria. These include the product's materials, whether it can be rented or repaired, and if it can be easily disassembled into components or materials for reuse or recycling. Kingfisher intends to share this tool with its suppliers.

Link these KPIs to staff incentives

This is crucial for inducing behavioural change at every level and ensuring that those changes stick. Human resources heads must be involved and might even drive the process.

*

Many companies have implemented one or other of the above, but few have done all three in an integrated way. Yet doing so is vital to accelerating change. Senior management should take responsibility, but other managers also have an important role to play in executing organisation-wide sustainability. In addition to these three strategic steps, there are other actions that functional managers can undertake.

Substitute abundant new resources for scarce resources

R&D managers should constantly look at how substitution might improve overall performance. In the automotive sector, for example, electric motors are more efficient, safer and faster than the traditional internal-combustion engines. Carbon fibre is lighter and allows companies to build quieter, more efficient, comfortable and beautiful cars (as in Tesla's case – see Chapter 7) or aircraft (as with Boeing's Dreamliner). Apple and GE have considered all the elements of the periodic table, identified which ones pose the biggest risks for supply, costs and regulation, and developed substitution opportunities for the riskier elements.

Factor in sustainability during the design phase

When making decisions, R&D engineers and scientists should use new tools like Autodesk's sustainability solutions to evaluate and reduce the environmental impact of new products over their life cycle as well as assess the impact of design decisions on the triple bottom line: people, planet and profits.

Use existing assets to scale up sustainable business models

Operations managers of energy, logistics or other asset-intensive companies often fret about upgrading or replacing costly physical infrastructure as part of a sustainability agenda. However, they can often find clever ways to reuse existing assets quite cheaply. For example, in 2012, France's La Poste launched Recy'Go, which collects and recycles used office paper and documents in small and medium-sized businesses. Recy'Go needed little capital to do this since the staff, trucks and bins used to distribute mail could also collect used paper from their clients. The only cost was the time and effort required to train the staff and set up a new information system. As Sophie-Noëlle Nemo, vice-president at La Poste and head of Recy'Go, points out:[12] "We didn't invent anything new. We merely connected a world of needs with a world of (existing) solutions." In 2014, employing only five full-time staff, Recy'Go served some 2,500 clients, mostly small and medium-sized enterprises, and collected over 13,000 tonnes of waste paper. By 2018, it aims to serve 50,000 clients, collect 50,000 tonnes of waste paper and generate €50 million ($60 million) in revenue for La Poste. The market potential is huge given that only 40% of paper in France is recycled (compared with 70% in Germany). Recy'Go will soon recycle printer cartridges as well. La Poste, whose core mail-delivery service has halved in recent years, certainly needs the extra revenues.

Combine technology with design to make sustainability cool

R&D managers and marketers should seek ways of beautifying waste through design. The trick is to find ways to appeal to customers in the developed world who want eco-friendly, high-quality, trendy products and services. Upcyling may be a new concept for business, but designers, artists and architects have been practising it for decades. In the 1950s, Bruno Munari, an Italian artist and designer, drew on Constructivist principles to transform basic materials such as wire, paper, bamboo and broken electrical components into elegant, witty and useful objects. Munari used cardboard for an ingenious sun visor that Dwight Eisenhower wore on his US presidential campaign trail. Similarly, Shigeru Ban, a Japanese architect who won the 2014 Pritzker Prize, has repurposed inexpensive materials to build cheap housing in communities struck by natural disasters. He even built a cardboard cathedral in Christchurch, New Zealand following the deadly 2011 earthquake. If companies can combine their left-brain R&D skills with right-brain design sensibilities, sustainability can be both frugal and aesthetically pleasing.

CASE STUDY 3

Unilever: sustainable solutions

Sustainability is increasingly on companies' agendas, but only a handful think of CSR as a strategic priority. Unilever, an Anglo-Dutch multinational consumer-goods company, belongs in the latter camp. It is at the forefront of *Fortune* 500 companies that place sustainability at the heart of everything they do.

This strategic initiative has come from the top. When Paul Polman became the firm's CEO in January 2009, after many years with P&G and Nestlé, he introduced an ambitious environmental, social and business agenda, manifested in the November 2010 launch of the Sustainable Living Plan. The plan aimed to double sales and halve the company's environmental impact by 2020. This is no small undertaking. Unilever owns and operates 260 factories and 460 warehouses in 90 countries, serving 2 billion consumers worldwide. It plans to add a further 2 billion consumers over the next decade, mostly in emerging markets, and still reduce its carbon footprint. The Sustainable Living Plan also includes social goals, such as improving both the nutritional value of its food products and the livelihoods of over 500,000 smallholder farmers and distributors that it works with worldwide.

David Blanchard, Unilever's chief R&D officer, says of the plan:[13]

This was frugal innovation by definition … We either say "I don't know how to do that" or use the plan as a way to challenge ourselves to think and act differently.

The Sustainable Living Plan's three pillars are: to help over 1 billion people improve health and hygiene; to halve the environmental footprint; and to acquire all agricultural raw materials from sustainable sources, all by 2020. The strategy is organised into seven distinct areas: health and hygiene; nutrition; greenhouse gases; water use; waste and packaging; sustainable sourcing; and better livelihoods. Blanchard says:

The Sustainable Living Plan acts as a rallying cry and a compass for everything the firm now does. It informs a lot of our innovation and operation initiatives and helps us approach things differently across the spectrum.

And the company has had some notable successes.

Thinking differently about hygiene

Lifebuoy, Unilever's well-known Asian soap brand, was transformed by the Sustainable Living Plan. The company began by considering the overarching importance of hand washing: every few seconds, someone somewhere dies as a result of not washing their hands. Although the recommended time for washing hands is 30 seconds, most people spend about 10 seconds doing so. The challenge, therefore, was to make sure that people get the right kind of microbial-kill during the shorter wash time. The R&D team invented a new technology called terpineol and/or thymol, a combination of natural activities whose germ-kill is ten times faster than other anti-microbials. The next challenge was to put that into a soap bar that could sell in India for Rs5 (10 cents). Unilever had to radically rethink how it made a bar of soap – how to structure the bar, how to get it to lather, how to get it to smell nice – and it had to be done cheaply. Its success means that Lifebuoy is now one of the fastest-growing Unilever brands, with sales up 10% year on year in 2013. Today, 111 families buy a Lifebuoy product every second.

Deodorants and reducing greenhouse gases

Unilever is a global market leader in deodorants, with well-known brands such as AXE, Lynx and Dove. It has a 40% market share globally, with its biggest markets in western Europe, North America and Latin America. It makes three different types of antiperspirant: deodorant sticks, which sell mainly in the US, and roll-ons and aerosols which sell in Europe and Latin America. Following the Sustainable Living Plan, it was clear that the aerosol business posed a particular challenge for Unilever. Aerosols in deodorant cans contribute to greenhouse emissions because of the gas they use as a propellant, and the aluminium cans require a lot of energy to manufacture. Researchers began by asking consumers how much their buying decisions were influenced by a product's sustainability, and discovered that this was not a priority. What mattered was performance: whether the aerosol would keep them dry and fresh. Customers were not prepared to trade performance for sustainability, nor were they willing to pay more. The challenge therefore was to give the same or better performance but in a more sustainable way. Achieving that is often all it takes for a consumer to choose one product over another. Unilever set out to produce more concentrated cans, which it achieved as a result of innovation in its laundry detergents business.

Persil and concentrated detergents

In 2007, Unilever launched concentrated detergents in the US. One of these products was the 25-wash Persil Small and Mighty. These "three times concentrates" replaced what Unilever used to call its "dilutes" business, whose packs were twice as high and twice as heavy. Even before the Sustainable Living Plan, the company regarded concentration as a way to increase value for money and lessen their environmental impact. But motivated by the need to be more sustainable at a lower price, it ended up with a product that also performed better. As Blanchard notes:

> This wasn't necessarily something we were expecting. As it turns out, as you concentrate, it actually becomes easier for the actives in the detergent to get at the dirt.

Concentration has had other environmental and cost benefits. The smaller pack sizes reduced distribution costs, allowing Unilever to cut its truck fleet by 20%. The innovation led to reductions in transport, packaging and waste to landfills, and much of the savings can be passed on to consumers.

"We realised, if you can concentrate a laundry detergent, you can do the same with aerosols," says Blanchard.

Lynx, AXE and concentrated aerosol deodorants

When Unilever applied the concentration model to aerosols it was able to put the contents of a 150ml can into a 75ml can. But this resulted in a new challenge: consumers were unconvinced that they were getting the same value, until Unilever introduced a new valve and a radically re-engineered actuator that maintained the performance. The concentration strategy, which was used for the Lynx brand, has since been applied to Dove, AXE, Rexona and Vaseline, and the company is looking to spread this know-how across all its businesses.

Sustainability throughout the organisational DNA

In many respects, sustainability is not new to Unilever. Its social and environmental commitment dates back to the founding mission in 1885 when William Hesketh Lever founded the Sunlight brand to create affordable hygiene in Manchester. At this time the Dutch side of the firm, Margarine Unie, was producing affordable nutrition in margarine and dairy products. In many ways, the Sustainable Living Plan has simply drawn upon Unilever's fundamental operating principles.

All this effort is beginning to pay dividends for the company. The 2014 Sustainable Living Plan reports progress against its targets including "48% of agricultural raw materials from sustainable sources, up from 14% in 2010" and success in helping "303 million people improve their health and well-being through Lifebuoy, Signal, Pureit and Dove brands, up from 52 million in 2010".

Conclusion

A few pioneering Western firms are making sustainability a strategic objective. New approaches such as cradle-to-cradle and collaborative consumption are both causes and consequences of this shift; and these trends will drive the frugal innovation revolution in the West.

Unilever, Marks & Spencer and Kingfisher have made impressive progress in reducing their environmental footprint, but they face another big challenge in extending sustainability to consumers. As the UK's *Daily Telegraph* reported in 2013:

> *Two-thirds of the greenhouse-gas emissions from Unilever's products – and half the water consumption – come not from manufacture or transport, but from their use. So if Unilever wants to cut its environmental footprint, it has to change the way consumers use its products.*

Such concerns are echoed by other consumer companies. As a senior manager at a leading fast-moving consumer goods company says:

> *The big leap will come when we can get consumers to change their behaviour, for instance, when we can get them to stop boiling an entire kettle of water every time they want to make a single cup of coffee.*

The way a company produces and sells its products is only one side of the frugal innovation equation. Equally important is the consumer's role. The next chapter explains how companies can shape consumer behaviour to achieve more frugal outcomes.

5   Principle four: shape customer behaviour

If I had asked people what they wanted, they would have said faster horses.

Henry Ford

We are all responsible for everyone else – but I am more responsible than all the others.

Fyodor Dostoyevsky, The Brothers Karamazov

MOST WESTERN HOMES have thermostats. These devices are so common we have ceased to pay them much attention. But they do matter: they control half a typical home's energy use (more than all appliances and lighting combined) and account for half the average energy bill. Properly programming thermostats can save up to 20% in heating and cooling costs, yet over 85% of us never do so. This is often because we are intimidated by their complicated interfaces, some of which seem to need a PhD to crack.

The electric thermostat was invented by Warren Johnson of Wisconsin in 1883, but its design has not changed much since. Until, that is, 2011 when Nest Labs, a Silicon Valley start-up, launched its "learning thermostat". This Wi-Fi-enabled device learns and monitors the user's habits, schedules and temperature preferences. With this information and real-time data from its integrated sensors, which track humidity, activity and light, the Nest device adjusts itself, for instance by reducing heating when the sun is out or turning off the cooling when no one is at home. Essentially, the device can reprogramme itself. Boasting an elegant, simple, intuitive user interface – only current room temperature is displayed in bold font – the device can be set up in just 1 minute and controlled remotely through a smartphone.

The device's plug-and-play ease of use is no accident. Nest was co-founded by Tony Fadell, who created the iPod while at Apple. Although the Nest costs $250, it saves users an average of $173 annually in energy bills. Furthermore, a Nest-commissioned study found that southern Californians who used the learning thermostats saved over 11% of alternating current (AC)-related energy. The Nest device helps consumers adopt more eco-friendly behaviour by:

- **E-mailing users a monthly energy report.** This details how much energy has been consumed and saved, and offers tips for doing better. (Messages include: "Changing the temperature just 1° can cut your energy use up to 10%.") It shows users the points (called "leafs") they earn every time they choose an energy-efficient temperature. It also shows users how they score relative to other Nest owners, fostering a healthy energy-saving rivalry, with messages like: "Your away temperature is 57°F. The average for the US is 59.3°F."

- **Allowing remote control through a smartphone app.** This allows users who are, say, driving home earlier than planned on a cold evening to inform the Nest device to gradually warm up the living room in time for their arrival. The smartphone also reminds users when to replace a system's air filter (as dirty filters can increase energy bills by 5%).

- **Offering "rush hour" rewards for moderate energy use.** By working with US energy utilities, Nest allows owners to earn money or credit by reducing energy use during peak periods. This feature has achieved an incredible 55% decrease in energy consumption at peak times. When, for example, temperatures rose to over 100°F in Austin, Texas, on June 27th 2013, Nest thermostats helped cut energy use by 56% on average during the hottest part of the day.

Through these initiatives, services and tools, Nest's customers have the power to save power – and combat climate change from their living rooms. Unsurprisingly, Nest's growth has been amazing. By January 2014, the company was selling an average of 50,000 devices a month, when Google offered \$3.2 billion to buy it as part of its planned expansion into the internet-connected home-appliances market. Not to be outdone, Apple announced in June 2014 that it was planning a new software platform that would enable iPhone users to remotely control the lights, security systems and appliances in their homes.

As noted in Chapter 4, large companies increasingly recognise that there is only so much they alone can do to become sustainable. Customers must also learn to do better with less. This is especially important because customers are often more wasteful than their suppliers. Unilever's chief supply chain officer, Pier Luigi Sigismondi, estimates that half the water consumption, and 68% of a Unilever product's total carbon footprint, relates to how consumers use it. Similarly, Michael Kobori, Levi Strauss's vice-president of global sustainability, observes that 58% of the energy used during the lifetime of a pair of Levi's 501 jeans occurs during the customer-use phase as a result of washing and drying them. Given this, Sigismondi and Kobori note that if their respective companies are to become truly frugal, they must first encourage their customers to change their habits.

It is hard to get consumers to be frugal – and to like doing so. But as the Nest story shows, these challenges provide opportunities to innovate frugally in a way that encourages customers to do likewise. Companies can empower and even delight their customers with simplified products that let them measure, visualise and monitor their behaviour and help change it for the better.

Drawing on the pioneering work of companies such as Barclays, Johnson & Johnson, IKEA, Philips, Progressive, Toyota and Unilever, as well as several visionary start-ups, this chapter shows how companies across many industries can pull, nudge or shove consumers into behaving differently. It also shows how firms can improve brand loyalty and market share by tailoring products to the way customers actually live and use products. One approach is to give consumers a sense that they are spending or using less because they choose to, not because they have to. In short, customers must truly believe that less is more.

This chapter outlines the challenges involved in changing consumer behaviour, and the behavioural techniques and tools that a few pioneering companies use to do so.

Three contradictions of contemporary consumption

Consumers care about the environment and yet are profligate with resources

In survey after survey, Western consumers say they care about the environment and that they would like to be more prosocial (voluntary behaviour intended to benefit others). Yet data on their actual behaviour (for example, their energy and water use) suggests that these noble-minded consumers frequently allow behavioural, economic and technical barriers to get in the way.

For example, in the GfK Roper Yale 2008 survey on environmental issues a majority of Americans said that "it is important that the products they purchase be environmentally friendly". Specifically, when buying cars, laundry detergent and computer-printer paper, 66%, 62% and 51% of respondents respectively said that environmental concerns are important or essential to their decisions. Furthermore, many said that they are willing to pay more for green products. Specifically, around half said that they would "definitely" or "probably" pay 15% more for eco-friendly laundry detergent or an automobile, while around 40% said that they would spend 15% more on green computer-printer paper or wood furniture.

Similarly, the GfK Roper Consulting Green Gauge 2011 US survey found that:

> In spite of rising economic concerns, Americans still want companies to go green, and there is evidence that they give credit to companies that do so.

Specifically, 74% agreed that a manufacturer that reduces the environmental impact of its production is making a smart business decision. The 2012 Edelman's Good Purpose Survey found that 76% of global consumers are willing to buy from companies that support a good cause, while the 2013 Havas Media's Meaningful Brands

Survey found that 71% of consumers want companies to solve social problems.

The data on actual behaviour, however, are different. *National Geographic* magazine, along with GlobeScan, publishes Greendex, a biannual survey of actual household behaviour in 17 countries worldwide in areas such as housing, transport, food and consumer goods. The Greendex 2012 survey, which covers developed and developing countries, found that developed-world consumers are the least environmentally friendly. The survey concluded:

> *American consumers' behaviour still ranks as the least sustainable of all countries surveyed since the inception of the study, followed by Canadian, Japanese and French consumers.*

The survey also noted that "environmentally friendly behaviour among consumers has increased from 2010 in only five of 17 countries surveyed". (Interestingly, consumers in India, China and Brazil fared best.)

This bleak view is reinforced by the research of large consumer-goods companies. Tesco, a UK retailer, calculated that two-thirds of its products' carbon emissions occur at the end of the food chain: in homes or on trips to their stores. So too with fast-moving consumer goods (FMCG) companies. In 2007, Reckitt Benckiser, which produces Dettol, Clearasil and Strepsils, was one of the first FMCG companies to launch a full life cycle carbon-reduction programme. It set out to reduce its total carbon footprint by 20% by 2020, a target achieved in 2012. Reckitt Benckiser realised that its customers were responsible for two-thirds of its products' greenhouse-gas emissions, so it redesigned its products to have a lower impact once in the customers' hands. The company understood that it may not be sufficient to rely on what consumers say they want, but rather to respond to what they *do*, and then help them change.

Consumers are powerful – but not enough to change

In the 20th century consumer power rose steadily, particularly in free-market economies. With continuously rising incomes and greater competition among firms, today's consumers are more powerful than ever. Their spending drives over 70% of the US economy. The internet and mobile telephony are further enhancing consumer power by creating more informed buyer communities. Government regulation has also helped. The European Commission has emphasised the need for more consumer choice, better information and stronger rights as it builds its single EU market.

Is all this working? The European Commission's Consumer Empowerment Index, based on a Eurobarometer survey of 50,000 consumers in 29 countries in 2010, examined consumer skills, awareness and engagement. The index found that consumers in Norway, Finland and Germany scored highly, while those from Belgium, France and the UK were on average 13% lower; the gap between the top group and Poles and Romanians was 31%. Italy, Portugal and Spain also scored poorly, especially in consumer skills, where the gap with the top performers was 30%. Women scored worse than men; the old were less empowered than the young; and poorer and less educated consumers also scored relatively badly. Among the least empowered were those without internet access.

Therefore, even consumers in advanced economies lack information, opportunity or motivation to consider issues around sustainable consumption. Evidently, green or sustainable consumption remains a niche, discouraging firms from making more than incremental improvements to their products. Most importantly, consumers may not get the right information to make optimal choices.

Energy companies are an example. Consumers typically waste energy when heating, cooling and lighting their homes. But as the Nest case shows, most homes are not equipped with devices that can provide clear, usable and actionable information to reduce bills. And if they do, consumers lack the technical means to act on it. For instance, consumers cannot typically monitor and control energy use while at work or travelling, so the lights and heating are left on unnecessarily. Yet Opower, a Virginia-based software company that partners with utility companies to promote energy efficiency, estimates that US customers could, with the right data and tools, reduce annual electricity consumption by 18 million megawatt-hours – equivalent to 10 million metric tonnes of carbon emissions – saving $2.2 billion annually.

Once again, therefore, the onus falls on companies to take the lead. If Unilever, for example, wants to meet its target of getting 200 million people to use and heat less water, it will have to persuade consumers to take shorter showers. It is trying to do this with an easy-rinse shampoo. David Blanchard explains the problem:[1]

> One of the biggest challenges for us is showers. No matter what you say to some consumers, they like their eight to nine minutes in the morning: three minutes to get clean and five to face the challenges of another day. Twelve minutes in case of a big meeting! And because showering is not a core competency for Unilever, we have to set up an open innovation website and invite experts who are working on showers to say how we can co-create solutions with them to help reduce water use while enhancing the shower experience.

Importantly, companies also benefit when customers use fewer resources. A 2014 American Council for an Energy-Efficient Economy (ACEEE) study estimates that reducing electricity consumption by 1 kilowatt-hour costs utilities just 2.8 cents; up to one-third of the cost to generate 1 kilowatt-hour of electricity at a power plant.

Consumption is important for well-being but can erode it

For most of the 20th century, the West's dominant economic model placed consumption at the heart of growth. Since the Bretton Woods Conference in 1944, a nation's gross domestic product (GDP) has become the benchmark for measuring economic health and progress. Consumption is normally the largest component of GDP, consisting of household expenditure on durable and non-durable goods and services. From this viewpoint, the more people consume, the greater the incentive for firms to produce. The more firms produce, the more the economy grows and the better off people are.

This consumption-based approach to welfare has its critics. E.F. Schumacher, an Anglo-German economist and author of *Small is Beautiful*, argued that pure consumption may not necessarily improve quality of life. Indeed, consumption for its own sake could degrade quality of life. Schumacher did not believe that growth was always good, or that bigger was always better. He claimed that GDP was a poor measure of well-being and argued that consumption is merely a means to human well-being. According to him, societies should aim to achieve the "maximum amount of well-being with the minimum amount of consumption".[2]

Such ideas are echoed by more recent thinkers, such as John Ehrenfeld and Andrew Hoffman. In *Flourishing: A Frank Conversation about Sustainability*, they counter the conventional view that the role of business is to provide ever more material wealth as a means to increase well-being. They question how growth can be sustained, and whether it is possible for a large, growing population to maintain its current lifestyles:[3]

> *Given any reasonable forecast of future eco-efficiency gains, growth will have to stop, leaving us mired along the way, if we are to avoid the depletion of all ecosystems on this planet.*

For Ehrenfeld and Hoffman, the growth-oriented view of sustainability is leading to "growing human suffering and environmental degradation". They conclude:[4]

> *Growth is, ultimately, a measure of quantity; we suggest instead a measure of quality ... Business's primary role is to help people flourish.*

In the world of Schumacher, Ehrenfeld and Hoffman, corporate strategies would shift from compelling people to consume more to encouraging them to consume better, as profit takes a back seat to a firm's contribution to flourishing. Modern consumers are conflicted. On the one hand, they worry about the environment and rising living costs, and possess greater empowerment and connectivity. On the other hand, they battle self-interest, inertia and their inability to make a difference. The challenges facing firms therefore are: to influence consumers' behaviour without making them feel manipulated; to help consumers balance self-interest with their concern for the planet; and to balance frugality with a sense of abundance.

Some pioneering firms are already resolving these dilemmas using two distinct approaches: motivational and empowerment. Motivational approaches use techniques from the behavioural sciences to nudge or pull consumers towards different behaviour. These approaches help people overcome cognitive and behavioural biases such as limited attention, cognitive overload, procrastination, discounting the future, sticking to the status quo, and so on. Motivational approaches mobilise consumers using a variety of tools, such as linking their behaviour with outcomes, commitment techniques (such as promises and pledges), social comparisons, aspirational appeals, reminders, anchors, feedback and fun.

Empowerment approaches provide consumers with the technical tools that can measure, monitor and manage their behaviour over time. They take advantage of the increasing ubiquity of smartphones, sensors in devices, the internet and social media to create apps that enable real-time monitoring and visualisation of behaviour. All this in turn enables consumers to become more aware of the causes and consequences of their behaviour and compare it with that of others. The most significant development here is the "Internet of Things", that is, the equipping of everyday objects – watches, fridges, cars – with tiny, interconnected identifying devices that allow continuous, unobtrusive measuring, monitoring and regulation of behaviour on the web.

Most efforts to shape consumer behaviour use a combination of both approaches, and are becoming increasingly widespread in areas as diverse as energy, education, finance and health.

Shaping consumers' energy use

Visualisation

Better visualisation can help consumers be more frugal in their energy use. For instance, S-Oil, a South Korean petroleum company, recently ran a balloon campaign to help people find a parking space, with the motto: "Save oil, save time, save money." When a car enters a parking space, the car pushes a balloon marked "here" out of sight. When the car leaves, the "here" balloon rises back into view. Drivers can spot balloons from afar, and so find spaces without wandering about the car park. Finding quick parking saves oil. In a single day, about 700 cars benefit and together save about 23 litres of oil, which when multiplied by 365 days is a significant saving in a year.

In a similar vein, Toyota Sweden launched its "A Glass of Water" campaign in mid-2010, based on the idea that calmer driving saves fuel and reduces carbon emissions. The problem is that driving is often associated with speed, acceleration and risk taking. So Toyota asked drivers to place a glass of water on the dashboard and drive without spilling a drop. In this way, drivers reduced fuel consumption by up to 10%. Of course, driving with an actual glass of water on the dashboard is not practical. So in July 2010, Toyota Sweden launched an iPhone app that looks and acts like a glass of water. The iPhone's accelerometer and GPS (global positioning system) enable the app to visualise how much virtual water is spilled during a journey as well as record the car's speed and distance over time. The app is also integrated with Google maps, so it can track the driver's route and where the water was spilled. At the end of the journey, drivers can see the results, including how much fuel was used. Further, the data is automatically uploaded to the "A Glass of Water" website, so drivers can analyse their driving in detail using maps and graphical tools. Drivers can also challenge their friends to take the test, and share and compare their progress on Facebook. During the campaign, over 95,000 people downloaded the app, making it the third most popular free app at that time. Since then, over 678,000 kilometres have been driven wisely and sustainably under the scheme.

Meanwhile, at MIT's SENSEable City Lab, engineers, designers and scientists are developing interactive tools that will empower city dwellers and make many dimensions of urban life more enjoyable and sustainable.[5] Carlo Ratti, director of the lab, points out that although cities cover only 2% of the earth's crust they account for half of the world's population and consume three-quarters of the world's energy.[6] With six out of ten people expected to live in cities by 2030 (and 6.5 billion urban dwellers by 2050), Ratti believes scientists, designers and urban planners must collaboratively prepare citizens for more sustainable lifestyles. In a Seattle project called TrashTrack, Ratti's team tracked 3,000 pieces of rubbish to show how far these items travel. In one case, a discarded inkjet printer ended a 4,000-mile journey in Baja California in Mexico. In other words, the removal chain that processes discarded products creates as much waste as the supply chain that manufactures and distributes them. After seeing the whole system visualised, Ratti believes that consumers may be less inclined to leave plastic bottles in a dump.

Another project entitled HubCab involves an interactive

visualisation tool that explores the routes of over 170 million taxi trips in New York City in a given year. Paolo Santi, a senior researcher on the project, explained that HubCab aims to contribute to the science of sharing – that is, using big data to model and optimise the nascent sharing economy – by quantifying and depicting the actual benefits of trip-sharing. For instance, HubCab data shows that if New Yorkers were willing to wait no more than an extra five minutes for a taxi, nearly 95% of all trips could be shared with another person heading in the same direction. Such an optimal combination of trips would cut total travel time by 40% and yield similar reductions in operational costs, gas emissions and traffic congestion. Santi aims to make HubCab available as a smartphone app not just for New York, but for other cities too.

Gamification

In March 2009, IKEA France launched a car-sharing website for customers. The idea was to help get people to IKEA and reduce energy use. As IKEA put it: "Everybody wins: drivers, passengers and the environment." The only problem was that too few drivers registered; someone needed to give car-owning IKEA customers a helpful nudge.

In April 2011, with the help of La Chose, an advertising agency, IKEA France launched the "Mysterious Passenger" campaign to encourage people to car share. Launched to coincide with sustainable development week, La Chose created a character ("a real guy from real life") who they called the mysterious passenger. They shot footage of this person (suitably disguised) in an IKEA car park and featured this in their advertising. The car sharer who picked up the mysterious passenger would receive €1,000 ($1,300) to spend at IKEA.

The campaign ran for three weeks, during which time the trailer was viewed more than 700,000 times on YouTube, pushing up website registrations fivefold on the entire year. Site visits increased by 600%. Some 4,000 people offered to share rides with other IKEA customers, leading to 2,000 car-shared journeys. The campaign made clever and frugal use of YouTube and social media to make consumers themselves more frugal. On the one hand it promoted eco-friendly behaviour; on the other it helped IKEA build its brand.

Social comparison

Most mainstream economists would argue that the best way to get consumers to regulate their use of energy is through pricing or subsidies. But less conventional behavioural economics has encouraged more psychological approaches. Opower mails a regular home-energy report (HER) to customers comparing their energy use with that of their neighbours. In this way, consumers can be goaded towards frugality. Opower now works with 93 utility partners in 35 states and eight countries around the world to reach over 32 million households and businesses. A study by ideas42, a behavioural economics consultancy, found that "the HERs programme on average reduces energy consumption by 2%". Furthermore, based on data from over 600,000 treatment and control households, the study concluded that this 2% reduction is equivalent to a short-run increase of 11–20% in the electricity price. The cost-effectiveness of the approach was comparable to traditional energy conservation programmes, with annual savings of $300 million.

DIY health care

In coming decades, health-care costs in the West are poised to rocket because of ageing populations and the explosion of lifestyle-related and chronic diseases. To defuse this ticking time bomb, forward-thinking health providers – ranging from Silicon Valley start-ups to health maintenance organisations (HMOs) and health insurance companies – are collaborating with governments and employers to usher in the "consumerisation" of health care. This new trend aims to give individuals a more active role in managing their own health care, from seeking out providers to choosing treatments. But consumerisation is also about shifting from cure to prevention. The idea is for consumers to manage their health by focusing on wellness. According to a 2012 Wolters Kluwer Health survey, 76% of respondents are prepared to make proactive health decisions. Many now have access to affordable and easy-to-use technologies, such as mobile health (m-health) and social-media tools, which put them more in charge. Such solutions can be classified into three categories.

Self-monitoring

In recent years there has been a huge increase in wearable devices such as Jawbone's UP fitness tracker: a wristband designed by Yves Behar that tracks and quantifies your steps, distance, calories, active and idle time, thus helping you understand how you eat, move and sleep, and make healthier lifestyle choices. Over 17 million wrist-worn activity trackers like Jawbone's were expected to be sold in 2014. Health-care providers are seeking to influence how consumers regulate and manage their health by integrating data from these wearable devices into their own mobile apps.

Remote diagnosis and treatment

By 2025, the US health-care system will be short of nearly 65,000 non-primary-care specialists. To deal with this, more hospitals and clinics are using telemedicine solutions like interactive video consultations, especially for elderly or rural patients. The Commonwealth Fund, a private foundation that supports independent research on health and social issues, estimates that using telemedicine for after-hours care in nursing homes can dramatically reduce hospitalisation rates and save Medicare, a US social insurance programme for older people, $151,000 per nursing home. In 21 US states, private insurers are already required to cover remote consultations. Telemedicine also offers privacy to patients, such as those suffering from mental illness, who wish to avoid visiting medical centres. Although telemedicine has traditionally been dominated by large technology providers such as Cisco, several digital start-ups are now jumping in. CellScope, a University of California, Berkeley, spin-off, makes an optical attachment that can convert a smartphone into an auriscope (known in the US as an otoscope). Parents can insert the device into their child's ears, take photos of the interior and e-mail them to the family doctor, who can quickly spot any infection. Another CellScope accessory converts a smartphone into a dermascope, to check skin conditions. Both attachments cost a fraction of the professional test devices used by physicians.

Adherence to treatment

Another big concern in health care is patients' failure to use medicines properly. They typically fail to take their initial prescription or the first refill or to take their medicine regularly or on time. For instance, 50% of patients in the US do not take their medication as prescribed. Such non-adherence imposes major health-care and social costs. A 2005 *New England Journal of Medicine* review of adherence research over the past half-century found that non-adherence costs $100 billion–$300 billion annually. This includes the costs of avoidable hospitalisation, nursing-home admission and premature death. The report called for greater efforts to "stimulate better prescribing of, and adherence to, essential medications". *The Economist* estimates that the average annual cost of non-adherence by those with high blood pressure is "nearly $4,000 more than the cost of treating those who pop their pills reliably".[7]

Technology and clever motivational techniques can be used to make sure that patients take their medicines properly. For instance, Janssen Healthcare Innovation, an entrepreneurial unit within Johnson & Johnson's Janssen Research & Development, has developed Care4Today Mobile Health Manager, a free mobile app that helps people stay on schedule with their medication. In particular, it enables friends and family to monitor usage. Care4Today even offers to support a charity of the patients' choice for every day that they take their medication. Likewise, Propeller Health makes a monitoring device that fits on asthma inhalers. Vitality markets GlowCap Connect, a web-connected bottle cap that glows and plays music to remind patients that it is time to take their pills. The device keeps track of daily doses by counting the number of times the cap is opened, and sends this data to a Vitality-hosted database that e-mails patients if they miss a dose. The system also alerts a designated friend or relative who can nudge the patient to act. Lastly, the pharmacy can send a message to the patient when it is time for a refill.

All this is possible because more than 120 million Americans own a smartphone and nearly one-fifth of these have at least one health app. These mobile health (m-health) apps and devices are frugal for several reasons. First, they allow doctors and nurses to monitor and treat patients remotely, thus saving time and travel costs. Second, they reduce the costs of collecting real-time, unobtrusive data that can then be used to judge the efficacy of treatments. Third, and most importantly, they are a cheap but powerful way of helping patients help themselves, even before they get ill.

Thus the true frugal benefit is long term: namely, prevention being better (and cheaper) than cure. As Don Jones of Qualcomm Life puts it, m-health innovations "give people dashboards, gauges and alarm signals" to help them (and doctors) monitor what is happening to them in real time. Such information could help patients avoid being hospitalised, thus saving the $4,000 average daily cost of a US hospital bed.

Socialising education

As discussed in Chapter 3, the internet and high-speed broadband are ushering in a frugal revolution in education. The rise of massive open online courses (MOOCs) means that educators can now reach vast numbers of students in far-flung locations, at relatively little cost. Conversely, from the students' perspective, many more can now access quality teaching at little or no cost.

This is not all. Clever design and use of technology and motivational techniques are changing how students learn. For instance, MOOCs let students learn at their own pace and from peers, and this discourages them from dropping out. Specifically, platforms such as FutureLearn, Coursera, EdEx and Udacity typically use visible learning, social learning, storytelling and gamification to promote effective learning.

Visible learning

Online courses are designed to make the learning process visible to users. Students are typically given signposts at every stage to help them assess their progress. They are made aware of where they are in a course, how much they have completed and what they can expect next. For instance, FutureLearn uses a "to do" list to show students their activities for the week, while a profile page provides a summary of activities including courses taken and comments made. Most platforms also allow students to test their new knowledge using quizzes that give them helpful responses and allow them to try again if they answer incorrectly.

Social learning

Perhaps the best (and most frugal) source of learning on MOOCs is other students. The number and variety of people taking an online course opens up a range of different experiences and knowledge, as students learn through sharing and debate. FutureLearn courses enable sharing by allowing students to add comments alongside course content. Individual students can build their own reputations in the process: more trusted and popular commenters can be "followed" by others; and students can search comments to facilitate learning and reputation building. The idea is to make learning more informal and enjoyable.

MOOCs also save on the cost of employing tutors by using online support from the student community. Motivating students to help one another gives them a chance to test their skills. MOOCs can also offer students social rewards by allowing others to vote on the quality of their comments, allowing the more engaged learners to build a reputation for being helpful or expert. The quality and frequency of their comments can even be included in their course assessment.

As Simon Nelson, head of FutureLearn, puts it:[8] "We believe that much of the learning comes from the discussion. Nearly 40% of our learners are actively commenting."

Storytelling and games

Online courses are typically presented by leading academics in their field. But instead of filming them ploughing through a long, live classroom session, courses feature short, well-edited videos in which the tutor talks through a single theme in an engaging and entertaining way. Increasingly, online platforms have co-opted scripting and editing techniques from the news and entertainment businesses (such as the BBC in the UK) to raise content quality and user participation.

Such platforms also use ideas from the gaming world. Salman Khan, an online education pioneer, believes in the power of games to motivate children to learn. His Khan Academy has experimented with game mechanics in its online courses. Students can accumulate points for their work, are awarded badges and get on leader boards. The academy's experiments show that the wording of badges or the use of points can have a dramatic effect on learning. In some cases, tens of thousands of students can go in a particular direction depending on the nature of the badges. In general, "gamifying" educational content through the use of on-demand video tutorials has made content more engaging for "digital natives" around the world.

Despite the hype about MOOCs, however, many experience poor student engagement and knowledge retention. University of Pennsylvania research in 2013 shows that only half of registered students ever view a single lecture, and only 4% complete a course. A separate study by researchers at the university concludes that MOOCs are taken by an "educated few and are not reaching the disadvantaged". To address this issue, Prabhu Subramanian, a UK-based entrepreneur, has developed a free, web-based collaborative learning platform called CoLearnr to encourage student collaboration and participation during and after a course. He says:[9]

> In order to truly teach millions of learners, you really have to teach only 100 learners; then provide these learners [with] the tools to teach more learners.

Guided by this principle, CoLearnr has now developed a portable, battery-powered Learnbox, which can run the entire platform, supporting up to 50 students. Students can access the box from any device including $30 tablets that are common in emerging countries. The Learnbox requires no access to a network or the internet, and can store Wikipedia, the Khan Academy and more open educational resources (OER). Subramanian believes that such innovations make collaborative learning work at scale:

> You can teach 100 learners online or in blended form, provide them [with] a "Learnbox" and let them teach in thousands. This is how you can innovate in a frugal way and yet make a true impact.

Breaking (bad) financial habits

The rise of a credit and consumption culture in the West in the late 20th century led to rising household debt. Even after it all came to a head in 2008, signs of consumer profligacy remain. US credit-card debt rose by 8% in 2013 to $38.2 billion, and UK savings fell to 5.4% of household net disposable income in 2013 from 7.8% in 2009 – a serious worry for governments and lenders.

Barclays Bank, a UK multinational banking and financial services company, reports that people tend to have little consideration for "rainy days". Most have no significant savings, spending what they earn and getting by only as long as they have a job. More worryingly, some customers face severe financial strain, typically use payday loans, are late with repayments and withdraw cash on credit cards. This latter group might be expected to reduce spending on non-essentials, but they actually spend more than average, precisely when they are in financial trouble. Worried that such behaviour on a large scale could harm the bank and the economy, Barclays has begun to look at how it might turn around its profligate customers.

One approach is through its financial health programme, which helps customers visualise their financial behaviour and meet savings targets. The programme also empowers Barclays' customers to connect with friends, family and peers to motivate better financial behaviour. For instance, Barclays has a simple pencil-and-paper tool to display on a kitchen fridge, showing daily and weekly expenditure by key categories. The bank also works with its branch staff to get them to engage more with their clients, and help clients in turn to engage more with their finances.

Barclays' personalised debit card initiative helps customers improve their financial habits by personalising their debit cards with motivational messages and imagery that remind them of their financial aspirations. Appeals include: "I sometimes forget I am spending real money when I use my card" (with cash pictured on the card); "Reminding me that one less drink at the pub gets me closer to my big holiday" (accompanied by pictures of that holiday destination); and "Pound by pound, brick by brick, saving for my dream home" (with a house pictured on the card).

There is a similar innovation explosion in the insurance sector which makes insuring a car, a house, or health more affordable. According to research by the Boston Consulting Group, in 2020 around half of all cars will have telematic monitoring equipment which tracks the number of journeys made, the time of day, and driving behaviour such as speed and braking. Although telematics services currently mainly include safety, roadside assistance and entertainment, car insurers such as Progressive and AXA are using such services to shift their business model from punishing drivers for bad driving habits to rewarding them for good behaviour. In 2012, Progressive launched SnapShot, a pay-as-you-drive (PAYD) car-insurance programme. Once users sign up (for free), they receive a monitoring device that plugs into the dashboard. During a 30-day trial, the device tracks how far and well users drive by measuring, for example, how often and how hard they brake. Progressive then uses the data to produce quotes with discounts of up to 30% for responsible drivers. Some 70% of those who try out the plan get discounts. Once users sign up for the plan, the device stays in the car, and the rate is reviewed every six months. SnapShot has signed up more than 1 million customers.

The lure of cost savings in such usage-based insurance plans improves even the most aggressive drivers' behaviour. According to the Brookings Institution, a US think-tank, if all US drivers opted for PAYD plans, two-thirds of US households would save around $270 per car. Even better, total mileage would decrease by 8%, resulting in annual savings of over $50 billion from reduced traffic, oil consumption and pollution.[10] And highway accidents, which killed more than 30,000 people in 2013 in the US, would also be dramatically reduced.

Recommendations for managers

Companies cannot expect consumers to change their behaviour by themselves or overnight. In many cases, companies must take the lead. First, though, managers must change their own behaviour. Those in customer-facing roles, namely sales and marketing, should re-examine the 4Ps of marketing – product, place, promotion and price – and recast them for an age of austerity. This means doing fewer multimillion-dollar Super-Bowl-style promotions aimed at buying ever more stuff, and emphasising more flexible pricing and clever positioning that will nudge customers towards frugal behaviour, so they feel richer even as they consume less. In particular, marketing and sales managers must do the following.

Segment customers according to their motivation for change

In most markets, some consumers are innovators and early adopters, and the majority are followers or laggards. Marketing managers should begin with consumers who are most willing and able to change. These consumers are also most likely to be able to influence others to change. While identifying and targeting this segment may once have been difficult, time consuming and expensive, the advent of connected devices and big data have made tracking and targeting much easier. As noted above, Barclays Bank's financial health programme, for example, can draw on customer-account data to ascertain profiles of early adopters of new savings programmes.

Organise the sales force for frugal customers and solutions

Sales managers may fear that frugal products will cannibalise or even destroy their high-end, profitable products. Even if this is not the case, sales teams are typically encouraged to sell big-ticket items. Thus medical-device sales staff, for instance, may prefer to pitch a high-end ECG machine costing $100,000 rather than a low-cost ECG device costing $5,000. To address this cannibalisation conundrum, firms should organise and manage their sales force accordingly. One option is to form two separate sales teams: one dedicated to frugal products and the other to high-end products. This is what Procter & Gamble and Renault have done in their respective sectors: they each have a separate sales force for their entry-level products. The other option is to exploit synergies between high-end and frugal products and encourage the sales force to cross-sell across these product lines. This is what Siemens is doing with its medical devices. It sells its entry-level M3 devices to more cost-conscious consumers – small clinics, say – with a view to then upselling when these consumers are ready to buy more high-end M2 and M1 devices. In some cases, firms may even downsell. For example, when large hospitals, seeking to be more prudent with their budgets, look for more affordable devices, Siemens may be able to hold on to these customers by offering M3 instead of the M2 or M1 devices that they used to buy in the past.

Use financial measurements to change customers' own business model

Asking customers to dramatically change their behaviour is akin to asking a company to change its business model. This only happens if the new model might significantly improve the bottom line. Changing a business model also requires investment, which must come with an attractive return.

This analogy can help frugal producers convince customers to change their personal business model by showing them the relevant return on investment. For example, gThrive, a Silicon Valley start-up, offers precision agriculture services to farmers in drought-prone California. It sells gStakes, maintenance-free wireless sensors designed like a lightweight plastic ruler, which, when inserted in various parts of a field, frequently measure and track soil and environmental conditions (moisture, air temperature, sunlight). This detailed data can be monitored remotely from a website, smartphone or tablet.

This affordable, easy-to-use system has several benefits. It acts as a GPS by precisely identifying the good and bad parts of a field, thus helping farmers optimise their use of crops, water, energy, fertiliser and labour, and as a predictive-maintenance tool by warning farmers when there is a looming problem with soil conditions or environment (such as too little light or water). Despite these clear benefits, Joop Verbaken, gThrive's co-founder, says that it is not easy to convince farmers to make the switch:[11]

> Initially farmers were sceptical about our solution – because adopting it meant changing their business model. But once they saw how our analytical tools could help them reduce water and fertiliser use, eliminate weeds and diseases and increase yields and product quality, they realised that ... they could recoup their gStakes investment within a few months.

Use social pressure

At TED 2013 (a global conference on world-changing ideas), Alex Laskey, CEO of Opower, described how a group of graduate students tested one of the following three messages to encourage people to save energy: "You can save $54 this month"; "You can save the planet"; "You can be a good citizen". None of them worked. Then Opower's team added a fourth message – "Your neighbours are doing better than you" – and magic happened. People who found out that 77% of their neighbours had turned down their air conditioners, turned down their own. Laskey commented:[12] "If something is inconvenient, even if we believe it, persuasion won't work. But social pressure? That's powerful stuff." With $40 billion of energy wasted in the US annually, Laskey believes that leveraging the power of the crowd could induce a collective shift in people's behaviour and save two terawatts of energy annually, enough to power all homes in Salt Lake City and St Louis for more than a year.

Social media now make this cheap and sometimes fun to do. For example, PiggyMojo, an online savings tool, switches customers from impulse spending to impulse saving. It helps users set a savings objective such as "go to college" and then start saving towards that goal. Whenever users overcome an urge to buy something, such as a $4 cappuccino, they text or tweet "I just saved $4" to family and friends, who "favourite" them and cheer them up. Users also get a message when those close to them also save, setting off a virtuous cycle that sustains thrifty behaviour in the community.

Make frugality aspirational

Tata Motors' $2,500 Nano car, launched in India in 2009, was meant to encourage low-income Indian families to swap their motorcycles and scooters for a first-time car – one that was affordable, eco-friendly, comfortable and safe. Despite being a technological breakthrough, the Nano failed to sell as well as its creators had hoped. This was largely because Tata Motors did not fully appreciate the aspirations of low-income Indians. They did not want to be seen driving "the world's cheapest car", as the Nano had been dubbed. By contrast, the SMART car, which in some ways looks similar to the Nano, has been highly successful in the US and Europe partly because it has been cleverly branded as a sleek car that offers "maximum comfort, agility, ecology and driving fun". The SMART car is not just affordable; it is affordable luxury. Marketers should take their cue from the SMART car when positioning frugal products or seeking to stimulate and shape frugal consumer behaviour.

*

The engineers, scientists and designers who make up company R&D teams must also play their part in helping customers adopt and sustain frugal behaviour. In particular, R&D managers can do the following.

Use design constraints and affordances to induce sustainable change

In 1977, James Gibson, a perceptual psychologist, coined the term "affordances" to designate all possible actions in an environment. Some years later, Donald Norman, a cognitive scientist and design theorist, expanded the definition of affordance to include "the perceived and actual properties" of an object that directly influence and determine how this object can possibly be used (for example, a knob suggests turning, whereas a slot implies that something must be inserted). Affordances make a product easier to use, thus encouraging its adoption; but constraints make a product harder to use. So, for example, small rubbish bins sensitise users to how much waste they produce (by forcing them to take the rubbish out more often). Other tricks include:

- placing electricity meters where people can see and therefore monitor them;
- designing detergent tablets (instead of powder) to make sure that users do not use more detergent than required;
- making washing machines that weigh the clothes and adjust the water required automatically;
- using smaller plates so people do not serve themselves more than they can eat.

Designers should always ask how they can encourage good and deter bad behaviour in users. They should also make sure that customers are repeatedly informed about how they can make better decisions.

Design for longevity, not obsolescence

Consumer electronics are often designed to be replaced every few months or, at most, every couple of years. Such so-called planned obsolescence is a major contributor to the 20–50 million tonnes of e-waste produced annually worldwide (a volume that is growing at 8% a year). The same applies to consumer durables such as cars, washing machines and some industrial products. To help reduce waste, R&D teams must design longer-lasting products, for which even cost-conscious customers would be willing to pay.

Expliseat, a start-up founded by two young French engineers, is a good example. It makes the world's lightest aircraft seats entirely out of titanium, each weighing just 4 kilograms. The seats can save an airline up to $500,000 per plane per year on fuel cost alone. Although an Expliseat costs more than rival products, each seat can be assembled and installed within minutes and can be used 100,000 times without deteriorating. Furthermore, its ergonomic design and lower bulk provide an extra 5 centimetres of legroom and better shock absorption. Although Expliseat's economy-class seats may not match the $400,000 business-class seats for comfort, low-cost airlines are eager to offer something extra for those on a tight budget.

Design for next-generation customers

Tim Brown, CEO of IDEO, an international design and consulting company, challenges designers to "invent for the future consumer". For example, Carrefour, one of the world's largest retailers, hired InProcess, an innovation consultancy, to reinvent the iconic 1960s shopping trolley still in use to serve the needs of today's customers better.[13]

InProcess's ethnographers studied how customers with different demographic profiles actually did their grocery shopping, from the time they entered a store to when they went through check-out, loaded and unloaded their cars, and stored their groceries in their homes. They discovered that a growing number of customers, especially women and younger shoppers, were bringing their own reusable bags to stores. These bags did not fit easily in a shopping trolley. Based on their findings, the company's designers created an eco-friendly trolley to promote the reuse of bags. Instead of a wire basket, the trolley has an open, flexible, modular structure, with a vertical hanger at the top on which customers can hang up to five reusable bags, and a bottom layer for carrying bulky items. Smaller items can be pre-sorted in bags to ease checking out and transport. A bar-code reader attached to the back of the trolley enables shoppers to scan their items and keep their shopping within budget. The trolley has been a hit among shoppers and has encouraged more to bring in reusable bags.

Commenting on this success, Carrefour's design director, Philippe Picaud, notes:

> Our supermarkets haven't kept up with dramatic changes in people's shopping habits in recent years. We are radically reinventing the end-to-end shopping experience to better serve increasingly frugal and eco-conscious customers.

*

Lastly, a company's senior management, including the CEO, should drive changes too.

Walk the walk to inspire customers

It would be hypocritical of chief executives to ask their customers to save energy while they criss-cross the world in private jets. Senior corporate leaders must also behave frugally if they are to inspire their customers to do the same. In May 2014, Levi Strauss's CEO, Chip Bergh, hit the headlines after admitting that he had not washed his jeans in a year. While many found his comment "shocking" and "disgusting", Bergh was making a valid point: you cannot ask Levi Strauss's customers to buy a pair of Water<Less jeans produced with less water and then waste gallons of water washing them every week. Indeed, 45% of water consumed during a pair of jeans' life cycle occurs after the customer buys them and starts washing them. Scientifically,

too, Bergh was correct: you do not need to wash your jeans that often (nor, for that matter, do you need to wash your bed sheets frequently). A 2011 University of Alberta study found no difference in bacterial levels between a pair of jeans that had not been washed for over a year and a pair that had been washed after two weeks. In this way, Bergh, who previously ran P&G's Tide detergent business, is encouraging his denim customers to wash less and save on water, energy and detergent. (He hand-washes and hang-dries his own jeans.) Other CEOs should follow suit. How many hotel-chain CEOs change their sheets less than once a week? And how many car share?

Explain to investors why selling less is good business

Here are three arguments to convince sceptical shareholders why selling less of the company's products can be a profitable strategy:

- "Our core business model, predicated on selling more and more, is unsustainable." Interface, one of the world's largest manufacturers of modular carpet, does not sell its carpet as a product, but rather leases it as a service. Under its Evergreen Lease programme, Interface installs, maintains and replaces the carpet for customers who pay a monthly fee to keep it fresh and clean. Because its carpet is modular, Interface selectively replaces only 10–20% of worn or damaged carpet at a time, reducing the use of new carpet material by 80%. It also recycles the maximum amount of post-consumer material into new products. Similarly, instead of selling light bulbs, Philips now offers "lighting as a service" to business customers and municipalities by signing a performance-based contract. For instance, in Washington, DC, Philips upgraded over 13,000 lighting fixtures to LEDs in the city's car parks at no upfront cost. Under a ten-year service contract, Philips is paid from the $2 million in energy savings that LEDs yield annually. Bruno Biasiotta, CEO of Philips Lighting Americas, says:[14]

  > With digital lighting systems, we really need to break with conventional thinking and look to the services and delivery models of the software industry to understand the future of lighting.

- "Customers are more likely to buy, and promote, our products if they last longer." Customers want to buy durable goods – cars, appliances and even light bulbs – that last longer and can be easily repaired. Companies will gain in customer loyalty if they oblige. Also, the aftermarket business of maintenance, repair, and service is lucrative. With the rise of the sharing economy, customers are more likely to buy more durable products which they can share after initial use. Clothes company Patagonia saw its reputation soar after encouraging customers to exchange their used Patagonia items with one another.

- "We need to attract and retain young customers and employees." Young people aged under 35 are not as interested as the previous generation was in owning material possessions. That is not to suggest they are less materialistic, only that they prefer the flexibility of, say, renting or sharing a car rather than buying and owning one. To attract these younger customers, companies must offer on-demand services to a customer community and not just single products to individuals. By encouraging customers to buy less and share more, companies will also attract next-generation employees who want to work for a socially and environmentally responsible organisation.

CASE STUDY 4

Simple Bank: shaping financial behaviour

Simple Bank has taken online financial management a step further. Launched by Alex Payne, Joshua Reich and Shamir Karkal in the US in summer 2012 as a "worry-free alternative to traditional banking", it uses mobile apps to help customers manage their money better.[15]

Customers can view their budgets, savings and spending in their current account. Any spending on their debit card is quickly reflected in their account; they get push notifications of this spending too. The bank uses customer data to provide them with an instantaneous view of their spending patterns. Simple uses the data generated when a card purchase is made – such as location, time, type of merchant – to help customers budget automatically. For instance, the Interactive Reports feature helps customers track spending over time. They can break down their spending by category and merchant and use this insight to spend more intelligently.

Simple's Search feature also helps customers search for expenditure pointers such as "weekday lunch", "in New York", or "dinner in Portland". The Goals feature helps customers balance income with monthly expenses and major purchases. Typical goals include save for a vacation, create a grocery budget and set aside money for bills. Simple finds that "customers who save and budget with Goals save twice as much as other customers". The Safe-to-Spend feature takes their balance and factors in upcoming bills, pending transactions and any saving goals. With Safe-to-Spend, customers "get a much more accurate picture of what you can really spend today without hurting yourself tomorrow".

Other apps help customers activate cards, block (or unblock) cards, change their PIN, access the in-app Knowledge Base or reach customer support. For instance, the Allpoint app helps users find the nearest ATMs with their smartphone; Photo Check Deposit allows them to deposit a cheque wherever they are; and Send Money allows them to transfer money with no charge. They can also block a lost or stolen card using a mobile app. In many ways, by doing what online financial aggregators such as Mint.com in the US and Money Dashboard in the UK also do, Simple has the potential to shake up the sleepy retail banking sector. In February 2014, BBVA, Spain's second-largest bank, acquired Simple for $117 million.

Conclusion

Changing deeply entrenched customer behaviour can be difficult. All kinds of cognitive and psychological biases intervene and scupper even the best intentions of conscientious consumers. There are ways companies can help overcome their customers' profligacy; and many of them will be more than willing to try.

Indeed, the most powerful allies among consumers are prosumers: customers so motivated and empowered that they become involved in the creation of frugal products and services, straddling the traditional boundary between supply and demand. The next chapter considers these prosumers, and the fifth principle of frugal innovation: co-create value with prosumers.

6   Principle five: co-create value with prosumers

When playing with Lego you are not a consumer, you are a producer.

Olafur Eliasson, Danish-Icelandic artist

IN SPRING 2014, French multinational retailer Auchan rolled out four new products. One was a teapot that automatically removes tea leaves after they have infused in hot water; another was a device that helps balance a cake on a car seat while driving. These products were not developed by a well-known consumer goods brand; they were conceived by Auchan's customers.

In September 2013, Auchan set up a website inviting customers to submit innovative product ideas. The site was powered by Quirky, a crowdsourcing platform launched by a 22-year-old, Ben Kaufman, in 2009. Over the next 2 months, customers submitted 800 ideas, from which 4 were shortlisted, based on the results of interactive voting by Auchan shoppers and Quirky's community of designers and inventors. This expert network then helped convert the winning ideas into viable products, which eventually appeared on Auchan's shelves in April 2014. Since then, Auchan has rolled out a range of consumer products designed by, or with, customers. As Vianney Mulliez, Auchan's CEO, points out:

We want to embed our customers deeply into our value chain as active partners – starting with the design of our products.

Auchan is owned by the Mulliez family, which also has interests in Decathlon, a sporting-goods chain operating in 33 countries and known for its innovative, high-quality, affordable products. Most of these are private-label goods developed in-house. The company employs 150 designers and even has an R&D department (a possible first for the retail industry), employing around 50 scientists and 530 engineers. Its innovation team has traditionally collected new product insights from professional athletes as well as its 50,000 employees, many of whom are avid sports fans who understand their customers' changing needs. These insights have helped the team produce numerous innovations, one example being a tent that can be erected in just two seconds.

In 2013, in an effort to democratise the innovation process and make its products more accessible and affordable, Decathlon got the public more involved in developing new ideas. It asked customers to vote on new product concepts developed by its in-house team, and the winning ideas made it into the stores. In early 2014, it launched a co-creation platform, which allowed end users to express their real needs, suggest improvements to existing Decathlon products and even propose new products. As Vincent Textoris, open innovation manager at Oxylane Group (which runs the Decathlon stores), explained: "The notion of client has disappeared. Now we talk about members (of a community)."

The Mulliez family also owns ADEO Group, one of the world's largest home-improvement chains. Its flagship brand is Leroy Merlin, a global leader in DIY products. ADEO's Lille headquarters is an impressive, energy-positive building. It uses no air conditioning or heating, instead making intelligent use of natural air flow to modulate the indoor temperature. Having revolutionised its building design, ADEO is about to revolutionise its business model.

Leroy Merlin was founded in 1923 by Adolphe Leroy and Rose Merlin to sell US army surplus left behind after the first world war. Stéphane Calmes, who is in charge of corporate training within ADEO's HR group, recalls:

> Good customer service has always been the lifeblood of our business since its inception nearly a century ago. But we always viewed and treated our clients as "buyers" since we perceived ourselves as "traders" (sellers). Hence our customer service long remained very transactional.

All this changed in 1997, when the group made customer satisfaction a top priority and began to engage clients more deeply by offering them personalised value-added services. In 2005, the group took its customer focus to the next level by recognising its clients, first and foremost, as "inhabitants". To understand their needs, it was necessary to visit them at home. Everyone from senior management to store managers began making house calls, resulting in more than 20,000 customer visits to date. What they learned surprised and humbled them. They discovered that customers used their products differently from how they were originally envisioned, and that only 20–30% of DIY products in any home were from Leroy Merlin. The company was potentially missing 70–80% of its customers' wallet share.

So ADEO is launching a new initiative to expand its retail stores by adding a physical "workspace", where customers can come not just to buy but also to make things, using traditional tools as well as cutting-edge automated 3D printers and CNC (computer numerical control) cutters. Customers will get training and support from ADEO's employees and be assisted by other expert users. The strategy is to evolve the buyer–seller relationship into a value co-creation model.

Calmes believes that this new model will also yield environmental and social benefits. For instance, when a washing machine breaks down because of a faulty part, rather than disposing of the whole appliance, the owner could walk into a Leroy Merlin store nearby and 3D-print a new spare part. Leroy Merlin is also planning to establish a community of customers who can volunteer to fix apartments in underprivileged neighbourhoods. As Calmes points out:

> We want to more deeply engage customers in all our activities by involving their entire being – their mind (creativity), heart (passion/compassion) and hands (skills) – in what we do. In a way, rather than telling our clients to "do it yourself" (DIY) we are proposing that they "do it with others" (DIWO).

Auchan, Decathlon and ADEO are visionary companies that have realised that the traditional notion of a value chain – of producers and consumers – is becoming obsolete. Many customers no longer want to be treated as passive buyers or "wallets on feet"; they want to actively participate in the design, production and even distribution of goods and services. Furthermore, customers want to contribute to the life cycle of the brands they consume. In sum, customers are becoming both consumers and producers, or prosumers. As a result, branded product and service suppliers as well as retailers must find ways to engage these prosumers and co-create value with them. By doing so, firms can lower the overall cost of innovation, develop and market products and services faster and better, delight customers with tailored experiences and boost customer loyalty.

The rise and rise of the prosumer

Several factors account for the rise of prosumers, including the following.

Consumers increasingly seek personalised solutions

Henry Ford reportedly told prospective customers: "You can have a car of any colour as long as it is black." But the golden era of mass production is long gone. Customers want personalised solutions for their unique needs and preferences. Some carmakers, such as Volkswagen, now offer customers the opportunity to configure cars to their personal tastes, using a vast palette of options. Others, such as Local Motors, go further, and allow customers to design and build their own vehicles from scratch. Founded in 2007, with headquarters in Phoenix, Arizona, Local Motors consists of a network of micro-factories that have popped up across the US. These micro-factories allow customers to build their own cars using open-source vehicle designs created – and continually improved – by a global community of 30,000 online auto aficionados from 130 countries.

Local Motors also sells open-source-designed products, ranging from the mighty Rally Fighter automobile (featured in the US version of *Top Gear*, a UK TV show) to the vintage-looking Cruiser motorised bicycle. The company's CEO, Jay Rogers, a Princeton-educated US Marine Corps veteran, estimates that it rolls out a new model for just $2 million in as little as 18 months (compared with 6 years and $200 million for major car companies). Local Motors wants to open 100 micro-factories around the world in the next 10 years.

If a car, which typically comprises 14,000 parts, can be

custom-built, then why not custom-build a mobile phone made of just 25 components? This question inspired Google to launch Project Ara, a free, open-source hardware platform that can be used to create highly modular smartphones. For $50, users will receive a kit containing a structural frame and modules (display, keyboard and battery) of their choice that can be snapped together like Lego blocks. Planned for launch in early 2015, Google's DIY phone, which will run on the open-source Android operating system, will provide longer life cycles for handsets as users will be able to upgrade individual components rather than having to buy an entire new phone. Google also wants to lower barriers to entry for phone hardware manufacturers by enabling hundreds of thousands of developers to design modules without having to pay a fee. All this is great news for the 1 billion smartphone users and 5 billion feature-rich phone users worldwide.

Consumers are increasingly dissatisfied with existing offerings

According to Eric Von Hippel, professor of technological innovation at MIT, customers who are frustrated with the limited functionality of existing products often tinker with them to extend their functionality and adapt them to fit their own needs.[1] While some companies may frown on such deviations from the product's originally intended use, others have come to view these MacGyvers (named after the improvising hero of the eponymous US TV series) as positive deviants and seek to harness their creativity. When developers hacked Microsoft's Kinect, a motion controller for video games, the company initially threatened to sue. But Microsoft soon realised that the hackers had helped identify Kinect's limitations and improve its functionality. Limor Fried, a New York-based hacker, had even offered a reward for the best hacked solution. In some cases, hackers devised original and practical applications for Kinect – such as a self-driving mini-car and an app that gives surgeons hands-free access to patients' MRI/CT scan data while operating – well beyond Kinect's original function in gaming. Humbled, Microsoft now actively involves hackers in its Kinect development process – a frugal alternative to the $10 billion it spends annually on R&D.[2]

In some cases, frustrated users create their own DIY solutions by legally hacking into everyday dumb objects like cars or consumer appliances. According to the US Census Bureau, nearly 11 million Americans commute an hour or more to work each day. That is over 440 million joyless hours wasted every month. But what if it were possible to make that commute as productive as using an iPhone? This was one aim of Automatic, a start-up that sells Link, a tiny accessory that plugs into a car's on-board computer and automatically boosts the vehicle's IQ. Link connects wirelessly with the driver's smartphone and sends subtle audio cues when it encounters bad driving habits such as rough braking and rapid acceleration that wastes petrol. It deciphers the annoyingly vague "check engine" alert and pinpoints the exact problem. It remembers where forgetful owners have parked their car, and can even detect when the car has crashed, alerting local authorities and loved ones.

Since the onset of the economic crisis, more cost-conscious and eco-aware citizens – especially those aged under 35 – prefer to renovate, fix or hack their products to upgrade their functionality and extend their usage. Thus they squeeze out more value from their existing investments, rather than systematically replacing ineffective products with new, costlier versions.

Consumers want a "conversation" with their brands

Customers who love their brands also like to play an active role in supporting them. They are willing to help design and produce them, and to share this passion with others. Such co-creation is not simply centred on the product itself, but also on the user experience and the lifestyle surrounding the product. And yet most companies continue their monologue marketing, pushing messages out to consumers rather than drawing in activist customers. This is despite the fact that 90% of consumers say they would rather buy products from brands with which they can "have a conversation". Some 40% of the tech-savvy millennial generation (those born between 1982 and 2004) wish to co-create products, services and experiences with desirable brands, especially via social-media channels. Firms that fail to engage in this way miss a powerful frugal opportunity to build and maintain their brands. In some cases, these firms also risk alienating their most loyal customers who, in searching for a more meaningful experience, may form their own powerful communities independent of the brand, which in some cases can even turn against it.

Consumers now design, build and sell products themselves

Some Eastern philosophy views creative expression as a basic human need on a par with food and shelter, a notion that is supported by Western psychology. In *Happy Money*, Michael Norton, associate professor of marketing at Harvard Business School, demonstrates that investing time, labour and money affects how people value products and people.[3] Norton's 2012 study with Daniel Mochon and Dan Ariely on the so-called IKEA effect shows that people value products much more when they assemble the products themselves.[4] Customers are increasingly able to express their creativity and emotional investment in physical objects by designing and building them.

The falling cost of 3D printers and personalisation platforms has made this easier and cheaper. For instance, the entry-level 3D printer from Replicator ("the Apple of 3D printing") sells for $1,375, but several crowdfunded start-ups such as New Matter and M3D intend to mass-market 3D printers that sell for as little as $149. Autodesk, a leader in computer-aided design software, has launched a consumer-friendly open-source 3D printer and 3D printing software in an effort to democratise manufacturing. Shapeways, a global network of large-scale 3D printing factories, allows people who do not want to print objects at home to upload their designs to a website and have 3D-printed versions delivered. Lastly, consumers can now not only design and build industrial-quality products themselves, but also sell these online. This is possible through online platforms such as Etsy, a leading e-commerce site that specialises in hand-made items and now boasts more than 1 million sellers and $1 billion in sales.

The desire of customers to create, especially in like-minded communities, and the existence of tools to help them do so, is driving a revolution in economic activity. Social networks and co-creation platforms are bringing together millions of disparate prosumers in creative communities, allowing them to collaborate in producing their own goods and services. In doing so, they are paving the way for what is being called the horizontal economy.

The rise of the horizontal economy

Vertically integrated value chains, controlled by companies that exclude customers, are being challenged by new value ecosystems orchestrated by customers themselves. The new ecosystems allow consumers to design, build, market, distribute and trade goods and services by and among themselves, without the need for intermediaries. This bottom-up approach is creating the horizontal economy. In a 1937 essay, Ronald Coase, a Nobel Prize-winning economist, argued that the reason Western economies are organised vertically – like a pyramid with a few large producers at the top and millions of passive consumers at the bottom – is because of transaction costs (the intangible costs associated with search, bargaining, decision-making and enforcement).[5] But with the explosion of the internet, mobile technologies and social media – think of the 1.3 billion interconnected Facebook users – these transaction costs have all but disappeared in many sectors. This has allowed a horizontal economy to emerge in the US, western Europe and Japan. The foundations of a new, self-sustaining commercial system are now being laid.

The building blocks of the horizontal economy include the following.

The "maker" movement: an army of tinkerers

The Maker Faire is an annual jamboree that originated in San Mateo, California, in 2006 to showcase the inventions of ordinary citizens, and offer workshops, demonstrations and competitions to help develop these ideas. In 2013, more than 120,000 people attended the San Mateo event. Maker Faires have been replicated across the US, for example, in Austin, Dearborn and New York (whose former mayor, Michael Bloomberg, declared September 24th–30th as Maker Week), as well as other parts of the world. When Rome hosted a Maker Faire in October 2013, parts of the city were shut down due to high participation in the event. Similarly, the June 2014 Paris Maker Faire was seen as a major event.

Now the mayors of every major city in the US and Europe want to host a Maker Faire, with some referring to them as a TEDx for MacGyvers – an event for tinkerers, not thinkers. On the occasion of the first White House Maker Faire in June 2014, President Barack Obama said:[6]

> *Our parents and our grandparents created the world's largest economy and strongest middle class not by buying stuff, but by building stuff – by making stuff, by tinkering and inventing and building. Today's DIY is tomorrow's "Made in America".*

Over several centuries, the US and Europe have sustained a grassroots culture of tinkering. Benjamin Franklin, one of the founding fathers of the United States, was a maker par excellence. A prolific inventor and an early open-source advocate, Franklin did not patent his inventions, but instead offered them freely to the public.

Today's makers are different from the lone geniuses of the past in one vital respect. As Dale Dougherty, the founder of Maker Faire, points out, we are witnessing the rise of "social tinkerers" who co-create as an integrated community online or in Fablabs and TechShops, thus generating a groundswell maker movement.

Fablabs and TechShops: DIY micro-factories that make anything

Conceived and launched by Neil Gershenfeld, a professor at MIT, a Fablab is a digital fabrication workshop, fully equipped with CNC machines, laser cutters and 3D printers, which is free and open to the public to tinker and make "almost anything". A Fablab has been described as a "factory in a box". Indeed, Fablabs' contents fit into a standard shipping container, allowing them to be easily transported and installed in any city around the world. There are currently more than 125 Fablabs in 34 countries.

TechShops are an advanced version of Fablabs where, for a $175 monthly fee, users get access to heavy-duty equipment for making industrial-calibre products. Mark Hatch, CEO of TechShop, says that many hardware start-ups are launched in his workshops and even use the TechShop location as their own office address. Interestingly, hardware products designed at TechShops are also beginning to revolutionise non-industrial sectors such as health care and financial services. For instance, Embrace, a $200 portable infant warmer developed by four Stanford graduates at TechShop, has already saved more than 50,000 premature babies' lives worldwide. Similarly, Jim McKelvey, a serial entrepreneur, used TechShop to design Square, a credit-card reader that enables anyone to accept payments on a smartphone or iPad. Square is a no-commitment, no-long-term-contract service that processed over $20 billion in transactions in 2013, and was expected to process $30 billion in 2014.

The lure of Fablabs and TechShops is that they provide not only (literally) cutting-edge tools, but also advice and support from staff and other tinkerers for first-time makers. Even neophytes can become expert tinkerers in no time.

Arduino and Raspberry Pi: low-cost building blocks of DIY products

It is becoming easier and cheaper to build your own electronic device or consumer appliance thanks to open-source hardware such as Arduino. Invented by Massimo Banzi, an Italian engineer, Arduino is a tiny, single-board micro-controller that amateurs and professionals can use to build devices that interact with their environment using sensors and actuators. These range from thermostats to automatic plant waterers and even art installations. Arduino's hardware design is freely available to anyone who wants to assemble a board manually. Costing just €20 ($27) as pre-assembled or DIY kits, nearly 1 million Arduino units have already been sold. As Banzi, a champion of open-source creativity, notes:[7] "You don't need anyone's permission to create something great."

Another frugal innovator, Eben Upton, along with colleagues at Cambridge University, created Raspberry Pi, a single-board, stripped-down, credit-card-sized computer – with a USB and Ethernet connector soldered on – that can connect to any monitor, mouse or keyboard to function as a desktop computer. Upton's team originally developed the Raspberry Pi to teach basic computer science to schoolchildren. However, soon after its launch in March 2012, scores of hobbyists and professionals began buying the micro-computer, priced at a mere £24 ($38), to create applications that extend well beyond education into agriculture, home automation, health care and communication. Raspberry Pi users worldwide have begun making everything from custom-made digital cameras to gaming devices to home alarm systems. One enthusiast, Dave Ackerman, even sent a weather balloon, equipped with a Raspberry Pi, 40 kilometres into the atmosphere where it survived −50°C temperatures to take detailed photos of the earth. The Raspberry Pi has been universally praised by experts (including Google's executive chairman, Eric Schmidt) for its affordability, usefulness and versatility. Not surprisingly, sales have rocketed, climbing from 20,000 units by May 2012 to 3 million units by May 2014.

Peer-to-peer sharing platforms

It is now increasingly easy for individuals to share their assets, products and skills without the need for (or interference of) intermediaries. In Germany, home-owners can generate their own solar energy and sell any excess into the grid. Perhaps more dramatically, since its inception in 2008, Airbnb (a community marketplace for short-let rentals) has established a presence in 190 countries with over 600,000 listings. (Over half of Airbnb hosts rely on this market to pay their rent or mortgage.) Already the world's fifth largest "hotel" chain (by number of beds), Airbnb is on its way to becoming the world's largest short-stay accommodation business, without owning a single building.

Similarly, Uber, a taxi service that connects users with drivers at the tap of a smartphone, has recently launched an extension called uberPOP in several European capitals. uberPOP is a peer-to-peer service that enables non-professional drivers to register their cars to transport individuals, thus earning extra income in their free time.

The initial value of the sharing economy – powered by providers like Airbnb and Uber – was in saving customers money; now it is being used to earn money by turning customers into prosumers. In 2013, the sharing economy generated revenues of around $3.5 billion, that went straight into prosumers' wallets. This is just the start. Growing at an annual rate of 25%, the sharing economy is expected to become a $110 billion market within a decade, without requiring any major investments. The European Commission predicts:[8]

> *At this rate, peer-to-peer sharing is transforming from an income boost through a stagnant wage market, into a disruptive economic force.*

Collective buying platforms that cut out middlemen and support small producers

Collective buying platforms help multiple buyers pool their demand in order to negotiate better prices. These platforms are especially relevant for consumers who want local produce, such as food. One successful example is La Ruche qui dit Oui (The Hive that says Yes), a French online marketplace for local, sustainable food producers targeting mainstream consumers. La Ruche's nationwide network of over 500 "hives" brings together a critical mass of local customers, giving them direct access to locally produced fresh, seasonal and eco-friendly foods. By cutting out the middleman, La Ruche's network connects 50,000 members directly to over 2,500 small farmers.

Large corporations and big-box retailers run global supply chains that deliver economies of scale that are increasingly unsustainable (such as selling bananas all year around). Collective buying platforms, by contrast, focus on large-scale localisation by supporting small-circuit supply chains that reduce time and distance between production and consumption, and are thus more sustainable environmentally, financially and socio-economically.

Crowdfunding platforms that finance new ventures

Platforms like Kickstarter, Indiegogo or KissKissBankBank enable lone inventors to raise funds to start and scale up an enterprise. This is particularly appealing to the millennial generation, who no longer trust the safety of a job. For instance, 40% of young millennials say that they want to be their own boss. But most banks and venture capitalists will not risk investing in start-ups launched by these 20-somethings. This doesn't bother the 20-somethings; they just try to emulate Eric Migicovsky who, aged 27, launched Pebble, a start-up that makes smart watches which connect to phones and notify users about e-mails, text messages, incoming calls and social-media alerts.

In early 2012, Migicovsky unveiled his project on Kickstarter, hoping to raise $100,000 in seed capital. Instead, he raised $10 million from over 68,000 backers, in just 4 weeks, making Pebble the largest crowdfunded project up to that point. Pebble has sold, mostly through its website, over 500,000 of its smart watches. To date, over 7 million individuals have pledged more than $1.3 billion to thousands of projects promoted on Kickstarter.

Technologists and artists no longer need to rely on wealthy philanthropists such as Warren Buffett or Bill Gates for support; crowdfunding platforms allow even modest earners to invest. One might refer to them as the "middle-class Medici" (a wealthy Renaissance-era Italian family that supported geniuses such as Michelangelo and Galileo). According to Amy Cortese, in her book *Locavesting:*[9]

> *If Americans shifted just 1% of the $30 trillion they hold in long-term investments to small businesses, it would amount to more than ten times the venture capital invested in all of 2011.*

This is what has led *Forbes*, a US business magazine, to predict that crowdfunding could go from being a $4 billion market today to a $1 trillion market in 2030.

Crowdfunding is also gaining support from politicians in the US and Europe. The US Securities and Exchange Commission (SEC) recently relaxed restrictions on crowdfunding, and France's Senate approved a law raising the cap on crowdfunding by small and medium-sized enterprises and start-ups. President Obama even lauded crowdfunding platforms like Indiegogo for bolstering the entrepreneurial ecosystem and unleashing a new wave of innovation in the US. It is not far-fetched to think that if President John Kennedy were to have sent a man to the moon today, he would have crowdfunded the entire space programme.

Some 80 million Americans (around one-quarter of the US population) and 23 million Britons (nearly one-third of the population) consider themselves sharers; and in France 48% consider themselves to be active participants in the collaborative economy. US and European customers, across the generations, are sharing and collaborating more than ever to get the products, services, knowledge or capital they want, faster, better and cheaper than from traditional sources.

The collaboration economy also gives consumers a more meaningful social experience. While baby-boomers and their offspring may view it as a cost-effective and convivial alternative to the brand-dominated mass-market economy, later generations see collaboration as the only way to consume. For them, sharing an apartment or a car with total strangers, or making their own products using open-source components, is the normal way to live. As such, economic power in almost all industries is shifting irrevocably from the supply side (producers) to the demand side (customers). Hence the horizontal economy is both a threat and an opportunity for traditional brands.

The crucial issue is whether corporate boards see their glass as half full or half empty. Even companies that feel threatened by these new communities of prosumers cannot afford to ignore them. As discussed below, older firms must consider how to integrate their own value chains into this horizontal economy.

Empowering and engaging prosumers

The term "co-creation" can be misleading; it implies that companies should merely engage customers to create products and services. There are two critical steps that precede and follow co-creation: the first identifies what product or service to design; and the second determines how to market and sell it. Therefore, companies must engage customers as partners in the three distinct phases: conception, development and commercialisation.

Phase 1: co-discovery of needs and dreams

For its 2014 Global Innovation Barometer, GE surveyed over 3,000 business executives from around the world. Of these, 84% stated that to innovate efficiently and successfully, it is critical for their company to understand customers and anticipate market evolution. Yet many companies continue to rely on expensive customer surveys and ineffective focus groups to collect market insights. Some visionary companies, however, have found a frugal way to identify customers' deeper wants and needs by involving the customers themselves. For instance, for over six years, Starbucks, a global coffee-house company, has run MyStarbucksIdea.com, where customers can express their needs by posting ideas for new products and better experiences (as well as building a sense of community). Other customers evaluate and vote for the most promising ideas, which Starbucks then puts into practice. So far Starbucks has collected, at virtually no cost to itself, more than 190,000 ideas and implemented over 300. These include a bold-tasting chai, faster Wi-Fi in stores, and providing a pump and a patch kit for cycling customers who get a flat tyre.

Similarly, to counter the onslaught of Airbnb, Marriott, one of the world's largest hotel companies with over 4,000 properties in over 80 countries, has launched Travel Brilliantly, a dedicated website where customers can submit – and vote for – innovative ideas for new services that can improve the experience of staying at Marriott hotels.

Manufacturers that sell physical products can now use crowdsourcing as a low-risk/high-return technique to reach non-traditional customer segments and assess the market potential for new products. For example, in June 2014, Harley-Davidson, a US motorcycle manufacturer, launched Project Livewire, a 30-city US tour to offer customers a test ride on the brand's first electric motorcycle. (Meanwhile, non-riders can try out Jumpstart, a simulated riding experience of the electric bike.) Although the company has no specific timeline for the development and launch of its electric bike, it expects Livewire to shed light on what it is about this type of vehicle that matters most to customers. The company is particularly keen on what it calls outreach groups – women, African-Americans, Hispanics and young adults – among whom demand is growing twice as fast as in its core market. Livewire is Harley-Davidson's strategy to engage future customers in defining what could become one of its core products.

Identifying customer needs is one thing. But what about sensing their dreams? As Bruce Nussbaum, author of *Creative Intelligence*, points out:[10]

> Ask people what they need and they'll give you a list of 10 or 20 things. The list will change from morning to night, from day to day. Ask people what they dream of, and they tell you one or two things that will never change.

This is especially true of millennials, 68% of whom want brands to be more active in solving social problems, and nearly half of whom want brands to provide simple ways for them to make a difference in the world, however small. Brands must provide an outlet for consumers, especially millennials, to express and share their aspirations, inspire bigger dreams, and co-create not just new products and services but positive change in society.

Phase 2: co-development of solutions

Customer involvement in the actual development process could range from validating new product concepts and features to co-designing an entirely new solution. For example, in the consumer-goods sector, despite the billions of dollars spent on R&D and market research, 90% of products fail at launch because they do not have the right mix of features that finicky customers want. Getting this mix right is tricky at the best of times, but especially when launching a first-of-a-kind product in an entirely new product category.

Marketers can, however, use social-media tools such as Affinnova to quickly test dozens of new product ideas with scores of customers online who can vote on their preferred features. In this way, they can help firms eliminate unviable ideas early in the development cycle and concentrate their efforts on honing and developing product concepts that customers most want. For example, when marketers at Dannon, the US subsidiary of Danone, a global food and beverage company, decided to launch a first-of-a-kind low-carb yogurt in the US, they had to choose from over 10,000 product ideas and countless combinations of names, positioning, serving sizes and packaging colours. Using Affinnova, Dannon identified the most critical product elements that mattered for most customers: a light yogurt with 25% fewer carbs (even if that meant a smaller serving size) and much less sugar (even if that meant less protein). Based on this input, Dannon launched Light 'n' Fit Carb & Sugar Control, a first in that product category. The product achieved sales of $75 million during its first year (and several hundred million since), helping Dannon to grab 11% of the light yogurt market.

In some instances, customers may hack a company's branded product and use it differently from its original purpose. Rather than being offended, brands should regard these hackers as an outsourced R&D team, celebrate their creative deviations and showcase them as clever inventions. IKEA has set up IKEAHackers.net, where it showcases useful solutions fabricated by ingenious customers jerry-rigging or combining IKEA products, such as a Grundtal toilet-roll holder converted into a headphone hanger, or Pax wardrobes fitted together to make display cabinets in a jewellery shop.

Co-development is not limited to consumer products and services. It can also be used in B2B industries. For instance, IBM has a programme called First of a Kind (FOAK) that brings together pioneering clients and IBM's R&D teams to co-invent breakthrough business solutions with cutting-edge technologies. To date, IBM has completed over 150 FOAK projects, ranging from improving access to health-care data without violating patient privacy to reducing the cost of electricity using smart grids. FOAK is a frugal way for IBM to test the market viability of new technologies with a leading client before commercialising them on a larger scale.

As stated earlier, however, customers – especially millennials – want not only to co-create branded products and services, but also to solve larger social problems. This is why Jez Frampton, CEO of Interbrand, a global branding consultancy, encourages brands to work with consumers to create shared value that helps society. Crowdsourcing platforms like OpenIDEO allow brands to organise challenges that engage thousands of existing and potential customers online to co-design such solutions. For instance, Steelcase, a global developer and manufacturer of office products and services, used OpenIDEO to find ways to revitalise cities in economic decline such as Detroit. Coca-Cola tapped OpenIDEO to identify techniques for encouraging households to recycle more. Similarly, Unilever has an online portal where it challenges the public to help solve social problems such as improving access to safe drinking water, reducing salt and sugar in food items, and storing renewable energy. Ideas from the public help Unilever develop better products and improve its business processes while contributing to society.

Phase 3: co-marketing, co-branding and co-distribution

Some 92% of consumers place more trust in suggestions and recommendations from friends and family than in advertisements. Indeed, only 10% of consumers trust brands at all. As a result, once a new product or service is available, companies need to mobilise communities of prosumers to create demand for it, by turning them into brand ambassadors who promote and even sell their favourite products and services. Unfortunately, marketing teams in large firms, accustomed to spending months on designing and launching marketing campaigns, are not organised to engage customers at Twitter-speed. This is why 59% of chief marketing officers view agile marketing processes as a top priority. To gain flexibility, marketing heads can use services from agile advertising agencies, such as Saatchi & Saatchi + Duke, which use social media as a cost-effective platform to launch word-of-mouth online marketing campaigns – and even flash mobs – within 24 hours.

Some clever companies are embedding customers into their value chains and providing them with incentives to perform specific tasks previously undertaken by the company. This is a win-win proposition: customers earn some money by testing and improving a product that they might later want to buy; and the company saves money by outsourcing work to customers, who can carry out the tasks faster, better and cheaper than the company itself could. DHL, a global logistics company, is doing precisely this. In September 2013 it launched MyWays, a platform that uses crowdsourcing to make last-mile deliveries in Stockholm. Buyers order products online and have them delivered by residents who have signed up to participate in the service. Buyers use a mobile app to connect to those who offer to deliver their packages in exchange for credits with monetary value.

Multiple customer roles

In the past, companies assigned customers to a single role: the passive buyer. Yet according to Forrester Research, 61% of US adults online are willing to co-create products and services with brands across industries. In the coming years, forward-thinking companies will probably be more like casting agents, learning to engage prosumers in various ways depending on the context and the task. Some potential roles that companies could invite helpful customers to play at different stages of a product's life cycle are as follows.

Dreamers

Customers can help brands dream up future scenarios or breakthrough products that may be unimaginable today. For example, Volkswagen held an online competition in China called the people's car project, which invited consumers to submit design ideas for futuristic cars they had dreamed about. Contributors could either tinker with concept designs available on Volkswagen's website or submit their own original designs. The winning idea came from Wan Jia, a student from Chengdu, who dreamed up a two-person, emissions-free hover car that uses magnetic levitation. Volkswagen then brought to life Jia's imaginary car by making a short video that shows her ecstatic parents proudly flying in the self-driving car that their daughter designed (the video has been viewed over 7.5 million times on YouTube).

Validators

Validators are customers who do not create anything themselves but help to validate new product ideas and prototypes. These customers can reduce thousands of potential options and features to a few that matter most to the majority of customers. For example, Hasbro, a US multinational toy and board-game company, invited thousands of customers on Facebook to vote on new house rules for its Monopoly game, such as "freezing your assets so you can't collect rent from other players while in jail". The rules with most votes are to be included in the main Monopoly game guide in 2015 (though these will be optional).

Ideators

Some customers go further and propose new ideas that can either improve a company's existing products, services and processes, or lead to entirely new solutions. For instance, Lego gives thousands of external programmers access to the code of its Mindstorm toy robot so they can develop new functions for it. Many of these have gone far beyond anything that Lego's R&D team imagined. Similarly, Jeppesen Sanderson, a Boeing subsidiary that develops navigational solutions, involved pilots in the design of its Mobile FliteDeck, a paperless navigation tool for the iPad – the aviation industry's first interactive mobile flight app.

Makers

These are the most hands-on, entrepreneurial customers, who create products themselves and are willing to partner with large companies to help to scale up the new idea. Through its Huggies MomInspired programme, Kimberly-Clark offers a $15,000 grant to DIY mothers with ingenious ideas to ease the burden on new parents. These "mompreneurs" use the grant money to launch start-ups that can build and market the products they have conceived. Past winners include Amy Oh, who designed the Grapple multi-toy tether that uses suction cups to hold toys – a boon for parents tired of picking up toys their kids are constantly dropping.

Evangelists

Loyal users, who love your products, can become brand advocates and preach the value of your existing and new products, helping to generate demand faster, better and cheaper than multimillion-dollar advertising campaigns. According to Steve Knox, senior adviser to Boston Consulting Group and a former director of customer marketing at P&G, brands need to establish deeper relationships with their strongest advocates, who typically form just 2% of the target audience. These hard-core fans wield the greatest influence in social networks and, according to Nielsen, a global information and measurement company, their ratings are trusted by 92% of all consumers. Frugal marketers can engage these self-motivated brand enthusiasts and use their social influence to generate buzz for free. For example, Intuit relies on a 500,000-strong army of brand advocates to share news and new product offers online with millions of small and medium-sized businesses. These prospective customers are hundreds of times more likely to check out the Intuit-related offers they receive from advocates than if they hear about them from other marketing channels.

Sales agents

In emerging markets in Africa, Brazil and India, multinationals solve the last-mile challenge (distributing products in far-flung areas with no organised retail distribution system) by recruiting people in local communities to act as their grassroots sales reps. This frugal, go-to-market strategy is more cost-effective and productive than setting up retail outlets. For instance, Essilor, an ophthalmic-lens producer, employs young people in rural India called "Eye Mitras" (friends of the eye) to go door-to-door in villages – where 70% of Indians live – to carry out eye tests. When needed, they also prescribe lenses that are manufactured locally at lower cost and sold cheaply to rural customers. This is part of Essilor's inclusive business initiative to bring affordable eye care to the 2.5 billion people worldwide who lack this essential service. Western companies can apply a similar strategy in developed economies by engaging customers as local salespeople in new market segments. Avon, a US manufacturer of beauty and personal care products, has been using this model for years. By selecting and training local women (and increasingly men) to sell its products door-to-door in their communities, Avon has long made frugal use of potential or existing customers as its sales force.

Fixers

Expert customers can act as companies' outsourced service units and help fix the problems of other customers, or address the needs of entire communities of users. For example, Yatango Mobile, an Australian telecoms company, offers phone credit to customers who provide technical support. Launched in February 2013 as a "social telco", the company is only open to Facebook users and offers up to $5 phone credit for customers who recruit friends on the social network. Furthermore, it has no call centres; all technical support is handed over to members in exchange for call credit. Yatango customers earn 10 cents in phone credit for every technical support question they answer on Yotango's online self-service forum.

CASE STUDY 5

giffgaff: the mobile network run by you

In 2008, Gav Thompson, head of brand strategy at O2, a UK mobile telecoms provider, attended a conference on social media in San Francisco. Hearing about Web 2.0 platforms such as Twitter inspired him to rethink how a mobile services provider might engage with its customers. He pondered whether his customers could be part of a community that helps run the company alongside employees. Thompson imagined a mobile network based on the principle of mutuality: customers would be rewarded for helping one another (and the firm). He wrote down "mutual, simple and fair" as its founding principles.

By November 2009, Thompson was ready to launch this new company, which he named giffgaff, an ancient Scottish term for "mutual giving". To contain start-up costs, it was launched as a mobile virtual network operator, owned by Spain's Telefónica and run on O2's network. The focus was on creating a mutually supportive consumer community. Members would post problems online that other members would solve, in return for "payback". For instance, when giffgaff switched to using new SIM cards, customers would either change the cards themselves by watching an instructional video on YouTube, or ask another customer to do this for them. In October 2010, the service was integrated with Facebook and Twitter, which then became alternative channels of customer support. The company also maintained a small customer-services team to solve giffgaff members' problems. To reflect the unique and central role of customers, giffgaff's slogan became: "the mobile network run by you".

Within a year of its launch, giffgaff had won the most innovative community award at the Social CRM Customer Excellence Awards, and the Forrester Groundswell Award. In June 2012, the Mobile Industry Awards voted giffgaff best mobile virtual network operator. Today giffgaff boasts over 1 million customers.

Rewards

The company's payback scheme provides a means to reward customers. For example, a customer can earn points for passing a SIM to a friend, who activates it. The friend receives points for topping up the phone with a credit card. Customers can also earn points for contributing to the giffgaff community. Sometimes, customers can earn points for promoting the company's service.

giffgaff's first payback was made in June 2010; in December 2012, it paid over £1.8 million to customers, including £15,600 to Teen Cancer Research.

And in June 2013, it paid almost £2 million to customers, including £12,200 to Great Ormond Street Hospital and £12,200 to Water Aid.[11]

New products

Many new product ideas come from the community's ideas board. giffgaff's labs develop and beta-test the ideas on selected community members. Those that pass are briefly opened up to the whole community, who decide either to implement the idea or drop it.

In September 2010, giffgaff introduced its first new product idea: a plan with 2 pence calls and 1 pence texts for a monthly payment of £5 ($7.50). It was withdrawn after trial. Three months later, giffgaff introduced a second product, nicknamed Hokey Cokey, which gave customers 60 minutes of talk time, 300 text messages and a free minute for every eligible incoming minute, all for £5 ($7.50). In June 2011, Hokey Cokey became an official product.

Apps

In July 2010, giffgaff released two iPhone apps and a Nokia app to help customers manage their accounts and access the community. All three applications were produced by community members rather than by giffgaff. It also invited members to develop similar apps for Android and Windows phones.

In May 2012, giffgaff promoted a member's idea for an app that gave users another way to top up their accounts. Six months later, it was released for the iPhone, and the community member who developed it became an employee.

Conclusion

Customers can be a powerful source of frugal innovation for companies. As this chapter has demonstrated, companies' most proactive customers – their prosumers – can help identify new ideas, validate and develop them into products and services, and commercialise them faster, better and cheaper. But customers are not the only external stakeholders that can help companies do better with less. Companies can also engage other external parties as part of their drive for frugality. These might be business partners such as suppliers or distributors. They can even be competitors, whether small, nimble, start-ups or large rivals. The next chapter looks at the sixth and final principle of frugal innovation: make innovative friends.

7   Principle six: make innovative friends

Ek aur ek gyarah hote hain. (*One and one make eleven.*)

Hindi proverb

THOMAS EDISON was a creative genius. A prolific inventor – perhaps most famous for inventing the light bulb – he single-handedly built the US's first and largest corporate R&D lab in the early 20th century. This lab became the technological foundation for General Electric (GE). For over a century, GE's leaders have striven to live up to Edison's high standards of innovation by investing massively in R&D and producing a stream of technological breakthroughs. These have included medical devices, aircraft engines, wind turbines, nuclear power plants, automated factories, and much more. By the end of the 20th century, GE, one of the world's most innovative companies, had achieved industrial leadership. Yet in 2012, its chief marketing officer, Beth Comstock, confessed:[1] "Our traditional teams are too slow. We are not innovating fast enough. We need to systematise change."

There are two reasons for this. First, GE's customers' needs have radically changed. Hospitals no longer just want to buy MRI (magnetic resonance imaging) devices from GE; they also want GE to help them serve patients better and more cost-effectively. Airlines want GE not just to deliver aircraft engines, but also to help them transport more passengers faster, more safely and more cheaply. In other words, customers do not just want sophisticated GE products; they also want personalised services that can help them run their businesses better.

Second, the competitive landscape is radically shifting. In the coming years, GE's toughest competitors will not be other industrial powerhouses such as Siemens or Schneider Electric, but the so-called GAFAs (Google, Apple, Facebook and Amazon). Indeed, as more physical devices – from giant power turbines to modest light bulbs – are connected to the Internet of Things, a torrent of big data will be unleashed on the world. If the GAFAs can gain access to the data generated by GE's industrial products, they can glean insights from that data to offer value-adding services to GE's customers. As the saying goes: "Whoever owns the customer's data owns the customer." More worryingly, GAFAs and other software firms are rapidly expanding into hardware; for example, Google and Apple are investing in connected consumer products and Amazon is getting into drones and robots.

Recognising these massive changes in customer needs and the competitive landscape, GE decided to radically transform its core business model. It is moving from being an industrial giant that sells technology products to customers to being an agile provider of integrated business solutions that can sense and respond to customers' needs. GE is keen to capitalise on its 130 years or so of domain expertise in the industrial sector – a key competitive differentiator vis-à-vis the GAFAs – while also adopting new tools and methods to innovate faster, better and more cost-effectively, not unlike a Silicon Valley start-up. As part of this strategy, GE decided to make innovative friends. As Comstock explains:[2]

There are millions of clever folks out there – restless entrepreneurs, ingenious tinkerers and passionate scientists – with brilliant ideas and solutions ... We want our R&D and marketing teams to tap into this "global brain".

In 2013, GE partnered with Quirky, a crowdsourcing platform (see Chapter 6), to make its patented technologies available to ordinary people to create internet-connected consumer products. Once someone conceives an innovative product, Quirky's in-house designers and engineers transform that invention into a practical product and help market it, all within a matter of weeks. If the product sells well, GE and Quirky share the profits after the inventor gets his cut. In early 2014, Garthen Leslie, a self-employed IT consultant in his

60s, proposed an idea for a smartphone-controlled, energy-efficient air conditioner. Based on that idea, in just three months Quirky had developed a workable product, Aros, which sells for $300 or less on Amazon and in major retail chains. Aros raked in $5 million just in pre-orders on Amazon, and thousands of units have been sold. Quirky, whose headquarters are in Manhattan, has opened an office close to GE's R&D headquarters in Schenectady, the city where Edison founded the company and gave the world electricity. Its proximity will allow GE engineers and scientists to work closely with Quirky staff to roll out new products fast. GE is also expanding in Silicon Valley, where Comstock frequently meets venture capitalists and entrepreneurs.

In 2013, Comstock helped launch GE Ventures, a $150 million fund that invests in promising Silicon Valley start-ups specialising in software, energy, health care and advanced manufacturing. GE Ventures' portfolio includes Rock Health (an accelerator of digital health-care start-ups), Stem (whose intelligent battery storage can reduce peak energy charges by 20%) and Mocana (a provider of embedded security systems for the industrial internet). Partnering with these start-ups not only gives GE access to disruptive technologies, but also creates a disruptive working culture. Comstock notes:

> Working with impatient 20-something entrepreneurs in T-shirts creates friction and tension within GE's buttoned-up corporate culture. But it's also energising. Start-ups' enthusiasm is contagious.

GE is also organising open innovation challenges, hosted on crowdsourcing platform NineSigma, inviting inventive minds worldwide to create affordable and sustainable solutions in its core health-care, energy and aviation businesses. Its Healthymagination programme, for example, is seeking new ways to fight breast cancer. The challenge received 500 proposals from 40 countries, from which 5 winners were each given $100,000 seed money, mentoring and access to GE's R&D resources. GE also launched the 3D Printing Design Quest to design lighter, next-generation aircraft engine brackets that can be 3D-printed. The winner, Arie Kurniawan, an engineer from Salatiga, Indonesia, beat 699 other entries from 56 countries. Kurniawan's bracket weighs 84% less than the original, but can withstand loads of 9,500lb or 4,310kg. Amazingly, Kurniawan had no aviation engineering experience, and it took him just a few weeks to create his ingenious solution.

Recognising the value of amateurs and tinkerers, GE has teamed up with TechShop to set up GE Garages, mobile units with advanced manufacturing labs fully equipped with 3D printers, CNC mills, laser cutters and injection moulders. These garages make innovation accessible to ordinary Americans by giving them hands-on experience using modern manufacturing tools to develop prototypes quickly. In GE Garages, people get training and support to turn their wildest ideas into products – whether for personal or wider use. More entrepreneurial people, who invent something relevant to GE, can access GE-supported crowdfunding and crowdsourcing platforms Indiegogo and Quirky to develop the idea commercially. Having travelled to New York, Washington and other major US cities, GE Garages were to visit Nigeria, Algeria and Turkey in 2014.

In mid-2014, GE also teamed up with Local Motors to launch FirstBuild, an open community of designers and engineers, to design, build and sell next-generation home appliances. These projects are often presented as mind-twisting challenges, such as how to convert a 7ft × 2ft (2.75m × 0.78m) space into a fully functioning kitchen. The most promising ideas – voted on online by the FirstBuild community – will be quickly prototyped, built and showcased in a Local Motors garage-sized micro-factory. Each micro-factory is equipped with rapid prototyping equipment such as 3D printers, welding and woodcarving tools, as well as manufacturing equipment that can produce customised goods in small batches to meet local demand. The micro-factory even has an embedded showroom to demonstrate and sell innovative products and get customer feedback. GE inaugurated its first FirstBuild micro-factory in Louisville, Kentucky, in July 2014. By setting up such micro-factories around the world, GE hopes to crowdsource cutting-edge ideas for its home-appliances business and move them faster from concept to showroom.

Despite spending around $6 billion on R&D each year, GE recognised the need for external partnerships, and is creating a lean, flexible, highly networked R&D operation accordingly. This chapter shows how, like GE, other companies can engage a global network of creative external partners (suppliers, universities, venture capitalists, start-ups, tinkerers, and so on) to co-develop frugal products, services and business models more efficiently.

The hyper-collaboration imperative

Olaf Groth, a professor at Hult International Business School in San Francisco, notes that businesses across industries in the developed world are now facing "wicked" problems, which by their very nature are complex and protracted.[3] These wicked problems are both social and economic. For instance, medical-device-makers and big pharma companies are being asked by the US and European governments to deliver high-quality health care to ever more people while reducing prices. Against the backdrop of rapid urbanisation and dwindling natural resources, city planners are calling on the construction industry to build smart, comfortable, energy-efficient cities. With an ageing industrial workforce and escalating raw materials costs, manufacturers – especially in Japan and Germany – are being asked to cut staff, increase productivity and produce affordable, eco-friendly products. Businesses cannot solve these complex problems alone. It is no longer the case that knowledge is power; now sharing knowledge is power.

Sceptical readers might ask: what's new? For at least a decade, businesses have embraced open innovation: the practice of opening up and networking R&D operations with external partners. By 2010, more than half of *Fortune* 500 companies had an open innovation strategy. In 2013 alone, many *Fortune* 500 companies launched innovation centres and immersive accelerator programmes in Silicon Valley to give their business managers the opportunity to "open up" and learn from nimble entrepreneurs. Which Western CEOs do not proudly talk about how their company is building "open innovation networks" and "partner ecosystems" to better serve their customers? However, the truth is that their innovation networks are not that open, and their partner ecosystems do not really serve customers.

First, when companies seek external know-how, they are disposed towards knowledge that reinforces rather than challenges their worldview. As Socrates pointed out, wisdom is about knowing that you don't know, not about believing that you know when you don't. He argued that wisdom could be cultivated by merely being curious: an unexamined life is not worth living. Sadly, as Tod Martin, CEO of Unboundary, an "intentionally small" consulting firm that advises *Fortune* 500 firms such as Coca-Cola, IBM and FedEx, points out:[4]

> *Curiosity is stifled in most large organisations, which tend to live by the proverb "Curiosity killed the cat". They prevent their own people from looking up and out and making sense of the world.*

He adds:[5]

> *They are open to new ideas as long as these come from others who resemble them. But they are not open to new perspectives, especially from those who are very different from them.*

The unexamined life which these uncurious organisations lead abruptly ends when the world suddenly and unexpectedly shifts. In other words, companies practise open innovation today mainly to become more efficient – by doing better what they already do – rather than to become more adaptable and agile – by unlearning what they already know and learning how to do new things. Unfortunately, only the most adaptable – not the most efficient – species survive. Indeed, organisations are dying earlier: the average lifespan of a company in Standard & Poor's 500 Index (the 500 leading publicly-traded firms in the US) shrank from 61 years in 1958 to 18 years in 2011, and will shrink further in the foreseeable future.

Second, when companies claim to be building partner ecosystems, they are doing little more than finding new ways to lock customers into their brands. They are replacing vertical integration with a vertical ecosystem. But a brand-specific approach is becoming irrelevant, even counterproductive, as customers are themselves able to create the products they want, independent of established brands. Instead, companies need to build horizontal ecosystems that integrate their brands with those of other firms – including their rivals – to provide customers with the rich choice and highly personalised experiences that they expect.

This new consumer-centric approach has been dubbed

"MEcosystems".[6] And although it threatens traditional bricks-and-mortar organisations such as GM and Bank of America, it is a boon for the GAFAs. Indeed, while GM is assembling a vertical partner ecosystem to build connected cars that run like "iPhones on wheels", Apple and Google are investing in a horizontal ecosystem to provide customers with seamless experiences across multiple devices, whether they are at home, at work, or driving between the two. Similarly, while Bank of America is busy beefing up its mobile banking capabilities, Google is attempting to become a virtual bank by filling its Google Wallet with plastic debit cards.

To win in this new context, companies must practise hyper-collaboration; that is, they must increase the breadth and depth of their partnerships in order to understand the real nature of so-called wicked problems and solutions. Hyper-collaboration will enhance companies' adaptability and resilience to better serve the MEcosystems. In doing so, they might foster truly open innovation ecosystems in which, as Groth puts it, "diverse sets of talents are induced to think like da Vinci, across disciplines".[7]

So how can business executives engage "Renaissance" thinkers and doers for an increasingly dynamic and unpredictable business environment?

Six ways to hyper-collaborate

Hyper-collaborative companies must make use of an eclectic group of partners to challenge senior-management thinking and encourage a continuous process of unlearning and relearning. This can be done in the following ways.

Talk to suppliers who think originally

As strategy consultants to large companies for a number of years, this book's authors have often informed senior executives about a breakthrough technology or solution developed by their suppliers. The usual response is: "That's an amazing invention. Why didn't our suppliers tell us about it?" But the suppliers did tell the company's purchasing managers, who showed no interest. And the purchasing managers cannot be blamed either; they are under pressure to cut costs, too often by squeezing their suppliers. Like the *Titanic*'s captain asking the mechanics to save coal as the ship headed for an iceberg, too many companies on a similar collision course are responding irrationally.

To change course, companies must now work more strategically with suppliers on new business models. For instance, in the late 2000s, many Western original equipment manufacturers (OEMs) – especially in Germany – dismissed the $2,500 Nano as a cheap car for the developing world. But now that Renault's low-cost Dacias are selling like hot cakes in core European markets, German carmakers are approaching auto suppliers such as Bosch (which developed the Nano's core engine and fuel-injection technologies) to explore how to leverage those frugal technologies to create affordable cars. Similarly, Marks & Spencer (M&S), a UK multinational retailer, hosts an annual conference of more than 1,000 of its global suppliers to learn how to implement its "Plan A" to become the world's most environmentally sustainable major retailer by 2020. It has dedicated websites for various supplier communities, such as the Food Supplier Exchange for its agricultural suppliers, where they can share best practices. Given that the supply chain accounts for 50% of its carbon footprint, M&S clearly cannot achieve its 2020 sustainability goals alone. As Mike Barry, director of Plan A at M&S, confesses:[8] "We won't change the world alone; in fact, we can't even change our own business alone."

Work with partners to serve MEcosystems

In developed economies, cost-conscious and eco-aware customers are assembling different products and services to meet their individual needs. Typically, these customers do not care if these products and services are branded. So companies must work with others in their sector (for example, carmakers, railways and airlines from the transport sector) to integrate their respective capabilities and provide their common clients with seamless experiences. For instance, French railway operator SNCF is collaborating with Renault on disruptive R&D projects to deliver affordable end-to-end transport solutions to shared customers. These frugal mobility solutions will seek either to optimise existing infrastructure – by, say, combining a long-distance train ride with last-mile travel in an electric vehicle – or to leverage radically new energy-efficient transport assets co-developed by SNCF and Renault. SNCF has also tied up with Orange and Total to launch Ecomobilité Ventures, Europe's first multi-corporate investment fund, which invests in a portfolio of promising start-ups that can collectively deliver end-to-end solutions in sustainable mobility.

Non-competing brands can also work together, not only to respond to the current needs of their shared customers, but also to anticipate their future needs. Simon Mulcahy, senior vice-president and managing director of financial services industry at Salesforce. com, which offers a customer relationship management platform based on cloud computing, encourages companies to adopt a wide lens to perceive their customer needs through the diverse perspectives of other industries, and to address these needs by borrowing best practices from other sectors.[9] For example, diverse industries such as construction, interior design and renovation, food, retail, entertainment, logistics, health, financial services, energy and communication all share a single customer in one particular location: their home. This is why Orange, Kingfisher, Carrefour, Legrand, La Poste, SEB and Pernod Ricard – seven leading companies in the above industries – have set up InHome, a cross-industry innovation incubator run by InProcess, an innovation consultancy.

Senior executives from these companies participate in a series of workshops facilitated by InProcess. There they gain deeper insights into the behaviour and needs of typical families who will be living in tomorrow's homes, and an understanding of new emerging usages and practices (from flat-sharing to living in contemporary yurts to hosting strangers at home) that reflect our rapidly changing lifestyles and values. (The workshop is itself based on a year-long, in-depth ethnographic study conducted by InProcess with real families.) During the workshop, each participant is asked to "get into the skin" of another participant and try to understand how his or her future needs can be met from another industry's perspective. Once empathy and trust have been established among participants, they consider scenarios in which they can integrate their respective offerings and capabilities to best serve their common customer.

At the end of these workshops, according to InProcess's CEO, Christophe Rebours:[10]

[Participants are] able to remove their "industry blinkers" and see things from their shared customer's viewpoint. The participants' motivation also shifts from maximising their individual share of what they believe is a fixed pie to maximising the size of the entire pie for the benefit of everyone.

For Rebours, InHome is successful because its members avoid the problem of a few big firms dominating smaller members. Instead, the Goliaths want to reinvent themselves as nimble Davids. Finally, collaborating companies reduce risk and save money because they invest in solutions collectively.

Engage competitors in realising big hairy audacious goals

Firms that hyper-collaborate pay heed to Sun Tzu's advice: "Keep your friends close but your enemies closer." This co-opetition among rival companies is a frugal strategy because by jointly investing in a high-risk/high-reward innovation project driven by a big hairy audacious goal (BHAG), they collectively reduce their risk exposure. Similarly, by working together they can help establish – and accelerate the adoption of – a new industry standard that could benefit them all.

For instance, the Natural Capital Leaders Platform is run by the University of Cambridge Institute for Sustainability Leadership (CISL) to address a BHAG: how to mitigate the rapid loss of natural capital, such as water and agricultural land. By 2030, the UK will be short of two-sevenths of the agricultural land needed for food, space and renewable energy. Similarly, it faces the paradoxical threat of both frequent flooding and severe drought. In 2020, if the UK were to face a dry year, it would be short of 120 billion litres (31.7 billion gallons) of water, equivalent to the amount used by farmers to irrigate crops in a typical year.

This looming land and water scarcity threatens to increase commodity prices and harm business. For this reason, arch rivals in the food industry, Nestlé, Mondelez and Mars, along with agribusinesses, such as Volac and Ingredion, and retailers, such as Kingfisher and ASDA, have joined the Natural Capital Leaders Platform. Their shared goal is to better understand and manage their impact and dependence on natural capital. Together, they hope to identify new business opportunities and frugal solutions, such as reducing waste and increasing farmland yields with less water.

Share assets and resources with other companies – and make big savings

Industrial firms should together implement the sharing and circular economy in two important ways. First, they should integrate their own value chain with those of other manufacturers, as often in business "one man's trash is another man's treasure". Second, they should monetise under-utilised assets by sharing them with companies that need them more. This dual strategy allows manufacturers to slash costs, maximise efficiency and generate new revenue streams. More importantly, it changes how a business is run, leading to lucrative opportunities in the process.

For example, by-product synergy (BPS) is a process of using the waste stream from one production process to produce either raw materials or finished products. As outlined by Deishin Lee, professor of operations management at Boston College's Carroll School of Management, BPS has been successfully adopted by Chaparral Steel, a Texan firm now part of Gerdau Corporation, which uses recycled steel to manufacture new products. Slag waste generated during the production process is sold to a nearby cement manufacturer, Texas Industries (which in 2014 merged with Martin Marietta), which uses it to make Portland cement. Lee discovered that this BPS strategy not only profits both manufacturers but also brings environmental benefits, by cutting carbon emissions by 10% and reducing energy consumption by up to 15% in the concrete production activity. This was possible largely because the steel slag had been pre-processed to add value to cement production. *Fortune* 500 companies are also now embracing industrial symbiosis, a large-scale version of BPS, which turns waste streams into profit centres. With the help of its partner Protomax, ASDA, a UK supermarket chain, upcycles its George plastic hangers and coffee waste into light, stable plastic panels to make the coffee tables used in its stores' cafés. The panels can be recycled later to make new panels.

Several Western governments and cities now encourage a similar systematic adoption of industrial symbiosis. Kalundborg in Denmark has pioneered industrial symbiosis since 1972, when Statoil, a Norwegian multinational energy company, supplied excess gas to Gyproc, a local gypsum producer, to dry plasterboard produced in its ovens. This practice has since evolved into Kalundborg Industrial Eco-Park, an interconnected web of nine leading private and public enterprises that exchange material waste, energy, water and information. Kalundborg's power plant manager, inspired by co-operative species, coined the term "industrial symbiosis" to describe this approach. He defines it as:[11]

Co-operation between different industries by which the presence of each ... increases the viability of the others, and by which the demands of society for resource savings and environmental protection are considered.

The Kalundborg ecosystem has already reduced annual carbon emissions by 240,000 tonnes and water use by 3 million cubic metres.

Kalundborg's success has also inspired other Western governments to encourage industrial symbiosis. In 2003, the UK government set up the National Industrial Symbiosis Programme (NISP) to consider industrial opportunities from sharing water, energy and waste materials. The NISP attracted 15,000 corporate members. Together, they reduced carbon emissions by 42 million tonnes and redirected 48 million tonnes of waste from landfills for reuse, reducing costs or generating income of more than £3 billion. The NISP has helped Michelin, a tyre manufacturer, reduce its landfill waste by 97% within just 3 years, 18 months ahead of schedule. It estimates that every tonne of carbon dioxide saved costs members merely around $1. This is a far more cost-effective approach than, say, carbon trading, with its high transaction cost. The OECD declared the NISP to be a game-changer in waste management. Its model is being replicated in 20 countries worldwide.

Sharing waste is only half the story

Companies can also share underused assets and resources. FLOOW2 is a business-to-business marketplace that enables companies to share and exchange under-utilised equipment, services, skills and knowledge. By tightly integrating their supply chains, companies can keep their fixed assets fully utilised and also save on costly raw materials and energy. For instance, in the logistics sector, Mars, a global food manufacturer, has developed a sustainable distribution network in Germany by sharing its vehicles with rivals.

Work with the social and public sectors

Large companies are facing growing pressure from governments, customers and employees to act as responsible corporate citizens by solving pressing social issues such as health-care access and financial exclusion. It is too often assumed that corporations are just profit-hungry monsters that ignore social problems. In fact many of them do care, but they lack the knowledge, skills, resources, or the right business model to tackle social challenges systematically and profitably. They may even be too proud to admit their ignorance or inexperience.

Fortunately, many other companies seek help from non-profit organisations to forge hybrid value chains (HVCs). HVC is a business model that aims to create affordable products and services for the poor. It is more than corporate social responsibility (CSR) or philanthropy, as it works in win-win partnership with all stakeholders. Businesses gain access to profitable new markets, while non-profit organisations achieve their desired social impact. In this way, multinationals such as Citigroup, Essilor, GE and Unilever have served bottom-of-pyramid (BOP) customers in Africa, Asia and Latin America. They are now looking to do the same in Europe and the US, where millions of citizens can no longer afford basic health care and financial services. For example, the FDIC estimates that nearly 70 million Americans currently have little or no access to basic financial services. Worse, the financially underserved were charged $89 billion in fees and interest in 2012. Indeed, low-income Americans incur nearly $40,000 of unnecessary fees during their lives.

Dan Schulman, group president for enterprise growth at American

Express (AmEx), a US multinational financial services corporation, sums it up succinctly:[12] "It's expensive to be poor." He reckons that steep banking fees, restrictions on minimum balance and inaccessible banking infrastructure have led millions of Americans to switch from traditional financial-services companies to a new generation of small, digitally savvy firms that provide affordable financial services. Two years ago, AmEx recognised that 70 million financially excluded Americans present a new market for frugal finance, and that its business model was ill-suited to serve these customers.

As a result, the famously exclusive service that did nicely for the affluent decided to reinvent itself as an inclusive brand for all. In 2012, AmEx launched two frugal solutions: Bluebird, a no-frills, low-fee checking and debit card service available through Walmart and online; and Serve, a prepaid card. In 2014, AmEx began developing HVCs comprising a multi-sectorial ecosystem of non-profit organisations, government agencies, advocacy groups, policy institutes and start-ups. It is also working with D2D Fund, a consultancy that uses behavioural science tools such as gamification to nudge consumers into healthier financial habits, to promote and advocate prize-based savings.

Similarly, to teach young people good financial habits, AmEx is piloting a project with non-profit organisations Moneythink and EveryoneOn to provide financial mentoring, free Wi-Fi and mobile-phone-based learning to students in Mississippi. Additionally, American Express Ventures, established in 2011 in Silicon Valley, will invest in early-stage start-ups to help people manage their finances better. In June 2014, AmEx launched a Financial Innovation Lab, where researchers and counsellors work together to support credit building and savings; the lab's results will be made publicly available. Through these multiple initiatives, AmEx is attempting to understand and solve a complex, multi-dimensional socio-economic problem. The unbanked and underbanked spend 10% of their $1 trillion disposable income on fees, the same amount as they spend on food. Schulman asks:[13] "Imagine if you could turn loose almost $100 billion back into the economy?"

Engage restless entrepreneurs, hackers and tinkerers

Airbnb, an online short-let rental company, was launched in 2008 by Brian Chesky and Joe Gebbia, two young people with no experience of the hotel industry. By 2014, Airbnb had become the fifth largest hotel chain in the world, filling more room nights than all the Hilton hotels put together (and Hilton began in 1919). Similarly, in 2006 Frédéric Mazzella and Nicolas Brusson founded BlaBlaCar which, by 2014, had emerged as Europe's largest car-sharing firm. BlaBlaCar now transports over 1 million passengers a month, which is more than Eurostar, a high-speed railway service connecting London with Paris and Brussels. The same applies to Uber, a mobile service directly connecting passengers with drivers for hire. Co-founded in 2009 by Garrett Camp and Travis Kalanick, Uber has disrupted the traditional taxi industry. In 2014 it was valued at $18.2 billion.

Neither Mazzella nor Brusson, nor Camp nor Kalanick, had any experience in the automotive or transport services sector, and yet they managed to disrupt both. How? They all confronted a pressing problem or critical need and after becoming frustrated with existing solutions decided to solve it themselves. Chesky and Gebbia were struggling to pay the rent on their San Francisco loft apartment when they hit upon the idea of turning their living room into a bed and breakfast. One Christmas, Mazzella couldn't get on a train to visit his family in the French countryside because they were all full. But he saw plenty of cars on the roads with single occupants. And so was born the idea of the BlaBlaCar car-sharing service. Late one December night in 2008, when Kalanick was unable to find a taxi in suburban Paris, he starting thinking of a mobile app that would connect him to a driver for hire at the touch of a button; and he came up with Uber.

Jacques Birol, a serial entrepreneur and strategy consultant who teaches and mentors entrepreneurs in France, explains:[14]

> Entrepreneurs are a frustrated and restless bunch who refuse to put up with the status quo. Adversity fuels their creativity. Unlike scientists, they create breakthrough solutions out of sheer (personal) necessity.

Birol notes that frustrated entrepreneurs think and act like problem experts who take over the entire issue with all their ingenuity and tenacity. They are willing to learn everything.

Conversely, in large companies in established industries, complacent executives operate as "experts of solutions" who seek to use what they already know or create needs for solutions they already have. They are ill-trained to unlearn. Liz Wiseman, a Thinkers50-ranked leadership expert and author of *Rookie Smarts: Why Learning Beats Knowing in the New Game of Work*, says:[15]

> *Inexperienced entrepreneurs are rookies (or first-timers) with sponge-like minds that absorb new knowledge quickly – whereas experienced executives tend to operate as if their minds are made of Teflon: no new knowledge sticks.*

The ever-frustrated and tireless rookies live by following Steve Jobs's adage: "Stay Hungry. Stay Foolish." It is time large companies began to inculcate this rookie mindset in their own executives.

To learn to transform adversity into opportunity, bricks-and-mortar Goliaths need to engage digital Davids not as opponents but as allies. For instance, Pearson, one of the world's leading publishing and education companies, founded in 1844, has recognised that digital learning tools and online educational solutions, such as MOOCs, the Raspberry Pi and Khan Academy, are not rivals to the conventional classroom-based learning models that Pearson's traditional products and services have always supported. Rather, digital learning tools and approaches present three major benefits for Pearson. First, they are better suited to the needs and preferences of digitally savvy young learners. Second, they represent a cost-effective way to scale up delivery of educational content to millions of knowledge-hungry students in fast-growing economies in Africa and Asia. Third, and most importantly, digital learning tools and data enable Pearson to better measure the effectiveness of education and improve learning outcomes.

Recognising these benefits, Pearson has stepped up its efforts to partner with innovative e-learning start-ups to collectively reinvent education for the digital age. For example, in 2013, it launched Pearson Catalyst for Education, selecting ten promising start-ups each year to work with Pearson's domain experts. The aim is to create innovative solutions that address ten key educational challenges identified by Pearson. In 2014, 215 start-ups from 30 countries applied for the programme. Pearson also linked up with educational technology incubators such as MindCET, based in Israel, which brings together entrepreneurs, educators and researchers to develop breakthrough educational technology, to help identify promising startups for the programme. Pearson believes that partnerships with nimble digital players will boost agility and innovation and enable it to create affordable educational solutions worldwide faster, better and more cost-effectively. Diana Stepner, vice-president of innovation partnerships and developer relations at Pearson, explains:[16]

> We believe that by partnering with the start-up community, together we can more quickly tackle true educational challenges and make a real impact in learners' lives.

While Pearson is engaging young tech start-ups to branch out beyond its analogue roots into the digital world, Ford Motor Company, which is over 110 years old, has linked up with a community of tinkerers to reconnect with its former tradition of crafting cars by hand. Indeed, engineers at major auto companies, including Ford, no longer make cars. The R&D teams use computer-aided design (CAD) software to design new cars. Large parts of the product development process are now carried out online (even crash tests are simulated in a virtual environment).

This is a far cry from 1896 when, in a tiny makeshift workshop behind his home, the 32-year-old Henry Ford manually built his first experimental gas-powered car from scratch, a vehicle he named the Quadricycle. At that time many experts scoffed at this horseless carriage, but Ford persevered. Even after establishing his company in 1903, he kept on tinkering, producing cars named the Model A, B, C and so forth before launching the legendary Model T in 1908. This became the US's first affordable, mass-produced car, which revolutionised transport worldwide. By the turn of the 21st century, however, Ford seemed to have lost touch with its entrepreneurial roots. With 175,000 employees across six continents, it had become bloated and unfocused, with too much bureaucracy and too many brands. Its innovation efforts were spread over too many car platforms to make the difference needed in a competitive market.

When Alan Mulally became CEO in 2006, Ford, which had lost 25% of its market share in the past 15 years, was haemorrhaging cash. It had trouble selling its numerous, dull, old-fashioned models. Mulally turned the company around by cutting unprofitable brands, eliminating duplicative vehicle programmes, uniting the company under the ONE Ford plan and shoring up R&D on promising new products. Ford survived and thrived. In 2008, it successfully weathered the economic crisis while GM and Chrysler filed for bankruptcy.

Managers across the company viewed Ford's near-death experience as a wake-up call. A number of innovation initiatives were launched to accelerate progress in order to become more agile to survive future crises. It would be quite a challenge to return Ford's culture to its roots of a nimble start-up. One way to encourage its R&D engineers to emulate Henry Ford, and think and act like ingenious entrepreneurs boldly pursuing unconventional ideas, would be to enable them to build things quickly with their hands again.

To realise this vision, Ford tied up with TechShop in 2012 and set up a 33,000 square foot DIY workshop and fabrication studio in Detroit equipped with 3D printers, laser cutters and machine tools. Located next to Ford's global R&D centre in Dearborn, Michigan, this giant playground for tinkerers is maintained by TechShop and is open to the public seven days a week. Its goal is to "democratise access to the tools of innovation" (membership costs $175 a month). Under Ford's Employee Patent Incentive Award programme, Ford R&D engineers who file a patent receive three months' free membership of this playground, where they can tinker, experiment, build prototypes and bring their ideas to life rapidly.

Since launching the DIY workshop, Ford has reaped several benefits:

- Ford's engineers find the unstructured environment bracing, as it enables them to dedicate time to projects about which they care personally.
- Having a new outlet for their ingenuity enables Ford engineers to be more creative and productive in their day-to-day R&D work.

- Since the DIY studio is open to the public, Ford employees get to socialise with MacGyvers and geeks from other industries, thus gaining new insights and perspectives to create new things.
- In this collaborative and non-hierarchical environment, new tools can be explored. For example, training events have been held to teach employees and external developers not only to build clever software apps using Ford's open-source OpenXC platform, but also to build a programmable gauge and test it on a real vehicle. As part of its OpenXC initiative, Ford is fully committed to making vehicle data widely accessible in an open-source format to external developers so they can easily integrate it in their innovative apps.

Within one year of its launch, more than 1,000 Ford employees had benefited from the TechShop membership. During this time, these tinkerers have helped Ford boost patentable ideas by over 100% (and the quality of patents has also risen) without having to spend significantly more on R&D. The more entrepreneurial and innovative culture has made Ford more open, agile and risk tolerant. Bill Coughlin, CEO of Ford Global Technologies (Ford's intellectual property arm), who made it all happen, explains how TechShop has radically shifted the corporate culture:[17]

> *There is now greater appreciation for the value of new inventions. Killing a concept that's only on paper is relatively easy, even a disruptive or breakthrough concept. But the chances of gaining serious consideration are markedly higher when you can quickly prototype it, such as at TechShop, and show it to others. Just watch how the future of mobility unfolds at Ford over the next few years.*

As described above, visionary companies such as SNCF, American Express, Pearson and Ford hyper-collaborate with a vast network of external partners to design and deliver breakthrough frugal solutions faster, better and cheaper. Other companies can learn to practise hyper-collaboration strategically by engaging suppliers, non-governmental organisations and even competitors. They can also reduce costs and generate new revenues by sharing assets and resources with other companies. And they can become agile and learn to innovate faster and more cheaply – as rookies do – by connecting their employees with nimble entrepreneurs and tinkerers. To make these external innovation partnerships really work, however, companies need to make relevant changes within their organisation.

Getting hyper-collaboration right

Companies must get their house in order before reaching out to external innovation partners, or else these partnerships will fail. To launch and sustain hyper-collaboration initiatives, companies need to take three critical steps.

Set up an innovation-brokering function

Companies need to invest in new skills to make sure that frugal partnerships work effectively. This innovation-brokering function can be assumed either by a dedicated team or by individuals within the R&D or technology departments. The broker's role is to identify, facilitate and nurture the company's partnerships with external innovators, be they suppliers, entrepreneurs, universities or social-sector players. Brokers must pull innovative ideas from the external ecosystem when they support the company's strategy, and push promising external ideas to their own senior managers. Brokers must be trilingual, understanding internal business units, external innovation partners and customers. They must be able to see the big picture and discern megatrends in technology, business and society; they must be doers, able to integrate external ideas into the company and bring them to market quickly; and they need to command the respect of the CEO and the board to get top-level buy-in.

An example is BNP Paribas, one of the world's leading financial services companies, which runs L'Atelier, an independently managed unit that tracks cutting-edge technology and market trends worldwide. With offices in three global technology hotspots – San Francisco, Paris and Shanghai – L'Atelier monitors how emerging technologies such as social media and mobile phones are changing customer needs and creating new business opportunities. L'Atelier's offices are deeply embedded in regional technological ecosystems and connected to hundreds of local entrepreneurs. The unit offers its innovation-brokering services – market knowledge, digital expertise and contacts – to BNP Paribas leaders and non-rival companies.

At BP, a UK multinational oil and gas company, the innovation-brokering function is assumed internally by the technology department, led by P.P. Darukhanavala (Daru), the chief technology officer. An engineer by training, Daru loves technology and tracks trends such as cloud computing and the Internet of Things through the firm's ecosystem of large tech vendors and digital start-ups. He also has enough business and diplomatic savvy to get buy-in from BP's business unit leaders for disruptive technologies that might improve BP's operational capabilities. Daru says that to become effective innovation brokers, R&D leaders and chief technology officers must think, feel and act like wise strategists who are "part business-minded, part diplomat, part parent and part psychologist".[18]

The brokering function is also relevant when sourcing ideas in fast-growing markets in Africa, India and China – regions that pioneered frugal innovation. For instance, Xerox Research Centre India, launched in 2010, enables Xerox scientists and engineers to partner with leading universities, research labs, start-ups and industry partners in India. As a result, they have co-created affordable, high-quality and innovative solutions for global markets, including video-based patient monitoring, remote document workflow solutions using mobile phones, and analytics and workflow solutions for health care, transport, education and customer care. According to Sophie Vandebroek, chief technology officer at Xerox:[19]

Within four years, our research centre in India – Xerox's first ever in an emerging market – has emerged as a major hub in Xerox's global innovation network.

Increase internal agility

It is not enough for large companies to access disruptive technologies and ideas from outside their organisation. They also need to increase their internal clock speed to keep up with the nimble entrepreneurs with whom they work. This means reducing bureaucracy and simplifying processes in design, production and delivery. In particular, as discussed in Chapter 3, rather than wasting resources trying to scale up new ideas that could quickly bomb, large companies must learn to scale down when seeking to test ideas in the market faster and cost-effectively.

At GE, the chief executive, Jeff Immelt, is attempting to boost the organisational agility of the company, which is over 130 years old, by inculcating what he calls "a culture of simplification". He wants his company to be leaner, faster and better connected to customers, and to leverage digital and IT tools cleverly so that it can, for instance, close deals 50% more quickly and introduce new products 30% faster. To that end, in 2013 GE launched its FastWorks, a set of tools and principles that is helping GE marry scale and innovation with speed and agility. It has trained about 40,000 employees using workshops and online tools to build minimum viable products that quickly solve well-defined customer needs. Rather than over-engineering for the optimal solution and crafting complex business models, GE's employees are learning to design and launch good-enough solutions, get quick customer feedback and then fine-tune them later as the teams learn more. In mid-2014, more than 300 projects across GE and around the world were using FastWorks. For example, GE used FastWorks to co-develop with Chevron and Los Alamos National Laboratory an innovative solution for flow metering in multiphase oil wells. The entire project – from problem statement to prototypes – was completed in less than a year, resulting in a commercial product, the Safire flow meter, that GE and Chevron intend to co-market to the whole oil and gas sector. Beth Comstock says:

> If you show some evidence that your disruptive idea actually works and that customers will buy it, even your most sceptical colleagues at GE will help you take your idea to the next level.

She adds that FastWorks validates dozens of breakthrough ideas simultaneously in the market before deciding which to scale up:

> We are learning to scale down first in order to scale up better later. Our goal is to build a new hybrid culture within GE.

Don't just protect intellectual capital – monetise it

Often, a company's first question about its external partnership is: "How do we protect our intellectual property (IP)?" But companies such as GE, Ford and IBM, which practise hyper-collaboration, ask a more pertinent question: "How can we maximise the value of our intellectual capital through partnerships?" The point is that companies invest billions of dollars in R&D, millions to patent their inventions, and yet more millions to defend them. And they need to invest even more to monetise their IP. For instance, the cost of launching a new consumer-packaged product quadrupled between 2007 and 2012. It costs big pharma companies over $1 billion to launch a new drug.

Yet most products either fail at launch or underperform initial expectations. According to *Forbes*, 250,000 new products are introduced around the world each year. But Booz & Company (now Strategy&) and innovation consultants Doblin (part of Deloitte, one of the big four professional services firms) claim that two-thirds of new products fail within two years and 96% do not generate enough sales to recoup their cost of capital. Indeed, the US generates intellectual property worth over $5 trillion, nearly 35% of its economy. But US firms waste over $1 trillion annually in underused IP – such as patents, copyrights and know-how – because they fail to extract maximum value from these intangible assets. BTG (British Technology Group), an international specialist health-care company, reports that over two-thirds of US firms own technologies they fail to exploit, and on average 35% of technologies patented by US companies are wasted because these organisations lack a clear commercial strategy.

It is time companies recognised that what matters is not how great their ideas are, but how quickly they can execute them. As Matt Bross, former chief technology officer at BT, put it: "There are no breakthrough technologies, only breakthrough market applications." Companies therefore need to open up their IP portfolio and share their intellectual assets with external partners with whom they can use the IP as the basis for co-creating new products better, faster and more cheaply. In doing so, companies can maximise the return on their intellectual capital while also generating new revenues from these products. IBM, which spends $6 billion on R&D each year, filed the most patents among all US companies in 2013, but that year it also generated $1 billion in revenue by licensing its patents to other companies, including early-stage start-ups funded by its venture capital arm.

Likewise, after spending millions on developing its Android operating system, Google gave away the technology so it could be incorporated into the maximum number of devices, thus securing a vast market for its search engine and other digital services. Google's open-source strategy paid off: Android is now available in over 1 billion devices, overtaking Apple's iOS as the world-leading mobile operating system.

In June 2014, Elon Musk, the iconoclastic founder of Tesla Motors, an electric car manufacturer, shocked the markets by announcing that he was giving away its core technology to all companies in the sector, including Tesla's rivals. Musk's decision is motivated by "enlightened self-interest"; by opening up Tesla's patent portfolio he can more rapidly expand the global market for electric cars – which today account for only 1% of US auto sales – and make electric vehicles more affordable and cost-effective to maintain. As Musk blogs:[20]

Given that annual new vehicle production is approaching 100 million per year and the global fleet is approximately 2 billion cars, it is impossible for Tesla to build electric cars fast enough to address the carbon crisis. Technology leadership is not defined by patents, which history has repeatedly shown to be small protection indeed against a determined competitor, but rather by the ability of a company to attract and motivate the world's most talented engineers. We believe that applying the open-source philosophy to our patents will strengthen rather than diminish Tesla's position in this regard.

CASE STUDY 6

Accor: hyper-collaborating without reservation

In the 1960s France's travel industry was growing rapidly, but most hotels were concentrated in urban areas. Sensing a huge opportunity, two dynamic entrepreneurs, Paul Dubrule and Gérard Pélisson, co-founded the SIEH hotel group in 1967 to build and operate US-style affordable hotels in suburban areas and along major highways. SIEH first launched the mid-scale Novotel brand, followed by Ibis, a budget hotel chain, and then another mid-range brand, Mercure, before buying the luxury Sofitel and Pullman. In 1983, SIEH was renamed Accor Group. Today Accor is the world's sixth largest hotel chain, with 3,600 hotels on five continents, with properties ranging from budget hotels to premium luxury accommodation. Over 60% of Accor's properties are franchised, and the company plans to raise this to 80% by the end of 2016.

After four decades of aggressive growth, Accor had become big and unwieldy. It was taken by surprise by the explosive growth of online travel booking services such as Expedia, Priceline and Orbitz, which disrupted the global hotel industry's traditional value chain. Accor began losing its competitive edge and was struggling to revive its innovative spirit. In 2013, Accor's new CEO, Sébastien Bazin, spent 100 days visiting various Accor properties around the world and meeting more than 1,000 staff members. He grimly concluded:[21] "We have built a Kafkaesque organisation that is too heavy and inflexible." He set out to make it more agile and entrepreneurial to out-innovate digital rivals such as Airbnb and Expedia, reinventing the entire hotel industry in the process. Bazin recognised that in order to innovate faster, better and more cost-effectively, Accor had to learn to partner extensively, especially with nimble entrepreneurs and creative small and medium-sized businesses (SMBs). Bazin wanted Accor to become a "caring elder brother" for innovative SMBs, with whom it could co-create cutting-edge solutions to deploy across the group. He appointed Yves Lacheret in early 2014 to the new post of senior vice-president of entrepreneurship advocacy, reporting directly to the CEO.

Lacheret has three core responsibilities. First, he seeks to connect Accor's functional heads and business-unit leaders, including franchise owners, with innovative SMBs that have a promising product, service or technology. By tying up with Accor, the SMBs – primarily based in France – get an opportunity to sell their solutions in all Accor's global markets. Once a suitable SMB is identified for a partnership, Lacheret's second responsibility is to shepherd the SMB through the initial phase of project collaboration with internal decision-makers to make sure that, as he puts it, "the body doesn't reject the transplanted innovation". Lacheret's role, however, is not limited to advocating partnership with entrepreneurial SMBs. He is also tasked with fostering an entrepreneurial culture within Accor. As such, Lacheret's third responsibility is to simplify processes, reduce bureaucracy, accelerate decision-making, and adopt test-and-learn and trial-and-error approaches to new innovation projects that involve SMBs.

Lacheret has the ideal background for an innovation broker. With 25 years of international experience in marketing and general management, he joined Accor in 2007 to run the Novotel hotels in France before assuming sales and marketing responsibilities for Europe. Lacheret says he has been an entrepreneur all his professional life, hands-on bootstrapping and scaling up new products and services or launching and growing new regional businesses for established brands, such as L'Oréal, Carrefour and now Accor:[22]

> At my very first meeting with an SMB, I could quickly pinpoint for them the specific area within Accor where their product or service could have the greatest impact. And since I report directly to our CEO, I could personally pitch an SMB's innovation solution to our Executive Committee and quickly get a go/no-go decision to pilot it. My job is to find the right ideas quickly and execute them rapidly so we can all get value faster.

Lacheret's search for innovative SMB partners focuses on Accor's needs in five strategic areas: digital guest rooms (enabled by internet-connected room appliances and electronics); food and beverages (which account for over 30% of Accor's total revenue); sales and marketing (for example, online reservation and price-comparison tools); human resources (to build a strong sense of community among Accor's 170,000 staff members and improve their well-being); and eco-friendly renovation and renewable energy. There are two main themes that cut across these five areas: digitisation and sustainability. Indeed, having missed the first internet revolution in the 2000s, Accor wants to ride the current digital wave enabled by the Internet of Things, mobile technologies and social media. For instance, 30% of the €300 billion ($380 billion) global hotel business is today conducted by online intermediaries such as Expedia and Travelocity, but mobile phones are expected to account for another 20–30% in coming years. Accor wants a slice of that too. To accelerate its digital transformation – and conquer the mobile services business – in March 2014 Accor hired Vivek Badrinath, a telecoms industry veteran, as its head of digital strategy.

Sustainability is another major area in Lacheret's innovation-brokering activities. In 2012, Accor launched Planet 21, an enterprise-wide initiative with 21 quantifiable commitments to integrate sustainable development by 2015. Planet 21 aims to boost Accor's sustainability performance in three areas: environment (for example, 10% reduction in CO_2 emissions and 15% reduction in water use between 2011 and 2015); society (70% of hotels to purchase products sourced locally by 2015); and people (for example,

75% of hotel managers to be promoted from within by 2015). Lacheret is actively exploring partnerships with several innovative SMBs to accelerate implementation. One SMB offers a solution that dehydrates organic waste (80% of organic waste is water), extracting from 100kg of waste 80 litres of water that can be used to water plants and clean rooms; the solid waste can be sold. Another SMB recycles used water and transforms it into energy. A third SMB recycles mattresses (which can be valuable to Accor, which has 350,000 hotel rooms). A fourth SMB has developed an ingenious solution to recycle waste from construction and renovation projects (this accounts for 70% of the total waste generated by Accor).

As well as boosting Accor's environmental credentials, these frugal solutions can save money, since heating, water and air conditioning together account for 7% or more of Accor's total costs. A core dimension of Planet 21 is talent sustainability: attracting and retaining diverse talent. Lacheret explains that even though Accor does not directly employ most of its hotels' staff, it still feels responsible for keeping frontline employees motivated and supporting their career growth. So he has teamed up with tech SMBs offering virtual communication and collaboration tools that allow Accor managers to remain in remote contact, track performance, provide feedback and offer career guidance to employees worldwide. To build stronger relationships among Accor's 170,000 employees, Lacheret has struck a deal with Corporate Home Exchange, a digital start-up that aspires to become the B2B version of Airbnb by enabling employees within a company to swap homes.

With 3.2 million SMBs in France alone, identifying the right SMBs and start-ups to partner with can be daunting. So Lacheret has teamed up with the Institute of Mentorship for Entrepreneurs (IME) of the French Chamber of Commerce and Industry (CCI). The IME connects high-potential SMBs with successful entrepreneurs and corporate leaders, who mentor the SMBs on how to achieve exponential growth. With the IME's help, Lacheret invites promising French SMBs to regular speed-dating events where they pitch their innovative products and services to a jury of Accor business-unit leaders, franchised hotel managers, and heads of purchasing and legal departments. The most innovative and useful pitches are selected for immediate implementation in a pilot project sponsored by an Accor leader. Lacheret plans to host similar speed-dating events in other tech hotspots, such as Silicon Valley and Singapore, and at major industry conferences such as the ITB Berlin Convention. He also plans to launch an online platform where innovative SMBs and start-ups can register themselves, pitch their products and services, and collaborate virtually with Accor.

Lacheret reckons that although Accor is slowly getting better at collaborating with innovative SMBs, there are three obstacles that can slow the process. First, he has to find a way to circumvent Accor's normal bidding process for larger suppliers. He is trying to convince purchasing departments to let an SMB idea initially be piloted in only half-a-dozen Accor hotels and, if successful, require the SMB to then enter a formal bidding process. Second, he must work with Accor's legal department to simplify the contracting process, which requires an SMB to sign a 40-page contract before it can start its collaboration. Lacheret would prefer a single-page contract signed at the speed-dating event itself. Third, he is working with Accor's accounts department to speed up the payment process – which typically takes months – as many SMBs are strapped for cash. When these issues are resolved, Lacheret expects a more agile Accor to be collaborating with hundreds of entrepreneurs and SMBs, and to reinvent the hotel industry.

Conclusion

Make innovative friends is the sixth and final principle of frugal innovation. Companies seeking to become frugal innovators can choose to implement some or all of the six principles analysed in previous chapters. Either way, reshaping a business around frugality requires significant change across the organisation. This change not only needs to be structural but also requires a shift in the corporate culture and way of thinking. How corporate leaders across sectors are changing the culture of their organisations as they strive to implement these principles is the subject of the next chapter.

One cannot solve a problem with the same kind of thinking that created it in the first place.

Albert Einstein

CHAPTERS 2–7 OUTLINED the six principles that collectively form a frugal innovation strategy, and explained how leaders can use these principles to reinvent their business model on the basis of frugality. They described how various functional leaders can restructure their divisions to enable the organisation to design, build and deliver affordable and sustainable solutions over the longer term. In the end, however, frugal innovation represents a new way of thinking and acting for all employees within an organisation. After all, it is people – not machines or processes – who innovate. And people (or employees, to be precise) collectively form the culture of a company.

Unfortunately, as the management dictum goes, "culture eats strategy for lunch"; and the wrong culture can kill even a great frugal innovation strategy. This chapter, therefore, discusses how corporate leaders can foster the right culture to embed frugal innovation within their organisations. They can do this by fundamentally shifting the mindset of all employees at all levels in the organisation, allowing them to create more value with less.

Evolutionary change

Change management in large companies is typically applied from the top down. Company transformations begin with the hiring of an army of management consultants, who create a roadmap to achieving a strategic goal. The roadmap alone might take two years to develop, and longer still to implement. Even before any results are visible, the environment has usually changed, requiring still further transformation. Conversely, some companies try to change too quickly, inducing only panic and stress in staff. It is hardly surprising, therefore, that nearly half of all change management programmes fail.

For organisational transformation to work, companies need to shift the thinking and behaviour of staff, at the right pace and the right cost. A frugal culture needs a frugal change management framework. Such a framework can be defined as one that enables companies to induce systemic and harmonious change and achieves the greatest and longest-lasting positive impact across the organisation and its ecosystem – and does so at an optimal pace, using minimum resources and mitigating negative side effects for all stakeholders involved.

The frugal framework must answer three interrelated questions:

- What is the ultimate goal?
- How do we achieve it cost-effectively (what are the processes, systems, technologies, perspectives, attitudes and personal qualities that need to be used)?
- Why should anyone in the company change?

The last question is crucial, as it addresses motivation and involves a mix of rewards and values.

Traditional change management programmes fail to incorporate the "what", "how" and "why" properly for three reasons:

- They are rarely transparent, leaving employees unsure as to why they should make the effort.
- They are typically pushed from the top down, with a take-it-or-leave-it attitude, spurring widespread resistance.
- They can be too inflexible, and assume that staff will be catapulted from one state to another with no deviation.

By contrast, a frugal change management framework ensures full transparency by actively involving employees, adjusting goals and tools as necessary throughout. It involves constant discovery and exploration. It emphasises trial and error and learning by doing. Most importantly, it does not view a corporate culture as inherently good or bad. As Peter Drucker, a management guru, famously said: "Company cultures are like country cultures. Never try to change one. Try, instead, to work with what you've got." Frugal leaders do not try to change what their company's culture is, but what it does.

In short, a frugal change management framework creates a learning organisation that thrives in a dynamic and complex environment by constantly iterating, experimenting, improvising and discovering.

The "what": bold commitment and dynamic goal setting

This involves properly defining and articulating the goal of a company's frugal innovation strategy. There might be a single, specific aim, such as putting a man on the moon, or in Renault's case designing and launching a $6,000 car. It might involve a new frugal product line or business. For instance, PepsiCo set up the Global Nutrition Group in 2010 to produce healthy and nutritious food and beverages (such as oatmeal and low-fat yogurt), which now account for 20% of the company's overall business. Other companies may want to incorporate frugality into all their products and functions. Unilever's Sustainable Living Plan aims to reinvent the company's entire product range and processes on the basis of sustainability, double sales to €80 billion ($96 billion) and halve its environmental footprint by 2020.

Whatever the goals, companies must make sure they have the following characteristics.

Bold, credible and aspirational

To grab internal and external stakeholders' attention, the goals should be bold. They can be so audacious that they challenge the dominant industry paradigm and force people to respond to the impossible challenge, saying: "Why not?" In 1999, Louis Schweitzer, then Renault's CEO, asked "Why not build a $6,000 car?" when others thought it impossible. The resulting Logan and Dacia brands now account for over 40% of Renault's global sales. In 2007, Stuart Rose, then CEO of Marks & Spencer (M&S), asked, "Why not build a green and profitable retailer?" He unveiled Plan A, a set of 100 ambitious goals – for waste reduction, energy efficiency, fair trade, sustainable sourcing, healthier lifestyle, work ethic and community engagement – in the company's factories, stores, products and suppliers that could not be dismissed as green-washing. Their credibility helped motivate M&S's 86,000 employees to find innovative solutions to meet these ambitious goals. Indeed, many new M&S recruits cite the audacious Plan A as a major reason to work there. Today, M&S boasts an 80% employee engagement rate, one of the highest among retailers globally. Investors also like the plan because it generates new revenues, and reduces waste and energy consumption.

Commitment at the top

Companies should not communicate their bold frugal innovation goals just through a press release. Instead, corporate leaders need to put their personal reputations on the line by making major public announcements about these goals and restating them constantly to employees, customers, investors and partners. In 2007, M&S's massive PR launch of its Plan A strategy had Rose appearing across media channels to underscore his commitment. He repeatedly used Plan A's tagline – "Because there is no Plan B" – to indicate that he and his senior management team saw no alternative to an environmentally frugal business model. Leaders must also stick to their commitment in the face of criticism and tougher periods. When M&S's 2008–09 profits fell by 40% during the depths of the recession, Rose held firm. He explained:[1]

> There will always be the Luddites, short-termists, sceptics, cynics, and not-in-my-back-yarders ... you can't back off just because things are tough.

By demonstrating their staying power, resilient leaders like Rose were able to entrench radical business models and cultural transformation in a way that will make it hard for others to reverse in future. Indeed, when Marc Bolland replaced Rose as M&S's CEO in 2010, the new leader continued, and improved, Plan A. His "Plan A 2020" unveiled in 2014 revises and augments the original 100 goals. For instance, Plan A

2020 increases the energy efficiency target from 35% to 50% per square foot, and aims to source 75% of all M&S-branded food from factories with the highest ecological and ethical standards. The revised plan, covering M&S's global operations, clarifies how the 100 goals will benefit customers, employees and partners. It also incorporates those goals into all communications and marketing activities.

Consistent but personalised

Companies need to ensure their frugal innovation goals are applied consistently across the organisation to induce enterprise-wide change. For instance, in 2011, to meet global demand for better-performing education services at lower cost, Pearson appointed Michael Barber as chief education advisor. An expert on education systems and reform, Barber had served as head of the UK Prime Minister's Delivery Unit under Tony Blair. At Pearson, he was tasked with implementing the company's frugal innovation strategy, built around one core objective: efficacy (or showing measurable results from learning). The concept derives from the pharmaceutical industry, which depends on systematic trials of new drugs. Pearson wants to bring the same rigour to education. This efficacy-focused strategy is intrinsically frugal, because by shifting the focus from inputs (designing and delivering educational content, tools and services) to outcomes (measurable impact on learners), Pearson is forced to do more with less – that is, deliver more rapidly the highest impact and value for its learners while maximising the value of its educational assets.

Barber runs a small, frugal team of highly engaged people who work with a network of efficacy champions across the business to embed the concept in Pearson's operating model. The idea is to ensure that every decision, action, process and investment that the company makes is informed by how the decision will achieve a measurable impact on learning outcomes. To drive this enterprise-wide cultural change, Barber's team worked with the company's leadership team to begin a conversation about efficacy within the company, and they are now actively working towards how the company should publicly report on its progress towards its efficacy goals alongside its financial results by 2018. Barber explains:

In shifting the conversation we wanted to ensure it was economical in the demands it made on time and resources, and also was as un-bureaucratic as possible. We adopted a frugal approach to innovation, and as a result, we developed efficacy as an improvisation – we found colleagues who wanted to learn about efficacy and become a part of a movement, and then, with these supporters, we built interest and intrigue in the benefits of efficacy across the rest of the organisation.

As part of this effort, Pearson has created a company-wide community with regional champions who work to embed efficacy wherever the company operates. For instance, if a team in the US is building a new product, the regional champion ensures that the team keeps the student's needs in mind at all times. (This might be done by making sure that the course will increase students' employability.) These company-wide conversations help identify areas that product teams can then refine. For instance, they might help improve how evidence is collected along the way, and how the students' goals are achieved.

In little over three years, this small community, working hand-in-hand with the leadership team, has had a significant impact on Pearson, a huge company with 40,000 employees. Output has included an efficacy framework, a decision support tool that helps the company's understanding of how learning products and services can achieve their expected outcomes or results. This tool is used internally – to, for instance, evaluate the efficacy of all investments over a value of $1 million – but it is also made available to all Pearson's institutional clients, such as schools, as well as tech vendors and start-ups to help them to create new educational materials and content that yield greater impact. Pearson will now make an acquisition only after the prospective asset has passed through an efficacy review that shows how acquiring it will maximise the impact on students.

Barber's frugal approach combined with the commitment of the leadership team has achieved an organisation-wide commitment to efficacy and the facilitation of a broader culture change within Pearson. As Vaithegi Vasanthakumar, a member of Barber's team, says:[2]

Pearson's mission to establish efficacy at the heart of the company began with a "start-up" approach which helped instigate a sea change in the company, for instance through ensuring a dedicated efficacy resource was embedded in each line of business and key geography. As a result, in a short period of time efficacy is no longer "at the edge of Pearson, pushing it forward", but is instead "at the heart of Pearson's core strategy, changing it from within".

While the change management programme's goals need to be consistent across business units and regions, they also need to be tailored to different contexts, regions, functions and even individuals. Marks & Spencer has mapped out the 100 commitments of Plan A to individual goals of all functions within the company and its suppliers. Munish Datta, head of Plan A delivery for M&S's worldwide properties, explains how his team tries to boost energy efficiency in M&S's 1,200 buildings (a total of 21 million square feet), including its global headquarters in London, which has over 4,000 occupants.[3] Since 2006, Datta's team has made M&S's facilities 34% more energy efficient and 27% more water efficient. In 2012, M&S unveiled a giant 151,000 square foot retail store in Chester, UK, said to be the world's greenest: 99% of the timber used is certified by the Forest Stewardship Council (FSC); 30% of the building is made of recycled materials; and its recycled aluminium ceiling is covered by a material made entirely of recycled glass bottles. It is 40% more energy efficient than other M&S stores, uses exclusively natural air conditioning and 70% of its heating comes from a biomass boiler plant, with nothing going to landfill. M&S calls the Chester outlet its "sustainable learning store", as 60% of its eco-friendly features set the standard for other M&S stores. Datta's team has saved M&S £114 million since 2006. During 2013, Datta's team's successful implementation of Plan A resulted in savings of £135 million.

Similarly, M&S is working with individual regional units to adapt and prioritise the 100 goals by factoring in local market needs, constraints and values, as Mike Barry, director of Plan A, explains:[4]

We've been working hard with our international business to roll out Plan A in the more than 50 countries where we have retail businesses. We cannot treat this roll-out as a standard set in London to be complied with elsewhere. We have to build the local capacity in our teams to work with their customers, employees and stakeholders on what matters to them locally.

Integrated and systemic

Although goals should be assigned for individuals – respecting the diversity of employees – they also need to be systemic to achieve maximum synergies. Specifically, they need to consider the interdependence of different functions and stakeholders. No one's goals should be set at the expense of another's, and everyone's goals need to be integrated into the larger system. In 2008 Franck Riboud, chairman of Danone, committed publicly to reduce its carbon footprint by 30% within five years. Danone's CEO, Emmanuel Faber, recounts:[5]

Many people at Danone felt the 30% goal was totally crazy ... Everyone had to come out of their comfort zone and learn to collaborate across functional, business, and regional boundaries to collectively achieve the 30% target.

Over 2,000 reduction plans were conceived across business units and subsidiaries, with clear goals for each of the five years. Some 110 "carbon masters" were put in charge of executing these plans and tracking outcomes, and 1,400 managers across R&D, sourcing, manufacturing and logistics had their bonuses tied to achieving the 30% target. By integrating their carbon-reduction efforts, the various business units and functions were able to create synergies and accelerate their innovation initiatives. In February 2013, Riboud proudly announced that Danone had cut its carbon intensity by 35.2% over the previous five years. But Danone is not resting on its laurels. Riboud has set a bolder target for his entire company: reduce carbon footprint by more than 50% by 2020 and stabilise CO_2 emissions while sustaining sales growth.

Measurable

The mantra "you can't improve what you can't measure" applies to frugality. Companies must tie their change management goals to specific key performance indicators (KPIs). KPIs enable employees at all levels to track performance against goals, and adjust individual or collective efforts accordingly. KPIs hold all employees, from senior managers to frontline workers, individually and collectively accountable for meeting their company's frugal goals. KPIs can act as milestones and signposts to measure progress, and boost morale at key stages. They also signal when progress is lagging.

In 2012, home-improvement retailer Kingfisher announced its goal to become "net positive" – that is, return more resources to the earth than it extracts and consumes – in response to forecasts of resource scarcity, social inequality and climate change. Its Net Positive plan has four priority areas – timber, energy, innovation and communities – and three related areas – employees, suppliers and the environment – for improvement. Kingfisher uses 50 KPIs, called the Foundations, to measure daily progress set against a 2012 baseline. Each KPI has a 2020 target and most must reach a 2015 milestone. Kingfisher tracks and reports progress every six months. According to Jamie Lawrence, senior sustainability adviser and in-house counsel to Kingfisher Group's Net Positive strategy:[6]

The KPIs also tell us where we need to collaborate more – internationally across business units as well as externally with suppliers and the government – to reach our 2020 targets.

The company is transparent about both its achievements and its setbacks. Its 2013/14 Net Positive Report, for instance, revealed that while 87% of the timber used in its products is responsibly sourced (against a target of 100% in 2020), it currently sells only 170 products with closed-loop (most eco-friendly) credentials against an ambitious target of 1,000 products by 2020. Richard Gillies, the company's sustainability director, admits that although Kingfisher is already generating £500 million ($790 million) in sales from its closed-loop products, the company is "still only scratching the surface of the commercial benefits that Net Positive can bring".[7] As former CEO Ian

Cheshire, who led the company until late 2014, notes:[8] "What we've learnt is that business 'unusual' isn't easy."

Many frugal innovation pioneers publish an audited annual report of progress made in meeting KPIs. These are also useful for motivating employees, and making everyone accountable for an organisation's frugal performance, especially if KPIs are linked to salaries and bonuses. Kingfisher will tie its Net Positive KPIs to the earnings of its top 250 managers by 2016/17, and to all relevant employees by 2020. At M&S, 20% of the CEO's and directors' bonuses are linked to progress on Plan A. Pearson has made the delivery of learning outcomes a central pillar of its HR policies, including recruitment, training, performance management and incentive systems. All Pearson's senior managers will eventually be measured – and rewarded – on learner outcome-oriented KPIs along with financial returns. Danone uses Danprint – a measurement tool co-developed with software provider SAP to track the carbon footprint of an entire product life cycle in every Danone subsidiary – to encourage its senior managers to perform better to meet the group's goal to stabilise CO_2 emissions while maintaining sales growth.

Dynamic and emergent

Frugal innovation goals should not be set in stone. What must remain constant is a company's vision to create ever more value for all stakeholders in an ever more socially and environmentally sustainable manner. As such, companies may need to revise initial goals as they shift their frugal innovation strategy to reflect changes in their market environment. Some ambitious companies might even decide to keep the pressure on by setting ever-tougher goals.

In 2010, M&S added 80 new commitments to its original 100, assigned them 2015 and 2020 deadlines, and followed this with an even bolder Plan A 2020, as part of a new collaborative business model. As Marc Bolland, CEO of M&S, explains:[9]

We know we can't deliver Plan A 2020 alone. That's why we're stepping up our efforts to "lead with others" by participating in broader coalitions to deliver sector-wide change.

Mike Barry adds: "We're creating resilience, flexibility and skills in our own workforce to take whichever route emerges as the right one." M&S has already met or exceeded 95 of its 100 original commitments and Plan A has brought the retailer £465 million ($735 million) of total benefit since 2007, and £145 million ($229 million) in savings in 2014 alone. More value is expected to emerge under its new collaborative approach.

Although M&S's Plan A has involved a clear, overarching strategy from the outset, other companies may prefer to start with a small project and modest goals, and to change just one part of their organisation or meet a specific market requirement. Once successfully completed, companies may then adopt new projects, initiated from any part of the business and supported by senior management. Siemens, for example, allowed its frugal innovation initiatives to emerge organically in emerging markets first before formalising them as a company-wide strategy. Founded in 1847, the German industrial conglomerate invests almost €4.29 billion ($5.15 billion) in R&D annually and employs nearly 30,000 engineers and developers worldwide who report 38 inventions every day (in mid-2014 the company held around 60,000 granted patents). In the early 2000s, as emerging economies such as India and China began their rapid growth, Siemens initially attempted to sell its sophisticated high-end products imported from Germany. But Indian and Chinese customers found them too expensive, and too complex to operate and maintain. Worse, these high-quality products often broke down because of local weather conditions and usage patterns, which harmed Siemens' image. In China, micro-particles from heavy dust pollution infiltrated the electronic circuits of Siemens' power converters and caused breakdowns. In India, regular power cuts and heavy-duty usage in crowded hospitals caused Siemens' medical devices to malfunction.[10] Christophe de Maistre, who ran several business units for Siemens in China in the mid-2000s and now heads its France and south-west Europe operations, confesses:[11]

We were humbled. For over a century Siemens equated quality with technological sophistication. China and India forced us to reframe the notion of quality in terms of value perceived by clients in a local context. We realised our Indian and Chinese clients wanted "good enough" products that are simpler and cost-effective to install, operate and maintain.

Siemens therefore decided to rethink its emerging markets innovation strategy. It began to use its Indian and Chinese R&D talent to design a new generation of simpler, more reliable, energy-efficient and user-friendly products. In China, it developed a robust and dependable converter suited to local weather conditions, which became a big hit. Similarly, Siemens' Indian R&D team developed a cost-effective, energy-saving waste-water treatment method, perfect for a country that generates over 40 billion litres of waste water daily, only 20% of which is treated.

Recognising that conventional waste-water treatment solutions are costly and energy intensive, Siemens' R&D engineers in India designed a bioreactor where certain bacteria and algae form a symbiotic relationship. The bacteria generate CO_2 that the algae use for photosynthesis. The algae in turn emit oxygen that the bacteria consume, thus forming a self-sustaining cycle. This sustainable water-treatment solution uses 60% less energy than conventional methods. In 2008, the growing success of these new products convinced Siemens' senior management to develop a formal frugal innovation strategy called SMART (simple, maintenance-friendly, affordable, reliable and timely-to-market) for a type of mid-range product line called M3, which complements Siemens' existing M1 and M2 premium product lines.

With emerging markets now accounting for over 30% of its global sales, Siemens wants to expand its M3 portfolio, and design, build and market its frugal SMART products worldwide. Over 15,000 Siemens engineers in India, China, Brazil, the US and Europe are now actively involved in SMART product development projects. Siemens today boasts over 150 SMART products, and has launched more than 30 in India alone, with another 30 in the pipeline.

SMART products have a positive impact on Siemens' top and bottom lines: they generate significant revenues and cost up to 50% less compared with more sophisticated products. Riding on the rapid market adoption of SMART products, Siemens sees huge business opportunities in this field – especially in emerging economies, where the M3 market is often bigger than the market for high-end products. It also sells its M3 products to cost-conscious European and US clients. Siemens invented an easy-to-use, 16-slice computer tomography device in China that delivers valuable day-to-day clinical data at an affordable price. The US is now its biggest market.

The dynamic nature of the frugal market is evidently not lost on Siemens. It believes that the SMART strategy is a global game-changer for the entire industrial sector. Accordingly, it hopes its M3 product line will fend off cost-competitive rivals from India and China that are more used to a frugal business environment. Siemens' home market, Germany, for example, has 2,000 hospitals and 90,000 private practices – a huge mass market for frugal products – and competition can be expected.

But Siemens also sees commercial synergies between its M1, M2 and M3 product lines as its SMART products could open doors to underserved mass markets – in both emerging and mature economies – where it might later upsell its premium products as customer needs evolve. Hermann Requardt, CEO of Siemens' €13.6 billion ($16 billion) health-care unit, which is leading the company's frugal innovation strategy, explains:[12]

> Our goal is also to be among the top players in the mass market. That's where our good-enough products come in and are playing a bigger and bigger role.

Siemens has set up an internal consulting group to train its various business units on frugal innovation so they can rapidly learn how to systematically design, build and deliver simple and affordable solutions across geographical areas.[13]

The "how": adopting disruptive business and mental models

As well as setting bold goals, companies must also consider how these can be met; and this means deciding what tools to use. Getting the right tools into employees' hands will increase their frugal intensity (FI), as noted in Chapter 1. FI is the innate capacity of an enterprise to generate ever more sustainable value while at the same time minimising the use of scarce resources (capital, raw materials and time). Chapters 3 and 4 showed how companies can flex their operating assets and make their products and services self-sustaining.

But it is also necessary for companies to boost the frugal intensity of their entire business model if they are to generate more value for all stakeholders in a cost-effective, resource-efficient and eco-responsible manner. PepsiCo and Kingfisher provide excellent examples of how this can be done.

Changing business models

PepsiCo operates in a hypercompetitive, fast-paced industry where each segment faces many unique growth challenges. PepsiCo's value chain is highly complex, as its production and distribution systems need to deal with stringent safety and health requirements, rapid shifts in customer demand and a constantly evolving mix of multiple stock-keeping units. PepsiCo is currently facing big challenges but also huge opportunities. On the one hand, with escalating energy and raw-material costs, it must make its existing business model, and value chain, extremely cost-efficient. On the other hand, it can see huge opportunities in the underserved emerging economies and untapped demand for healthier food and beverages in developed economies. To seize these high-stakes opportunities, however, PepsiCo needs to reinvent its business model.

In 2010, PepsiCo set up the Global Value Innovation Centre (GVIC). Based in India, the GVIC has a global remit to identify frugal business practices that will have a significant positive impact on PepsiCo's revenues and costs worldwide. Tanmaya Vats, an industry veteran who heads the GVIC, explained that its strategic mandate is twofold. First, PepsiCo must develop disruptive new business models that it can use to penetrate and win in unserved and underserved markets, and to do so cost competitively. Second, it must find ways to boost its frugal performance in mature markets such as the US and Europe. As Vats puts it, the GVIC's goal is to "make the pie bigger while also making it more lucrative for PepsiCo".[14]

The GVIC's structure is itself frugal, built on hyper-collaboration.

It is staffed by only a dozen industry experts who work closely with academic partners, start-ups and domain experts worldwide to co-create innovative solutions. Its primary focus is to reduce the capital intensity in PepsiCo's value chain, specifically by overhauling capital expenditure. In particular, the GVIC is developing cost-effective and flexible manufacturing, logistics and dispensing systems for producing, distributing and serving food and beverages faster, better and cheaper. For instance, the GVIC is concept testing low-cost cooling and dispensing systems in India and the Philippines. These low-cost coolers deliver exceptional value compared with existing systems with similar throughput. They are also visually appealing and deliver just-in-time chilling, which is four times faster than the current standard while being energy efficient. The dispensers are not only significantly cheaper than other available options but can also support multiple formats of beverages, ranging from hot and cold to beverages based on powders and concentrates. They also allow customers to change the beverages served by season, ensuring that revenues are maximised throughout the year. They have smart features that can be programmed to auto-sanitise the equipment and stop dispensing if the source water falls below the prescribed standard.

The GVIC calls these innovative systems "disruptive value solutions" because they not only cost 40–60% less than existing options, but they also deliver matching or better features, functionalities, safety, performance and aesthetics. Thus they create greater value for PepsiCo and its customers with a lot less.

Six unique features differentiate the GVIC's approach to frugal innovation from those of others:

■ The GVIC does not work in an ivory tower. Every innovation project must be sponsored by a PepsiCo business unit, which is closely involved in it. If early results look promising, the business unit commits to scaling up the GVIC's solution.

■ The solutions are all based on a strong business case. They must solve a big business need or address critical customer needs in existing or new markets.

■ The GVIC only accepts projects with a big hairy audacious goal (BHAG), such as at least reducing operating costs by half, that requires a radically different solution. "The BHAG motivates our disruptive innovation teams," says Vats.

- The GVIC applies the engage and iterate principle (see Chapter 2) for rapid prototyping, market trial and customer feedback.
- Every disruptive value solution must involve all PepsiCo's functions – from R&D to marketing – in its implementation.
- Frugal solutions and business models are first tested in some of the world's most complex and resource-constrained emerging markets before they are deployed globally.

These unique attributes of the GVIC's operating model boost the success rate and impact of its frugal innovation projects.

The GVIC is blazing a trail for companies in business model innovation (BMI). Although BMI is the starting point for frugal innovation, most large companies begin on the wrong foot. They first try to reduce the fat from their existing bloated businesses using techniques such as value engineering, business process re-engineering and lean manufacturing. This subtractive approach has two limitations: first, there is only so much waste that can be removed; and second, the leaner business model may still not address the real needs of the firm's targeted customers. You cannot re-engineer a company to death; you need a new model. This is why the GVIC's BMI initiatives, which lead to disruptive value solutions, start from scratch and consider customers' most critical needs.

In a commoditised industry such as food and beverages, PepsiCo has to keep moving up the value ladder in the face of low-cost competition. The GVIC is helping the company disrupt itself before its rivals do. It is developing frugal business models that allow PepsiCo to penetrate and lead new unserved markets as well as boost its performance in mature markets.

Kingfisher's Net Positive strategy provides other valuable lessons in how to disrupt an old business model. Its goal is to sell 1,000 products with closed-loop credentials by 2020. But its existing supply chains cannot cope. So it is building an entirely new supply chain and new supplier partnerships. Kingfisher's Jamie Lawrence says:

We could have just focused on designing one sexy, newsy "closed-loop" product which didn't sell a lot. Or we could have focused on 1,000 products that don't sell well. But such products wouldn't fundamentally affect our supply chain and would just remain niche. So instead we are focusing on designing ten entirely new supply chains as opposed to products. The question we are asking ourselves is: Can we get 10 supply chains to be circular and from that get 1,000 new products?

To make this happen, Kingfisher is working with a coalition of the willing. For instance, it decided to use recycled plastics and pallet wood, which is usually thrown away after several shipments, to make worktops in kitchens. When its existing supplier of pallet wood did not want to comply with the new plan – since that would mean less pallet wood to sell – Kingfisher simply switched supplier.

Changing mental models

By adopting new business models designed from scratch, based on the principles of frugal innovation, companies can start upgrading the "hardware" component of their corporate culture. But to embed frugality in their corporate DNA, companies must also upgrade the "software" component of their culture: the mental models of their employees. This might be called mental model disruption.

Companies must get staff to think differently about their role in the business world. One way is to get them to consider the customer of the future, 5, 10 or 20 years hence. For instance, the Collaborating Centre on Sustainable Consumption and Production (CSCP), a think-and-do-tank based in Germany, conducts visioning sessions in which senior managers at large US and European companies have immersive experiences to explore the possible world of 2025 or 2035. In these sessions, participants are introduced to the personas of future consumers from different socio-economic and cultural backgrounds. Each persona is described with real data about his or her behaviour, perceptions, values and motivations. Despite their diversity, future consumers all share one important value: they aspire to lead a good life by consuming better rather than consuming more. That means sharing cars and bikes, growing their own food, and working and living in energy-efficient buildings. Participants are encouraged to think about how they might satisfy these future consumers' frugal needs and lifestyles.

The CSCP has conducted several visioning sessions, with participants from the World Economic Forum, the World Business Council for Sustainable Development, PepsiCo, Puma, IKEA, Nestlé and Deutsche Telekom. Michael Kuhndt, the CSCP's CEO, explains how senior managers "are first shocked to discover that their future customers have fundamentally different lifestyles and values than current customers". They soon realise that most of their existing products and services need to be reinvented to cater for future needs.

Customers of the future will also be older, especially in the developed economies of western Europe, Japan and the US. There are already 130 million people aged over 50 in the EU; by 2020 one in two EU adults will be over this age; and by 2050 one-fifth of the US population will be 65 or older. This ageing baby-boomer generation – which will control 70% of US disposable income by 2017 – represents a huge "silver market": the longevity economy will almost double from $7.1 trillion today to $13.5 trillion by 2032 (equivalent to the combined GDP of Japan, Germany, France and the UK).

Given their physical limitations, these rapidly ageing customers will demand accessible and affordable solutions, and corporate R&D teams will need to shift their mental models accordingly. They will have to develop products with minimal, user-friendly functionality, rather than complex products overloaded with features. Simplicity is the lynchpin of inclusive design, defined by the British Standards Institute in 2005 as:

> *The design of mainstream products and/or services that are accessible to, and usable by, as many people as reasonably possible ... without the need for special adaptation or specialised design.*

Cambridge University's Engineering Design Centre (EDC) has developed an inclusive design toolkit to help R&D teams develop simpler, better, more accessible and cost-effective products for consumers with particular needs. For example, the toolkit features simulation glasses that replicate various levels of visual impairment, so designers can develop products that are visually clear for 99% of the population, not just the well-sighted. It also includes simulation gloves that mimic arthritis of the knuckle joints, so designers can develop products such as food packaging and garden tools that can be used without putting too much pressure on the fingers. These simulation tools were developed by Sam Waller, an inclusive design researcher at the EDC, who wants to see his inventions used by mass-market manufacturers so they can make better decisions when developing new products. He wants to avoid the false assumption made by too many manufacturers: "If I can use it, everyone can."

According to the EDC's research, developing a new product based on inclusive design principles does not increase costs, and could even lower them by eliminating non-essential features that hinder usability. By developing more inclusive mainstream products, manufacturers can also reach a wider market. As Ian Hosking, a senior researcher at the EDC, explains:[15]

> If manufacturers and retailers were to adopt inclusive design as a "normal" R&D practice, they could become industry leaders by cost-effectively developing products and services with high usability.

Hosking and other EDC researchers are collaborating with leading organisations, including Procter & Gamble, Stora Enso, Transport for London, Heathrow Airport and John Lewis, which have joined the Inclusive Design Consortium. Nestlé's R&D teams have used EDC tools, such as the special gloves, to redesign some of the company's packaging for easier use. For Nestlé, these tools elevate its product packaging from good to great design, and give the brand a competitive advantage. As Anne Roulin, Nestlé's global head of packaging and design, explains:[16]

> Putting the consumer at the centre of packaging development means creating products and packaging that are easy to use regardless of age, disability or physical condition.

Western economies are becoming not only more inclusive but also more circular, as eco-aware customers aspire to live and work in energy-positive buildings and consume eco-friendly, recyclable products. To succeed in the emerging circular economy, companies must consider sustainability in their design decisions. They must reframe sustainability as being "more good" rather than "less bad". Customers will chafe at the car company that buys carbon offsets while manufacturing gas-guzzlers, or the furniture supplier that campaigns to save the Amazon rainforest while depleting Indonesian forests to make its furniture.

Greg Norris, a professor at Harvard School of Public Health, wants companies to increase their "handprint" – that is, the direct positive impact they can have (for example, generating potable water as a production by-product). For manufacturers, the product design phase – where over 70% of a product's life-cycle costs are determined – offers the best opportunities for reducing their environmental impact, by saving materials and energy and increasing their handprint (by opting for renewable energy and choosing recyclable materials). For example, architecture, engineering and construction firms' US, European and Japanese corporate clients want greener buildings. The life cycle of US buildings accounts for nearly 40% of all energy use, 72% of electricity consumption, 14% of potable water use, nearly 40% of CO_2 emissions and 30% of waste output. As a result, developed-country regulators are imposing increasingly stringent environmental standards on new construction.

To comply with – and even exceed – these exacting regulations, architects and engineers need tools like Tally, an application provided by Autodesk, a design software vendor, to perform a life-cycle assessment (LCA) of building materials before they are selected. LCA is a process of quantifying the full environmental impact of a building design – based on all the materials used – in terms of its total energy footprint, water consumption, greenhouse gases and waste generated over its entire life cycle.[17] The LCA is a prerequisite for lessening the environmental impact of a building. Yet in practice LCA is rarely done, and those firms that attempt it do so with spreadsheets and duct tape, an error-prone and time-consuming process. Tally was developed by KieranTimberlake, an architecture firm, with Autodesk and PE International, a consultancy. It automates the LCA process, making it faster, more reliable and more cost-effective. Emma Stewart, head of sustainability solutions at Autodesk, explains:[18]

Rather than acting as specialists focused on the design of a building, architects and engineers can use Tally to see the entire system, how the different elements of a building interact and affect its environmental performance over its life cycle. That systemic view empowers them to make optimal design decisions and materials selection that would reduce the overall environmental impact of new buildings.

In addition to Tally, Autodesk offers other solutions to help manufacturers design energy-efficient factories, as well as eco-friendly products such as fuel-efficient, lighter and more aerodynamic cars. In the coming years, Stewart expects more Autodesk clients to design buildings, factories and products that generate more energy and resources than they consume. Stewart, who has a PhD in environmental science and management from Stanford University, notes that enlightened companies know instinctively that they are doing the right thing for society and the environment, but they cannot quantify the financial return to investors. To address this issue, her team has partnered with Impact Infrastructure, a start-up that focuses on automating triple-bottom-line accounting. Its tool, AutoCASE, is a cloud-based business-case analysis tool to automatically calculate the sustainable return on investment (SROI) of infrastructure and building projects throughout their design phase. The SROI includes the financial ROI as well as the non-financial benefits for the local community, government and the environment. Chief financial officers can use the SROI analysis results to convince investors that their sustainable investments not only pay back financially, but also deliver benefits to a broader range of stakeholders who, as Stewart notes, "give the company the 'licence to operate'".

Senior managers in Western companies need to reframe their mental models not only to serve ageing and environmentally conscious consumers in developed economies but also to meet the needs of billions of frugal consumers in emerging markets such as India, China, Brazil and Africa. Today, two-thirds of the world's middle-class consumers live in the US and Europe. By 2030, nearly two-thirds will live in Asia. Africa's middle class – currently around 350 million – is the fastest growing in the world, with Nigeria's consumer market alone poised to reach $1.4 trillion by 2030. Emerging markets are full of paradoxes likely to baffle the savviest Western R&D and marketing managers. For instance, although middle-class consumers in India and Africa earn much less than their Western counterparts, they have equally high aspirations for themselves and their children. They want high-quality products but expect these to be affordable.

Emerging markets also suffer from deficient infrastructure (40% of Indian villages lack all-weather roads) and underdeveloped health-care, education and finance sectors (40% of rural Chinese lack access to decent health care, while over 75% of adults in sub-Saharan Africa do not have bank accounts). Yet these markets also boast world-class mobile communication networks, enabling them to leapfrog developed nations in mobile phone adoption. In early 2014, India and China together had approximately 2.2 billion mobile subscribers. China already boasts 92% smartphone penetration; and mobile internet use in Africa is expected to increase 20-fold by 2020.

Western companies may be daunted by emerging markets, but they cannot ignore the opportunities. To compete and win they will have to unlearn much of their R&D, manufacturing, sales and marketing practices, and rebuild them around frugality. Specifically, Western managers need to adopt a frugal mindset. If they can learn how to develop and market affordable high-quality products to billions of demanding consumers in unpredictable and resource-constrained economies, they can apply that mindset anywhere in the world.

This frugal mindset is what inspired Carlos Ghosn, the Brazilian-born CEO of Renault-Nissan, to send Gérard Detourbet, a seasoned engineer who co-led the development of Renault's entry-level vehicles such as the Logan, to the south Indian city of Chennai (see Chapter 1). Having succeeded in engineering a €5,000 ($6,000) car, Detourbet's team at the Renault Nissan Technology and Business Centre India (RNTBCI) is building its new CMF-A platform for a wide range of low- and ultra-low-cost vehicles. These are aimed at first-time buyers in India and other emerging markets, who will account for 60% of global auto sales in 2015 and around 66% of the global car industry's profits by 2020. Vehicles built on CMF-A will deliver extreme affordability backed by high performance and reliability. As Ghosn points out:[19]

Emerging consumers want real cars, not modified rickshaws or cheaper versions of cars from other countries. They want cars that are modern, robust and desirable; products they are proud to own.

Renault and Nissan recognised early on that they could not meet the high standards of emerging-market consumers by selling outdated, stripped-down versions of vehicles designed in France or Japan. Instead, Detourbet decided to invent from scratch the CMF-A – by adding many innovative components such as a fuel-efficient engine and a robust chassis – which can produce simple, elegant, dependable cars that meet the unique transport needs of emerging-market drivers. Detourbet notes that several breakthrough ideas for the development of CMF-A in Chennai have come from his boldly inventive Indian engineers and local suppliers, who rely on *jugaad* (frugal ingenuity) to find clever ways to generate more value with fewer resources.

The RNTBCI's former managing director, Karim Mikkiche, who now heads Renault-Nissan's computer-aided engineering and testing worldwide, notes:[20]

When you put a limitation on resources, you remove the limitation on creativity. Nothing is forbidden. As you have nothing to lose you boldly challenge the status quo. That's how you come up with disruptive innovation.

Renault and Nissan plan to launch the first vehicles built using the CMF-A platform in India in 2015 and later in other emerging markets, including Brazil and Africa. Their success could attract more Renault and Nissan managers from the US, Europe and Japan to RNTBCI for a crash course on frugal innovation. As Mikkiche points out:[21]

Once you tackle the contradictions of the complex Indian market, you can use the frugal and flexible mindset acquired here to satisfy customers anywhere in the world.

Like Renault-Nissan, IBM is attempting to reinvent its business model, and its senior managers' mental models, by gradually shifting its innovation focus to emerging Asia and Africa. In 2011, IBM's head of research and technology, John Kelly, asked Robert Morris if he would be interested in moving to Asia to run IBM's Global Research Labs from a non-US point of view. Morris, who had run IBM's research lab in Almaden, California, and subsequently IBM's services research, jumped at the opportunity and moved his family to Shanghai. From his new base, Morris took over the labs in India, China, Brazil, Africa, Australia and Japan, and is always looking to expand geographically. He recounts:[22]

> *During the first 100 years of its existence, IBM's main customers were in the US, Europe and Japan. Twenty years from now, most of IBM's customers will be based in Asia and Africa. Our goal is to boost our R&D and leadership capabilities and rapidly expand our partner ecosystems in emerging markets to capitalise on the huge growth opportunities there.*

Morris also sees Asia and Africa as emerging sources of innovation, showing how to innovate faster, better, and cheaper using the principles of frugal innovation. IBM's scientists and engineers in China innovate and complete their R&D projects at great speed. They design and launch good-enough solutions and then continually improve them based on further market input – using an iterative launch–test–improve cycle – thus drastically reducing time-to-market and gaining a first-mover advantage.[23]

Chinese innovators also excel at *jiejian chuangxin* (resource-saving innovation) and are finding ingenious ways to minimise costs and reuse materials and technologies. IBM's R&D team is using these rapid, resource-saving innovation techniques to tackle a massive problem in China: air pollution. The Green Horizon initiative, on which IBM is working with the Chinese government, aims to predict pollutant flows and quickly compute the impact of shutting down a source such as a coal-burning power station.

In India, IBM researchers found that most banks do not have centralised data warehouses, so they developed edge analytics, which scrape all the data from the end points in transaction flows and use it to build risk models.

Morris is even more excited about Africa's innovation potential, which IBM deems a super strategic continent that is ahead of the curve. In November 2013, IBM inaugurated its first African R&D lab in Nairobi, Kenya – a Silicon Savannah – a frugal innovation hotbed that draws on mobile phone technology. Nearly 20 million Kenyans now use M-Pesa, a mobile-based money transfer service whose users do not need a bank account (indeed, many Kenyans may decide that they will never need one). Over 50% of Kenya's GDP flows through M-Pesa. Charles Graeber, a *Bloomberg BusinessWeek* contributor, spent ten days in Kenya with no cash or debit or credit card, relying on his phone to pay for taxis, food, accommodation and even safari tours. He concluded:[24] "I feel like a caveman who's just been handed a Bic lighter."

Increasingly, M-Pesa is becoming the source of other disruptive business models in energy, education and health care. M-KOPA, a solar lighting solution, allows Kenyans to lease the solar equipment and make micro-payments using M-Pesa. When all the instalments have been paid, consumers own the product and receive free, clean electricity. M-Pesa and M-KOPA embody *kanju*, an African "make do" attitude that makes the best use of what people already have – mobile interconnectivity and abundant sunshine.[25]

Researchers at IBM's Nairobi lab use *kanju* to improve the city's traffic congestion, which is among the worst in the world. They have adapted a clever solution, Megaffic, originated by their Japanese colleagues, which optimises traffic flows by predicting congestion points and offering drivers alternative routes. Rather than relying on costly roadside sensors, as in Western capitals, this frugal solution uses image processing and advanced analytics to detect traffic conditions from a small number of low-resolution webcams installed in roads in Nairobi. As Osamuyimen Stewart, co-founder and chief scientist at IBM Research – Africa, explains:[26]

> IBM couldn't come to Africa with a big technology armoury and ask local governments to invest billions of dollars in the costly solutions we sell in the West. We need to think on our feet and invent from scratch frugal solutions tailored to the African environment.

A Japanese research colleague was so excited about how his work was being used in Kenya that he moved to the Nairobi lab.

Stewart now oversees R&D teams that are developing cutting-edge solutions to tackle Africa's seven greatest challenges: agriculture, water, energy, education, health care, financial inclusion and mobility. Stewart's own interest is in studying the link between Ubuntu, a classical African philosophy which says that no one exists in isolation and everyone is interconnected, and IBM's Smarter Planet initiative, which uses data to solve fundamental world problems. IBM researchers in the US, Europe and Japan also want to get involved.

Western managers do not need to travel to Chennai, Shanghai or Nairobi to gain exposure to the frugal mindset of innovators in emerging markets. They can learn how to practise *jugaad*, *jiejian chuangxin* and *kanju* in new academic centres and industrial consortia in the US and Europe. These include MIT's Tata Centre for Technology and Design, Santa Clara University's Frugal Innovation Lab, the Centre for Frugal Innovation at Hamburg University of Technology, and the Nordic Frugal Innovation Society.

In 2014, UCLA Health's Institute for Innovation launched its Global Lab for Innovation. Its mission is to partner with health systems around the world to find proven health-care innovations that everyone can afford. These crowdsourced solutions are ranked according to their cost-effectiveness – they must be at least 20% cheaper than existing approaches – as well as appropriateness and scalability.

Molly Coye, chief innovation officer at UCLA Health, believes that the Global Lab she leads will demonstrate to US health-care decision-makers that there are other, cheaper ways of delivering quality care. Coye notes:[27]

Affordable access to health care has become a global preoccupation ... the US needs to reach out to other countries and build a global innovation network.

At the same time, she acknowledges home-grown frugal health-care solutions, such as Partners in Care Foundation, a California-based non-profit organisation. It has developed a low-cost, simple and safe programme to encourage the elderly to be more physically active at home in order to avoid falls, which now cost the US health-care system $30 billion annually.

Rather than bringing emerging markets solutions to the West – a process known as reverse innovation – the Global Lab wants to encourage multi-nodal innovation by connecting progressive health-system leaders, entrepreneurs, financiers and policymakers from around the world, so that they can learn from one another and co-create solutions that benefit everyone.[28] The Global Lab is supported by many leading organisations such as the Innovation Learning Network, an influential group of health-care systems, health foundations, safety-net providers, tech companies, and design and innovation firms that collectively strive to make health care better through good design.

The "why": the foundation of change management

This forms the foundation of the change management framework, as it addresses two fundamental questions that employees are bound to ask: "Why should we change our company's business model to make it more frugal?"; and, more importantly, "Why should I personally change and start thinking and acting frugally?" If companies cannot answer these questions fully, they will not be able to convince their employees to adopt and use the tools discussed above.

Leading from the top

Corporate leaders must respond to the "why" questions as follows: "If all of us as a company don't start changing now, we won't be in business tomorrow." This is what Unilever's CEO, Paul Polman, effectively said in 2010. When outlining the details of Unilever's Sustainable Living Plan, he asked all 170,000 employees to help double the company's revenues while halving its environmental footprint by 2020. Polman justified his plan first in purely business terms. On the one hand, he argued, by 2020 Unilever would need to reach 2 billion more customers, many of whom would be low-income consumers from emerging markets, in addition to the 2 billion consumers it already serves worldwide. On the other hand, to produce and deliver goods to these 4 billion consumers, Unilever would require access to increasingly costly and scarce natural resources such as water, agricultural land and energy. The company felt it had no choice but to find frugal solutions in order to deliver more value to more people and using fewer resources.

Polman then highlighted two intangible benefits: greater brand loyalty from increasingly eco-conscious consumers, and more interest among younger staff who want to work for socially responsible companies. He was conveying to his employees the fact that only frugality would secure the company's long-term viability.

But he wanted more. He told employees that their company had a moral obligation to tackle the world's pressing social and environmental problems; that it must lead the industry by raising the bar on sustainability. "Our purpose is to have a sustainable business model that is put at the service of the greater good," he asserted.[29] Polman was positioning Unilever's Sustainable Living Plan as a noble cause worth serving. He also confessed that he did not have all the answers on how to achieve the 2020 goals and that he could not do it alone anyway. This humility was appealing to Unilever's employees, who recognised that they would all have to play a part in embedding frugality in their jobs. Since 2010, Polman has travelled the world and imparted his vision at dozens of meetings in major Unilever regions and in hundreds of public speeches and media interviews.

It is important to convince employees, but it is equally important (and possibly harder) to convince shareholders and analysts of the need for change. In some cases, board members may worry that shareholders will punish the company for focusing on frugal products. To make a strategic shift, CEOs will need to take on hard-headed analysts and the board. Polman has done this in two ways. First, he made a case for reversing the traditional focus on shareholders rather than customers. He has gone on record as saying:[30]

> I don't think our fiduciary duty is to put shareholders first. I say the opposite. What we firmly believe is that if we focus our company on improving the lives of the world's citizens and come up with genuine sustainable solutions, we are more in synch with consumers and society and ultimately this will result in good shareholder returns.

Second, he placed a ban on quarterly reporting to the stock market and actively courted more long-term investors over short-term, speculative hedge funds. As a result, between 2009 and 2012, Unilever shares held by hedge funds went from 15% to less than 5%. Polman says:[31]

Historically, too many CEOs have just responded to shareholders instead of actively seeking out the right shareholders. Most CEOs go to visit their existing shareholders; we go to visit the ones we don't yet have.

Using customers to motivate employees

One highly effective way to convince employees about the need for change is to show them how their customers are changing. Nothing is more persuasive for employees than to hear the voice of the customer demanding frugal solutions. Leaders should therefore point to the changes in the values and needs of current and emerging customers as a core argument when making the case for cultivating a frugal culture within the organisation.

They can then call on employees to help bridge the perceived gap between customers' frugal expectations and the company's current business model and offerings. Air Liquide is a world-leading supplier of gases, technologies and services to the industrial and health sectors. The company, which generated €15 billion ($18 billion) in revenues in 2013, has a strong reputation in Western markets for technically sophisticated solutions. Air Liquide invests €265 million ($318 million) annually in innovation, and 6,200 employees, mostly scientists and engineers, contribute to its innovation projects worldwide. Most of its senior and middle managers are engineers and scientists by training. Air Liquide's profits have been healthy in recent years. Yet François Darchis, a senior vice-president who oversees innovation (which includes R&D and new business) and a member of the executive committee, is reminding researchers and managers that the company must shift to a frugal business model to meet its customers' need for simpler, affordable and sustainable products and services. This is especially the case in India and China, Air Liquide's fast-growing customer bases. Emerging markets already account for over 25% of the company's revenues, and this is expected to double within a decade.

Darchis reflected that although Air Liquide has mastered the art of doing more with more in developed markets (namely creating sophisticated and safe solutions that can also be expensive), its local competitors in India and China are experts at doing less for less (offering lower-quality but competitively priced products and services). To compete and win in emerging markets, Air Liquide must learn to do more with less, marrying quality, safety and affordability. This is why in July 2014 Darchis launched the company's Shanghai Research & Technology Centre (SRTC), which is dedicated to designing frugal technical solutions in such areas as energy efficiency, water management, food chilling and freezing, all tailored to the Chinese market's needs.

Darchis also foresees a big shift in the needs of developed-world clients. By 2025, as billions of industrial assets are connected to the internet, Air Liquide will need to expand its core business model. In addition to selling gases, it must start offering value-added services, such as data analytics, to help its business clients optimise the performance of their industrial assets. This means that it has gradually to let go of its industrial-era business processes and mental models and learn to innovate faster, better and cheaper to meet its customers' data-driven needs, just like Google or Amazon.

To help with this transition, or "enlightened self-disruption", as Darchis puts it, the company has set up i-Lab to identify opportunities for "greater value in a rapidly urbanising and globalised economy facing severe resource constraints". I-Lab is headed by Gregory Olocco, who reports to Olivier Delabroy, head of R&D at Air Liquide. Olocco has a doctorate in mathematics and Delabroy has a PhD in engineering; both have years of experience as general managers. Their dual background in technology and business has enabled them to collaborate effectively with Air Liquide's R&D teams and its business-unit leaders. According to Olocco and Delabroy, i-Lab enables Air Liquide to experiment with a frugal innovation culture built around agility, deep understanding of customer needs and usage patterns, and partnerships with start-ups.[32]

I-Lab does this in three ways. First, it serves as a think-tank for Air Liquide by forecasting customer needs and identifying long-term opportunities for various business units. Second, it acts as a corporate garage fully loaded with advanced technologies such as 3D printers to prototype breakthrough ideas, develop proof-of-concept and pilot projects within six months (unsuccessful projects are terminated immediately). Third, it is creating the blueprint for Air Liquide's social business model, which will enable the company to actively engage all stakeholders in local communities where it operates and co-create greater business and social value with them. For instance, in India and Morocco, i-Lab is piloting social business projects that train and use local entrepreneurs to supply Air Liquide's products and services at an affordable price to small businesses that operate at the bottom of the pyramid.

These pilot projects are testing frugal supply chain techniques to cost-effectively and safely produce good-quality industrial gases in small batches and deliver them fast and reliably to bottom-of-the-pyramid customers, despite underdeveloped infrastructure in these emerging markets. They also take advantage of mobile technologies – widely available in India and Morocco – to cost-effectively and securely manage financial transactions such as payables and receivables.

Delabroy believes that if the radically innovative and frugal supply chain and financial management solutions that i-Lab is piloting in India and Morocco are successful, Air Liquide could apply them in mature economies too. In doing so, it could not only bolster its social business credentials at home but also totally reinvent its manufacturing processes and logistics networks in developed markets.

In sum, i-Lab helps Air Liquide employees understand why their company must change its business model to adapt to new global market realities, and shows them how to enable that change. Darchis explains:[33]

> I continually remind my fellow leaders and even our board members that just because you have lived 113 years doesn't mean you are immortal ... To fight complacency, corporate leaders like myself must continually create constraints within their organisation and maintain a sense of urgency.

Using incentives

Constantly communicating the need to change now or lose badly tomorrow is crucial in getting employees to commit to change. But this is not enough. Intrinsic motivation factors such as "I am doing the right thing" or "I am helping save the planet" alone cannot sustain organisation-wide mindset and behaviour change. Extrinsic motivation factors such as rewards and incentives are also needed to ensure that employees remain fully engaged with the change process. Leaders must therefore set up organisation-wide incentive systems based on KPIs to reinforce new behaviour.

As Kingfisher's Jamie Lawrence puts it:

> There are 80,000 employees at Kingfisher. Internal engagement is a big task. When people are informed, there is a positive response. Creating such a positive atmosphere can be part of the solution. But the real challenge is affecting not just hearts but also minds. The big challenge is how to make Net Positive part of everyone's job description.

To achieve this objective, Kingfisher aims to make Net Positive targets a part of employees' bonuses. Doing so will require a change in the company's current compensation programmes. Buying teams, for example, are not yet measured on their commitment to Net Positive objectives. Nevertheless, Kingfisher does have a few sustainability teams backed by Véronique Laury, its committed CEO. And Net Positive is a key part of the company's business plans. As Lawrence says:

> The challenge is getting middle-management and director level support, creating rewards and making this part of the day job. We have the support of the top but we need to embed this in the organisation's middle management.

CASE STUDY 7

Aetna's frugal health-care strategy

In March 2010, President Barack Obama signed into law the Patient Protection and Affordable Care Act (PPACA). His goal was to rein in rocketing US health-care costs, which were expected to reach $4.6 trillion, or 20% of US GDP, by 2020. The president wanted to give "hard-working, middle-class families the health-care security they deserve" and bring affordable medical insurance to 50 million uninsured American citizens.[34]

Mark Bertolini, chairman and CEO of Aetna, one of the US's largest and oldest health insurers, is unconvinced. He believes that the Affordable Care Act, which could cost $1.3 trillion to implement, is putting the cart before the horse. It tackles the question of "how we pay for health insurance" without asking "what we pay for". Bertolini argues:[35]

> [US health-care delivery] has become too bloated and is accountable to no one. It charges patients and rewards care providers on services delivered, not patient outcome.

Although well intended, the act serves only to widen access to a broken system. A 2012 *Journal of the American Medical Association* article identified six major areas of waste in the US health-care system: over-treatment; poor care co-ordination; ineffective execution of care processes; administrative complexity; pricing failures; and fraud and abuse. This waste accounts for 20% (around $600 billion) of the system's annual expenditure. The article concluded:[36] "Reducing waste is by far the largest, and most humane, and smartest opportunity for evolving an affordable health-care system."

According to McKinsey, a consultancy, the most effective way to reduce waste is to reinvent US health care, discarding the current fee-for-service reimbursement model, which compensates providers for tasks they perform, in favour of one that rewards successful health outcomes for patients. The latter approach, if adopted widely and systemically, could save an estimated $1 trillion.[37] Pay-per-performance would also improve accountability and efficiency, by encouraging providers to deliver the best care for patients.

Aetna is playing a large part in such a transition. The company, which is over 160 years old, is radically transforming its bricks-and-mortar health-insurance business into a digital enabler of value-based care. Bertolini notes:

> To survive, most health insurers have only two options: either move up the health-care value chain, by exclusively serving the premium market, or move down the value chain by buying out hospitals and become vertically integrated. We chose neither, and instead decided to move deeper into the value chain by becoming the "Intel Inside" of the entire health-care system.

As part of this strategy, Aetna offers a comprehensive portfolio of technology solutions and value-added services to hospitals and other health-care providers so that they can shift to a value-based care model. Historically, providers and payers such as Aetna have been at odds, fighting over pricing, reimbursement and patient relationships. But now Aetna wants to empower providers with insights and technology solutions that yield an upside for both parties when patients get better care at a lower cost.

To achieve this, Aetna is supporting providers in establishing Accountable Care Organisations (ACOs). These are health-care providers, including primary-care physicians, specialists and hospitals, which collaborate and bear collective responsibility for the cost and quality of care.[38] By operating within an ACO, providers avoid redundant services, enhance co-ordination among care teams and improve patient compliance with care plans, while delivering the right care at the right time. With the rise of the ACO model, value-based payments are forecast to account for half of all US health-care spending (compared with 20% today) by 2020.

In 2011, Aetna launched a new business unit called Accountable Care Solutions to offer help, advice and population health management solutions to providers moving towards an ACO business model. In addition, Aetna jointly markets new health plan products with health systems where its members receive care from providers in the health system's ACO network. Aetna estimates that in the first year of such a plan, its customers save 8–15% on premiums, and providers save costs and generate more value. For example, Aetna's ACO relationship with Banner Health Network resulted in a 5% decrease in medical costs for its members in the ACO-based health plan in 2013. Quality also improved, as Aetna members served by Banner Health Network had improved cancer-screening rates and fewer avoidable hospital admissions, and diabetic members had better blood-sugar management. In 2014, 20–25% of Aetna's claim payments were made to doctors and other providers who deliver value-based care, and the company intends to increase this to 45% by 2017. Aetna expects to have 60 accountable care agreements in place by the end of 2014 and is in negotiations with an additional 200 health systems and provider organisations to expand its value-based network.

Aetna is also changing another staple of the industry: the corporate health-care plan. The company wants to be to health care what Expedia.com is to travel: that is, a platform for consumers to compare health plans and custom-build their own. Employers are increasingly eschewing standard benefits and offering their employees cash to buy the health-insurance products they want. This has spurred growth in private health-care exchanges that not only offer proprietary products from a single insurer, but also match consumers with appropriate products and plans offered by multiple insurers.

Aetna is participating in these private exchanges, where staff can choose or build their own health plan using products and services offered by multiple, competing insurance firms, of which Aetna is just one. It might look like a gamble, but Aetna is betting that employees and individual customers will choose its value-based products rather than rivals' fee-for-service products, not least because Aetna's products may be 10–12% cheaper. As more customers sign up, Aetna will be able to convince more providers to switch to a value-based care model.

To encourage collaboration among providers and give more power to consumers, Aetna needs new technological and consumer marketing skills. It has invested more than $1 billion in technologies to become the GAFAs (Google, Apple, Facebook, Amazon) of the health-care sector. For example, Aetna established Healthagen, a collection of population health management solutions, care management services and health information technologies as well as an incubator of disruptive digital health-care solutions. Headed by a physician-turned-serial-entrepreneur, Charles Saunders, Healthagen acquires high-growth businesses and invests in promising start-ups. It uses a high-velocity business incubation process to speed up the development, launch and growth of their solutions. Saunders says:[39]

> It usually costs millions of dollars and takes 4–5 years to launch a new tech company in health care. The whole process remains an art; at Healthagen we turned it into a science. We can get a new tech business up and running in fewer than 18 months.

Healthagen relies on a Concept Lab, which brings together designers, customers and industry experts to identify market needs and technology trends, and then brainstorms and co-creates market-relevant solutions to pressing health-care challenges. Saunders comments:

> All the businesses we incubate are purpose-built to address real market needs. Every pilot project we do is funded by a real customer – say, a Fortune 500 employer – who has a genuine interest in seeing the project succeed.

Healthagen serves four stakeholders – providers, employers, patients and insurers – and its portfolio includes several fast-growing businesses such as Accountable Care Solutions, ActiveHealth Management (which provides population health management solutions) and Medicity (the largest health information exchange in the US). Aetna also owns iTriage, a free mobile app that allows patients to manage their own health. iTriage users can search for the possible causes of multiple related symptoms, locate care, understand the price of the service and book an appointment, all within minutes. The app has been downloaded more than 10 million times.

Aetna also set up Aetna Innovation Labs, which identifies clinical, technology and mobile ideas two or three years ahead of the market, validates and measures their value through proof of concept, and can quickly launch and scale them up in the marketplace. Michael Palmer, Aetna's chief innovation and digital officer, who runs the Innovation Labs, is also responsible for setting and delivering the company's consumer digital strategies so it can execute the change from a B2B model to a B2C business. The Innovation Labs' mission, he says, is to find the holy grail of the medical field: personalised and preventive care.

Palmer is challenging two age-old principles in health care: to treat all patients equally, and "if it ain't broke, don't fix it":[40]

> We want to use personalised consumer data and predictive analytics to deliver tailored solutions to individual users. We want to empower consumers with digital tools they can use to identify potential health issues and take proactive steps to address them well before disease onset. Prevention is a lot less painful and much more cost-effective than cure – especially for chronic diseases (which could cost the US nearly $4 trillion by 2023).

For instance, Innovation Labs is piloting a solution with Newtopia, a personalised health coaching provider, to reduce health risks discerned from a person's unique genetic profile, such as metabolic syndrome, which can lead to diabetes, stroke and coronary heart disease.

Aetna is also hiring leading consumer marketing experts, and plans a strong marketing campaign for the retail market using mobile and social-media platforms to appeal directly to end users. For instance, in October 2013, Aetna appointed Dijuana Lewis, formerly a senior manager at Walmart, to lead a new consumer products and enterprise marketing organisation.

Bertolini believes that these new businesses and senior appointments will help Aetna's nearly 50,000 employees change to a more frugal mindset. Aetna has led by example, having already moved its own company health plan to a private exchange, and is piloting its customer-engagement tools – such as its metabolic syndrome risk-reduction solution – among staff.

The company has become a market leader in accountable care solutions and runs 47 ACOs serving more than 1 million patients nationwide. Aetna is trying to persuade the two-thirds of *Fortune* 100 companies that it serves to switch to Aetna-powered private health exchanges. At the same time, it will persuade more health providers to switch to an ACO model using Aetna's tech solutions and services, thereby creating a virtuous cycle in the health-care industry.

There are, of course, significant obstacles to realising this grand vision, in particular investor caution and industry vested interests. Aetna's traditional business model has generated record membership and revenue and strong profit growth for investors, so why change track, shareholders ask. Bertolini responds:

We are on the wrong track. Unless we quickly get on the right track and start running faster, we might as well forfeit the race.

He also fears that organisations that have long benefited from volume-based care will lobby hard to resist the shift to an outcomes-based system in the US. Indeed, the accountable care model that Aetna promotes may have a greater chance of success in China, the Middle East or South America, where lifestyle-related and chronic diseases have exploded, and health delivery and medical insurance systems are far less developed than in the US.

Nonetheless, Bertolini is optimistic:

Over the past 160 years, we have sustained an agile culture that anticipates changes and rapidly shifts strategies in order to maintain our legacy of creating value for society. Year after year, we need to prove our worthiness to earn our licence to do business. We can't take it for granted.

Conclusion

The order in which leaders seek to address the what, how and why of organisational change can vary across companies. For some, it may make sense to start with the why to create a sense of urgency and purpose for the hard graft that will follow. For example, Aetna, one of the world's largest health insurers, is using US health-care reform as the impetus to radically reinvent its business model to deliver quality care at lower cost to more Americans.

Other, more action-oriented, companies may prefer to start with the how to achieve quick wins before embarking on the why. Indeed, early signs of success could provide the incentive to do more.

For other companies, the what, how and why could feed off each other in an iterative cycle, with the what getting bigger and more ambitious as successes pile up. For example, Marks & Spencer's Plan A initiated in 2007 focused on defining the what (100 sustainability commitments) and identified a limited set of tools (a lightweight how) to achieve quick short-term wins and serve a modest why (reduce social and environmental footprint at the operational level). The next iteration of Plan A, initiated in 2010, broadened the what by adding another 80 commitments, and stepped up the how to address business model transformation to serve a more ambitious why (to become the world's most sustainable retailer). As Plan A began to deliver positive results, M&S became bolder. In 2014 it announced its audacious Plan A 2020, which drastically expands the what (by encompassing all employees, customers and suppliers worldwide), the how (launching whole new businesses rather than merely reinventing M&S's existing business model) and the why (to turn M&S into a catalytic change agent, rallying the entire retail and consumer-goods sector to co-build sustainable economies and societies).

In the end, however, the approach that works best for a company will depend on its existing culture, its current situation and its leaders. As pointed out at the start of this chapter, a truly frugal change management programme will seek to work with a company's existing culture rather than attempt to reinvent it. Regardless of the approach taken, the most important thing is to make a start.

9 Conclusion

THE WORLD OF BUSINESS is witnessing a frugal innovation revolution. In almost every industry a few, forward-thinking companies are championing the quest to do more, and better, with less. Whether it is Renault-Nissan in automotive, GE and Siemens in manufacturing, Unilever and PepsiCo in consumer goods, Marks & Spencer and Auchan in retail, Novartis and GSK in pharmaceuticals, Pearson in education, American Express and Barclays in finance, or Aetna in health care, these frugal innovation pioneers are rewriting the rules of the game; in some industries, they are changing the game entirely.

By being early movers, these innovators are consolidating their leadership and leaving their competitors behind. Like Renault-Nissan, GE and Siemens, they are shaping and leading completely new markets for affordable products and services. Like Aetna and PepsiCo, they have drastically lowered operating costs in their value chain. And like Unilever and Marks & Spencer, they have become standard bearers of sustainability. As well as reaping tangible financial benefits, these frugal forerunners are achieving intangible advantages in the increased brand recognition, customer loyalty (among cost-conscious and eco-aware consumers), higher employee engagement and more public goodwill that their new thinking has engendered.

We estimate that around 5% of companies in developed economies are advanced in their frugal innovation journey; 15% have adopted frugal innovation in some parts of their organisation but not organisation-wide; and the remaining 80% have yet to formulate a coherent and comprehensive frugal innovation strategy.

The 80% of companies in the US, Europe and Japan that have yet to embark on the frugal innovation journey, or have taken only a few small steps in that direction, should consider kick-starting their frugal innovation engines without delay for three reasons:

- Frugal products and services are rapidly evolving from niche markets into the mainstream in developed economies, as dwindling purchasing power drives millions of middle-class consumers to switch from premium to value-for-money products. Christophe de Maistre, president of Siemens, France and south-west Europe, predicts that there will only be two classes of products by 2020 – the A class, comprising high-end and expensive goods and services for the wealthier minority, and the B class, comprising good-quality and affordable products for the mainstream.

- US, European and Japanese regulators increasingly want companies to become more inclusive and sustainable by developing products and services that are more affordable, accessible and environmentally friendly.

- Companies across industries will soon face a plethora of frugal competitors whose cheaper, better-value products will start taking big chunks of the market from incumbents. These frugal rivals are coming from several directions. They include the GAFAs (Google, Apple, Facebook and Amazon); nimble tech start-ups; cost-competitive companies from emerging markets, especially India and China; and major corporations from other industries (such as Walmart, which is expanding into financial services and health care). Companies across all industries in developed markets therefore have little choice but to adopt a frugal approach to innovation, as quickly as possible.

Change will not be easy. Companies must be willing and able to overhaul every function from R&D to sales and marketing, reorganise the company structure, rethink human resources policies and incentives, and shift their business and mental model from doing more for more or less with less, to doing more with less and even better with less.

This transition will be particularly painful for North American firms that have yet to appreciate fully how dramatic shifts in consumer preferences, regulations, the competitive landscape and dwindling natural resources are swiftly and irrevocably propelling the developed world towards frugality. A Boston Consulting Group report published in *MIT Sloan Management Review* in 2013 shows that North American companies are much less willing than their European or Asian competitors to create a new, more sustainable business model. North American companies seem less aware of the planet's resource constraints, and so feel less compelled to learn more frugal ways of doing business. But if this complacency persists, they will soon find themselves at a huge competitive disadvantage, especially compared with frugal European and Asian competitors.

What matters most in the frugal innovation journey is not processes, strategy or structure, however, but leadership. Ultimately, frugal innovation is about people; it is human ingenuity that drives innovation, not software code or robotics. Corporate leaders inured to a command-and-control management style will stifle any form of innovation, frugal or otherwise. Senior leaders must recognise that they cannot manage frugal innovation in an organisation as if it were a predictable and mechanistic system. Rather, they must think and act like gardeners, preparing and tending the soil in their organisation, sowing the right frugal seeds and then backing away to allow frugal innovation to flourish, stepping in to tend the plants only when needed. When it comes to leading frugal innovation initiatives – as with gardening – less is more. This frugal leadership is about unleashing value from employees with minimum effort. Frugal leaders, such as Mark Bertolini (Aetna), Carlos Ghosn (Renault-Nissan), Jeffrey Immelt (GE), Joe Kaeser (Siemens), Indra Nooyi (PepsiCo), Paul Polman (Unilever), Franck Riboud (Danone) and Andrew Witty (GSK), foster change and grow their organisations by enabling creativity to emerge from the bottom up.

Implementing a frugal innovation strategy in any organisation can be daunting. There is no magic formula. But leaders might use the tools and techniques outlined in this book to set frugal innovation goals and priorities that match their company's unique culture and needs. The website www.frugalinnovationhub.com provides additional tools, case studies and best practices to transform your organisation into a frugal enterprise. It also enables you to join a community of like-minded people with whom you can collaborate and exchange ideas and solutions, thus allowing for faster progress on the frugal innovation journey.

For many companies in the US, Europe and Japan, accustomed to the world's most advanced R&D labs and the richest customers, the notion of frugal innovation may seem like an oxymoron: how can something frugal be considered as innovative; and how can you innovate in a frugal manner? In developed economies, frugality may even be construed as a step backward: an anti-modern notion that can hamper social progress and economic growth. Yet frugal innovation represents, in important ways, a return to the industrious roots of the advanced economies built on hard work and prudent use of resources.

As Benjamin Franklin, one of the founding fathers of the United States and a prolific innovator himself, put it:

> The way to wealth is as plain as the way to market. It depends chiefly on two words, industry and frugality: that is, waste neither time nor money, but make the best use of both. Without industry and frugality nothing will do, and with them everything.

Acknowledgements

WE WOULD LIKE TO THANK the many people who have made this book possible. Paul Lewis for believing in the idea, commissioning the book and sharpening our writing; our agent Bridget Wagner Matzie for helping us shape the proposal and hone the argument; Clare Grist Taylor for guiding us through the publishing process; Penny Williams and Paul Forty for their substantial help with editing the book; Valentina Zanca for proactively marketing it; and Arushi Saxena and Rémi Rongières for their excellent and thorough research assistance.

This book would not have been possible without the support of all the frugal innovators we interviewed. We thank them for sharing their stories and insights with us. We hope that the finished product does justice to their ingenuity and passion and the positive changes they are making in society.

We are grateful for the ideas, comments and case studies that were generously provided by Simon Francis and Kat Nielsen of Flock Associates, Conrad Chua of Cambridge Judge Business School, Polly Courtice of the Cambridge Institute for Sustainability Leadership, Venkata Gandikota at the Nordic Frugal Innovation Society, Leonardo Previ at Trivioquadrivio, Molly Coye at the University of California, Los Angeles, Elisabetta Osta at Barclays Bank, Rachel Konrad at Renault-Nissan, Nathalie de Baudry d'Asson at Le Lien Public, Mohi Ahmed at Fujitsu, Daniel Jasmin at ExploLab, Mark Hatch at TechShop, Miora Ranaivoarinosy and Olivier Maurel at Danone, Dominique Gibert at Diateino, Matthew Claudel at MIT, Philippe Mustar at Ecole des Mines ParisTech, Breck Garrett at Aetna, Leigh Farris at GE, Olivia Lisicki, Madjid Yahiaoui at CCI Paris, Vaithegi Vasanthakumar at Pearson, Elvire Meier-Comte at Siemens and Sami Ghazi at PepsiCo.

We also want to thank the public relations teams at the companies that appear in our case studies for arranging interviews with their corporate executives.

Lastly, we appreciate the care and support of our families and friends throughout the writing of this book. We couldn't have done any of this without them.

Notes and sources

Notes

1 Frugal innovation: a disruptive growth strategy

1 Rosemain, M., "Renault 2013 Sales Gain on Surging Demand for Dacia Cars", *Bloomberg*, January 21st 2014.

2 Piketty, T. and Goldhammer, A., *Capital in the Twenty-first Century*, Belknap Press, 2013.

3 Cone, C., global chair, Edelman Business + Social Purpose, interview with Navi Radjou, November 26th 2012.

4 European Commission, "Environment: New rules on e-waste to boost resource efficiency", press release, August 13th 2012.

5 Mainwaring, S., *We First: How Brands and Consumers Use Social Media to Build a Better World*, Palgrave Macmillan, 2011.

6 Hatch, M., *The Maker Movement Manifesto: Rules for Innovation in the New World of Crafters, Hackers, and Tinkerers*, McGraw-Hill, 2013.

7 Rifkin, J., *The Age of Access: The New Culture of Hypercapitalism, Where All of Life Is a Paid-for Experience*, J.P. Tarcher/Putnam, 2000.

8 Botsman, R. and Rogers, R., *What's Mine Is Yours: The Rise of Collaborative Consumption*, HarperBusiness, 2010.

9 Mulliez, V., CEO, Groupe Auchan, interview with Navi Radjou, October 8th 2013.

10 McQuivey, J., *Digital Disruption: Unleashing the next Wave of Innovation*, Forrester Research, 2013.

2 Principle one: engage and iterate

1 www.forbes.com/sites/bruceupbin/2012/09/04/intuit-the-30-year-old-startup/

2 www.linkedin.com/pulse/20121101134612-1940438-fall-in-love-with-the-problem-not-the-solution

3 "The History of Quicken", www.intuit.com.

4   Peters, T., *Thriving on Chaos: Handbook for a Management Revolution*, HarperBusiness, 1987.

5   Strategy& (formerly Booz & Company), *The 2014 Global Innovation 1000: Proven paths to innovation success (Media report)*, October 28th 2014.

6   Hewitt J., Campbell J. and Cacciotti, J., *Beyond the Shadow of a Drought*, Oliver Wyman, 2011.

7   Grogan, K., "Productivity of pharma R&D down 70% – study", *PharmaTimes*, December 2nd 2011.

8   Booz & Company, op. cit.

9   Prabhu, A., innovation and insights director, Lion Dairy & Drinks, interview with Jaideep Prabhu, February 23rd 2014.

10   Booz & Company, op. cit.

11   The case study on Fujitsu's work with farmers at Sawa Orchards in Wakayama, Japan, is based on interviews conducted by the authors with several senior executives at Fujitsu in the US and Japan.

12   Booz & Company, op. cit.

13   Ries, E., *The Lean Startup: How Today's Entrepreneurs Use Continuous Innovation to Create Radically Successful Businesses*, Crown Business, 2011.

14   Mayhew, S., head of R&D strategy development, GSK, interview with Jaideep Prabhu, February 17th 2014.

15   Cornillon, P., senior vice-president R&D, Arla Foods, interview with Jaideep Prabhu, February 28th 2014.

16   Radjou, N., *Transforming R&D Culture*, Forrester Research, March 20th 2006.

17   Scott, M., "The Payments Challenge for Mobile Carriers", *New York Times*, February 26th 2014.

18   Comstock, B., "We've learned these four lessons from startups, and we're using them to transform GE", LinkedIn, December 10th 2013.

19   Most of the material used in this case study comes from Radjou, N. and Prabhu, J., "Beating Competitors with High-Speed Innovation", *Strategy+Business*, December 18th 2013 (www.strategy-business.com).

3   Principle two: flex your assets

1   Anand, N. and Barsoux, J-L., *Quest: Leading Global Transformations*, IMD International, 2014.

2   Trout, B.L., director of the Novartis-MIT Center for Continuous Manufacturing, interview with Navi Radjou, May 9th 2014.

3   "RAF jets fly with 3D printed parts", BBC News, January 5th 2014.

4   "Peter Weijmarshausen: 3D Printing", etalks, April 2nd 2013.

5   This quote from Gérard Mestrallet, CEO of GDF-Suez, is slightly adapted
    from its original version that appeared in his interview with a French
    magazine, *L'Expansion*, in December 2013.
6   Dugan, J., *Caterpillar to Expand Manufacturing and Increase Employment
    in the United States with New Hydraulic Excavator Facility in Victoria,
    Texas,* Caterpillar press release, August 12th 2010.
7   Wong, H., Potter, A. and Naim, M., "Evaluation of postponement in
    the soluble coffee supply chain: A case study", *International Journal of
    Production Economics,* Vol. 131, Issue 1, May 2011, pp. 355–64.
8   O'Marah, K., chief content officer, SCM World, and senior research
    fellow at Stanford Global Supply Chain Management Forum, interview
    with Navi Radjou, March 11th 2014.
9   Beasty, C., "The Chain Gang", Destination CRM, October 2007.
10 Morieux, Y., "As work gets more complex, 6 rules to simplify", TED Talk,
    October 2013.
11 Lopez, M., CEO, Lopez Research, interview with Navi Radjou, March
    28th 2014.
12 O'Connell, A., "Lego CEO Jørgen Vig Knudstorp on leading through
    survival and growth", *Harvard Business Review,* January 2009.
13 "The Return to Apple", All About Steve Jobs: http://allaboutstevejobs.
    com/bio/longbio/longbio_08.php.
14 O'Connell, op. cit.
15 Francis, S., CEO, Flock Associates, and former head of Aegis Europe,
    interview with Jaideep Prabhu, January 27th 2014.
16 This case study is adapted from an original version that appeared
    in French in *L'Innovation Jugaad,* published by Diateino in 2013. It is
    published with the permission of Diateino.

4   Principle three: create sustainable solutions

1   "Tarkett joins the 'Circular Economy 100' program", Tarkett, February 8th
    2013.
2   "Fixing Capitalism: Paul Polman interview", Confederation of British
    Industry (CBI), November 14th 2012.
3   "A water warning", *The Economist,* November 19th 2008.
4   Kanani, R., "Why IKEA Thinks This Mega-Trend Will Define The Next 30
    Years Of Business", *Forbes,* February 7th 2014.
5   McDonough, W. and Braungart, M., *Cradle to Cradle: Remaking the Way
    We Make Things,* North Point, 2002.
6   Kobori, M., vice-president, global sustainability, Levi Strauss & Co,
    interview with Navi Radjou, May 21st 2014.
7   Ebner von Eschenbach, head of BMW Group's Financial Services
    Segment, interview with Jaideep Prabhu, April 7th 2014.

8   Walker, J., former head of innovation, Kingfisher, interview with Jaideep Prabhu, February 20th 2014.

9   Heck, S., Rogers, M. and Carroll, P., *Resource Revolution: How to Capture the Biggest Business Opportunity in a Century*, Melcher Media, 2014.

10 Mazoyer, E., deputy CEO, Bouygues Immobilier, interview with Navi Radjou, April 29th 2014.

11 Laville, E., CEO, Utopies, interview with Navi Radjou, March 28th 2014.

12 Nemo, S-N., vice-president, La Poste, and head of Recy'Go, interview with Navi Radjou, April 30th 2014.

13 Blanchard, D., chief R&D officer, Unilever, interview with Jaideep Prabhu, February 20th 2014.

5   Principle four: shape customer behaviour

1   Blanchard, D., chief R&D officer, Unilever, interview with Jaideep Prabhu, February 20th 2014.

2   Schumacher, E.F., *Small Is Beautiful: A Study of Economics as if People Mattered*, Harper & Row, 1973.

3   Ehrenfeld, J. and Hoffman, A.J., *Flourishing: A Frank Conversation about Sustainability*, Stanford Business Books, 2013.

4   Ibid.

5   MIT's SENSEable City Lab research team, interview with Navi Radjou, May 13th 2014.

6   Ratti, C. and Kloeckl, K., "Rise of the Asian Megacity", BBC, June 20th 2011.

7   "Health and appiness", *The Economist*, February 1st 2014.

8   Wilby, P., "Moocs, and the man leading the UK's charge", *Guardian*, August 18th 2014.

9   Subramanian, P., founder, CoLearnr, interview with Jaideep Prabhu, May 1st 2014.

10 Bordoff, J. and Pascal, N., *Pay-As-You-Drive Auto Insurance: A Simple Way to Reduce Driving-Related Harms and Increase Equity*, Brookings Institution, July 2008.

11 Verbaken, J., co-founder, gThrive, interview with Navi Radjou, August 18th 2014.

12 Laskey, A., CEO, Opower, "How behavioral science can lower your energy bill", talk at TED 2013.

13 Rebours, C., CEO, InProcess, interview with Navi Radjou, March 14th 2014.

14 "Philips Introduces 'Lighting as a Service'", SustainableBusiness.com, January 23rd 2014.

15 "Meet Simple; A Worry-Free Alternative To Traditional Banking", TraxonTech, March 14th 2013.

6 Principle five: co-create value with prosumers

1 Von Hippel, E., *Democratizing Innovation*, MIT Press, 2006.
2 "Samsung ranks second in R&D spending for 2013", GS Marena Blog, October 24th 2013.
3 Dunn, E. and Norton, M., *Happy Money: The Science of Smarter Spending*, Simon & Schuster, 2013.
4 Norton, M., Ariely, D. and Mochon, D., "The IKEA effect: When labor leads to love", *Journal of Consumer Psychology*, Vol. 22, 2012, pp. 453–60.
5 Coase, R., "The Nature of the Firm", *Economica* (Blackwell Publishing), Vol. 4, Issue 16, 1937, pp. 386–405.
6 White House, "Remarks by the President at the White House Maker Faire", Office of the Press Secretary, June 18th 2014.
7 Dutcher, J., "Massimo Banzi: How Arduino is Open-Sourcing Imagination", DataScience@Berkeley, April 22nd 2014.
8 European Commission, "The Sharing Economy: Accessibility Based Business Models for Peer-to-Peer Markets", Business Innovation Observatory, September 2013.
9 Cortese, A., *Locavesting: The Revolution in Local Investing and How to Profit from It*, John Wiley, 2011.
10 Nussbaum, B., *Creative Intelligence: Harnessing the Power to Create, Connect, and Inspire*, HarperBusiness, 2013.
11 "Giffgaff", *World Heritage Encyclopedia*, November 25th 2009.

7 Principle six: make innovative friends

1 Safian, R., "Generation Flux: Beth Comstock", *Fast Company*, January 2012.
2 Comstock, B., senior vice-president and chief marketing officer, GE, interview with Navi Radjou, April 7th 2014.
3 Groth, O., "Hacking Wicked Social Problems With Renaissance Thinkers and Gamers", *Huffington Post*, February 18th 2014.
4 Martin, T., "The (Un)examined Organization", *The Alpine Review*, Issue No. 2, 2014.
5 Martin, T., CEO, Unboundary, e-mail exchange with Navi Radjou, August 18th 2014.
6 "Four Disruption Themes for Business", The Altimeter Group, April 2013.
7 Groth, op. cit.
8 Marks & Spencer's Plan A Report, 2014.
9 Mulcahy, S., senior vice-president and managing director of financial services industry, Salesforce.com, interview with Navi Radjou, March 6th 2014.
10 Rebours, C., CEO, InProcess, interview with Navi Radjou, March 14th 2014.

11 Gertler, N., "Industrial Ecosystems: Developing Sustainable Industrial Structures", MIT master's thesis, Smart Communities Network, 1995.

12 Corkery, M., and Silver-Greenberg, J., "Lenders Offer Low-Cost Services for the Unbanked", *New York Times Dealbook*, July 22nd 2014.

13 Fera, R.A., "American Express Spotlights the Issue of Financial Exclusion in Davis Guggenheim Doc 'Spent'", *Fast Company*, March 2014.

14 Birol, J., serial entrepreneur and strategy consultant, interview with Navi Radjou, August 25th 2014.

15 Wiseman, L., Thinkers50-ranked leadership expert, interview with Navi Radjou, August 18th 2014.

16 "Pearson debuts new global accelerator class", *Pearson News*, June 16th 2014.

17 Coughlin, B., CEO, Ford Global Technologies, e-mail exchange with Navi Radjou, August 2014.

18 Radjou, N., "Innovation Networks: Global Progress Report 2006," Forrester Report, June 2006.

19 Vandebroek, S., chief technology officer, Xerox, interview with Navi Radjou, August 25th 2014.

20 Musk, E., "All Our Patent Are Belong To You", Tesla Blog, June 12th 2014.

21 Litzler, J-B., "Sébastien Bazin divise Accor en deux pour mieux le réveiller", *Le Figaro*, November 27th 2013.

22 Lacheret, Y., senior vice-president, entrepreneurship advocacy, Accor Group, interview with Navi Radjou, July 7th 2014.

8 Fostering a frugal culture

1 Hall, J., "Sir Stuart Rose on the ethical spirit of Marks & Spencer", *Daily Telegraph*, February 1st 2009.

2 Vasanthakumar, V., Senior Associate, Office of the Chief Education Adviser at Pearson, interview with Jaideep Pradhu, August 28th 2014.

3 Datta, M., head of Plan A delivery, Marks & Spencer's worldwide properties, interview with Jaideep Prabhu, May 9th 2014.

4 Marks & Spencer's Plan A Report, 2014.

5 Faber, E., CEO, Danone, e-mail exchange with Navi Radjou, August 2014.

6 Lawrence, J., senior sustainability adviser and in-house counsel to Kingfisher Group's Net Positive strategy, interview with Jaideep Prabhu, February 21st 2014.

7 Kingfisher, *Net Positive Report*, 2013/14.

8 Ibid.

9 Marks & Spencer, op. cit.

10 Radjou, N., Prabhu, J. and Ahuja, S., *L'Innovation Jugaad: Redevenons Ingénieux!*, Diateino, 2013.

11   De Maistre, C., president, south-west Europe and France, Siemens, interview with Navi Radjou, January 17th 2013.

12   *COO Insights*, Roland Berger Strategy Consultants, March 2014.

13   Meier-Comte, E., senior consultant, Siemens Corporate Technology, interview with Navi Radjou, July 25th 2014.

14   Vats, T., head of PepsiCo's Global Value Innovation Centre, interview with Navi Radjou, July 22nd 2014.

15   Hosking, I., senior researcher, Engineering Design Centre, University of Cambridge, interview with Jaideep Prabhu, July 2014.

16   "Nestlé's approach to packaging design aims to make its products easier to enjoy", www.nestle.com, January 20th 2012.

17   Life-cycle assessment, Wikipedia.org.

18   Stewart, E., head of sustainability solutions, Autodesk, interview with Navi Radjou, March 13th 2014.

19   Radjou, Prabhu and Ahuja, op. cit.

20   "Innovation for everyone", video produced by the Renault-Nissan Alliance, YouTube, July 11th 2013.

21   Ibid.

22   Morris, R., vice-president, Global Labs, IBM Research, interview with Navi Radjou, October 16th 2013.

23   Williamson, P.J. and Yin, E., "Accelerated Innovation: The New Challenge From China", *MIT Sloan Management Review*, Summer 2014.

24   Graeber, C., "Ten Days in Kenya With No Cash, Only a Phone", *BloombergBusinessweek*, June 5th 2014.

25   Olopade, D., *The Bright Continent: Breaking Rules and Making Change in Modern Africa*, Houghton Mifflin Harcourt, March 2014.

26   Stewart, O., co-founder and chief scientist, IBM Research – Africa, e-mail exchange with Navi Radjou, August 2014.

27   Coye, M., chief innovation officer, UCLA Health, interview with Navi Radjou, June 26th 2014.

28   Immelt, J.R., Govindarajan, V. and Trimble, C., "How GE is disrupting itself", *Harvard Business Review*, October 2009.

29   Gunther, M., "Unilever's CEO has a green thumb", *Fortune*, May 23rd 2013.

30   Cofino, J., "Unilever's Paul Polman: challenging the corporate status quo", *Guardian*, April 24th 2012.

31   Ibid.

32   Delabroy, O., head of R&D, and Olocco, G., head of i-Lab, Air Liquide, interviews with Navi Radjou, January 28th 2014.

33   Radjou, Prabhu and Ahuja, op. cit.

34   "Statement by the President on the Anniversary of the Affordable Care Act," White House press release, March 23rd 2013.

35   Bertolini, M., CEO, Aetna, interview with Navi Radjou, July 16th 2014.

36 Berwick, D.M. and Hackbarth, A.D., "Eliminating Waste in US Health Care", *Journal of the American Medical Association*, April 11th 2012.

37 Latkovic, T., "Claiming the $1 trillion prize in US health care", McKinsey & Company Insights & Publications, September 2013.

38 Accountable care organisation, Wikipedia.org.

39 Saunders, C., CEO, Healthagen, an Aetna company, interview with Navi Radjou, August 6th 2014.

40 Palmer, M., chief innovation and digital officer, Aetna, and head of Aetna Innovation Labs, interview with Navi Radjou, August 1st 2014.

Sources

The Renault-Nissan, SNCF, Pearson and Siemens cases featured in Chapters 1, 2 and 8 are based on blogs the authors wrote for the strategy+business website, published by PwC Strategy& Inc (www.strategy-business.com/16239054/32414715), © 2013 PwC, and republished here with permission. PwC refers to the PwC network and/or one or more of its member firms, each of which is a separate legal entity. Please see www.pwc.com/structure for further details.

Index